A NEW DISPENSATION

(Plain Talk for Confusing Times)

Kryon
Book 10

88 International Kryon Books
See [www.kryon.com] for more info

Spanish
Kryon Books - One, Two, Three, The Parables, The Journey Home, Kryon Book Six and Seven

Spanish
Kryon Books 8 and The Indigo Children books

Italian
Indigo Children

Hebrew
Kryon Books - One, Two, Three

Hebrew
Kryon Books - The Parables of Kryon, The Journey Home, Books Six, Seven, Eight, Nine, and The Indigo Children

Hebrew
Indigo Celebration

Italian
Kryon Parables, Book One, & Book Two (not shown)

Finnish
Book One, Two, Three, & Indigo Children

Turkish
Kryon Books - One, Two, Three, Six, Seven, Eight, and Nine

Turkish
Kryon Parables, The Journey Home, and The Indigo Children

Greek
Kryon Books - Six, Seven, Eight, and Parables of Kryon

Slovene
Indigo Children

Greek
Book Six
(coming)

Greek
Books Seven and Eight
(coming)

Greek
Parables
(coming)

Slovene
Indigo Children
(coming)

Last-minute additions:
Estonian - Kryon Books One and Two

88 International Kryon Books
See [www.kryon.com] for more info

French
Kryon Books - One, Two, Three, The Journey Home, Kryon Book Six, Seven, and Eight

French
Kryon Book Nine and The Indigo Children and Indigo Celebration

Japanese
Kryon Book One & The Indigo

Russian
Indigo Children & Kryon Book

Hungarian
Kryon Books - One, Two, & The Indigo Children (8 & 9 coming)

Bulgarian
Books One & Two

German
Kryon Books - One, Two, Three, The Journey Home, and The Parables of Kryon and Kryon Book Six and Kryon Book Seven

German
Kryon Book Eight and The Indigo Children, and Indigo Celebration

Greek
Kryon Books - One, Two, Three, and Five (The Journey Home)

Danish
Kryon Book One

Chinese
Kryon Books - One, Two and Three (coming)

Dutch
Journey Home - Parables of Kryon - Indigo Children

In Loving Memory

In 2003 and 2004 we lost two great friends.
They were both healers and Human spiritual
guides. We miss them greatly.

Roger LaChance

Roger and his wife, Karen, developed The LaChance
Method—a type of healing used to this day by many
healers. It's a fast release of old patterns, allowing a
person to move on and heal themselves. Roger and
Karen presented with the Kryon team on many occasions in the early days of presenting Kryon with large
seminars around the United States.
Roger's laugh was unmistakable!

Halé Makua

Makua (as he was called), was a Hawaiian spiritual
leader, Indigenous Grandfather, wise man, and
mentor to us all. Many who took the Kryon Hawaiian
Cruise of 2003 will remember his loving and caring
personality as he introduced us to his ancestors on
the rim of the volcano crater on his beloved big island of Hawaii. Now he joins this group of Lemurians.
Makua, we will never forget you!

Dedicated to

Luise Hansen

*Our angel
in
Japan*

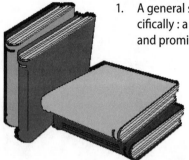

dis·pen·sa·tion - noun
1. A general state or ordering of things; specifically : a system of revealed commands and promises regulating human affairs.

2. A particular arrangement or provision especially of providence or nature.

A NEW DISPENSATION
Plain Talk for Confusing Times
Kryon Book 10

Publisher: The Kryon Writings, Inc.

1155 Camino Del Mar - #422
Del Mar, California 92014
[www.kryon.com]

Kryon books and tapes can be purchased in retail stores, by phone, or on the Internet at [www.kryon.com/store]. (800) 352-6657 - E-mail <kryonbooks@kryon.com>

Written by Lee Carroll
Editing by Jill Kramer
Copyright © 2004—Lee Carroll
Printed in the United States of America
First Edition—First Printing—June 2004

ISBN# 1-888053-14-3 : $14.98

Table of Contents

Table of Contents... continued

From the Writer
"Introduction"
Kryon Book 10

Lee Carroll

Introduction

Introduction
Kryon Book 10
by Lee Carroll

Greetings to the readers of the Kryon series, and also to those who are just beginning the Kryon experience. Okay... I always start that way. What can I do differently this time? This is the tenth Kryon book, and the twelfth book if you also count the two *Indigo Children* books co-written with Jan Tober (my spiritual partner and co-founder of the Kryon work). This is normally the time I greet readers and tell them what's in this book. So, I'll do that right now.

First: If you're one who questions channelling, then why are you looking at this page? Close the book! Don't you know that evil energies will capture you if you read further? After all, haven't you been told that you don't have any control over your spiritual intelligence or logic? Isn't it true that you were born in sin, and there are those "out there" who want your soul? Well, we may not agree with all that, but if that's what you believe, we'll honor it. So we strongly recommend that indeed, don't go further. It's not for you.

We don't have any desire to rip away anyone's faith. We don't have an organization to join, nor are we evangelistic. We don't wish to compete with organized religion, and we respect those who are anchored in their spiritual truth. What you should know about us is that we never ask for money, don't try to create followers, and don't even have a written doctrine. We just give information about our views of the love of God and let it present itself in whatever energy is appropriate. We also believe in channelling, and feel that it's the way in which Humans have *always* been given spiritual information, and yes... I was being facetious in the last paragraph. Our biggest spiritual truth is that God might be much bigger than we were all told. I believe that Humans are smart and should be able to weigh what they've been told against the real experiences that we're all having on this planet.

Second: If you're new to channelling and wish to know more about what we represent, you can read what we have to say about this completely and thoroughly in Kryon Book Seven, *Letters from Home*, Chapter 1, called "The New Age." It's also on our Website [www.kryon.com] under "Site Favorites." It's called, *What are you into?* This information really sums up what we're doing, and how special we feel humanity is at this time. The last Kryon book was released in 2002 and contained specific channellings from the previous two years. This book contains selected live channellings given since Kryon Book Nine. The time frame is from August 2002 through December 2003, with selected questions (last chapter) through March 2004.

Third: If you're a Kryon reader, thank you! You know what to expect. There is new and profound information in these pages, and also a very loving feeling to all of it, which is what we're all used to after 15 years of this Kryon experience. If this is your first Kryon book, it won't matter that you didn't read the others... there's something here for you!

However, perhaps this book might stimulate you to find the first nine Kryon books. If so, go backwards a book at a time and enjoy the history of the development of energy around humanity and the Kryon channelling. If you want to see how it all started, you can read Kryon Book One, the shortest of all, channelled back in 1989. This is when Kryon outlined what the potentials were of Earth. It now reads like prophecy, where Kryon spoke of much of what's going on today—magnetic shifts, unbalanced world leaders creating chaos, weather changes, and so on. As the books continued, more was validated in physics, biology and now (finally), astronomy. In subsequent books, Kryon spoke of a time when the religious leaders of Earth could no longer "say one thing and do another." This is now literally in our news! Kryon spoke of integrity becoming a "player" of importance on the planet, and now we've seen this in 2003 where Fortune-500 companies have fallen over, and even the FBI was shaken up due to this very issue! Who would have thought that could have happened? In an older energy, these things were just swept away... too much money or power was at stake.

This book covers one of the big questions: *With all this new spiritual energy, why does it look so bad right now?* It also covers more on becoming interdimensional and being able to capture the essence of master-hood and ascension. One of my favorite chapters is the channelling on Self-Worth (Chapter 9), where Kryon gives us the steps to help with this very large issue.

In 2003, Kryon started giving the spiritual attributes of DNA, including some of the names and energies of the interdimensional layers. This isn't the most practical information ever given by Kryon, but many of you who enjoy the esoteric will begin to have validation about what you've always "known" was really there. The difficult part for me was that the DNA layer-names Kryon gave were in Hebrew! This was tough, since I don't have a *Hebrew mouth!* I have a *Southern California mouth.* That means I can say things like "beach" and "dude" okay, but Hebrew words are really strange to me. So I got help.

One of the most fun things that has happened in the last four years is that when we visited Israel in 2000, our host, Ilan Vainer-Cohen, met and married Shana, the daughter of Peggy Phoenix Dubro, who was presenting with us. Peggy is the creator and steward of the EMF Balancing Technique,®which we support. Her work is now worldwide in almost 50 countries. You can find a 1999 article on her technique in Kryon Book Seven (*Letters from Home*), page 374.

Ilan came to America and now lives in New England. He has become my "Hebrew expert," since Hebrew is his first language. One of the things we noticed right away when we started publishing the DNA channellings on our Website was that we got letters from many wonderful Israeli Lightworkers trying to help us with the DNA layer spellings in Hebrew. It was very helpful, except that each had a different spelling to offer! So we've addressed this Hebrew spelling issue as an Appendix within this book, telling why we ended up spelling things the way we did, and also giving the Hebrew letters involved in each DNA name-phrase. When Kryon finishes with all 12 layers, I feel another book coming (maybe).

Policy: One of the things we decided about a year ago was to publish all of the current major channellings of Kryon on our Website. In the past, we only did a few, encouraging people to get a Kryon book or find the *Sedona Journal of Emergence* magazine, where the Kryon channellings are published each month. You see, the major content of all the Kryon books *are* these channellings, and by publishing them on the Web, we thought we might spoil the sales of subsequent books. Our decision to do it anyway is a statement that says that "book sales are secondary to getting the information out quickly." So the result is that what you're holding in your hand is a compilation of much of what has already been on our Website!

Many reminded us that Websites are temporary, but books can last a very long time (unless you have a dog). So it made us feel better about doing it all differently. Also, for those who printed all the channellings from the Kryon Website and have them in a binder somewhere... this book is much easier to take in the car, right? Just think, you also get the index, and the dog will find it harder to tear out the pages [smile]. I think that my friends are correct: Books just have a "feel" about them that no Website will ever capture. In addition, the other languages that will have this book don't have a Website.

Lee Carroll, Up-Close and Personal

I thought it would be interesting to some of you if I got more personal within the Introduction of this milestone book. I'm just like you. I've had my joys and my disappointments in the last two years. Also, some interesting and fun things have happened over the years within the Kryon work that I'd like to now share. So perhaps it's time to tell you more than I have in the past as the author/channel. I'll let you in on some things that irritate me, and some things that make me smile.

Disappointments:

War: I detest war, and everything that comes with it. That's just a statement, and not an indication of any of my political preferences. Sometimes war is the only way, and sometimes it isn't, but when it occurs, it's a tragedy no matter what the justifications. There are broken hearts and bodies, and lives that are impacted forever. So these are difficult times for me or anyone else to be going out into the world with a positive message. Kryon told me it would be this way, however, and warned me long ago to expect challenges on the planet. He has spoken for over a decade about a very real battle between the old and new energy. I think we're in the midst of it.

Loss of friends: Kryon also told me to expect betrayal and the loss of friends. From the mail I get, I'm not alone! This has indeed happened to many, and from unexpected corners. Some years ago Kryon indicated that there would be a time when humanity would be forced to "get off the fence" with respect to what they really felt. Many have, and within the process, I, and others around me, have lost friends. Take a look around. The U.S., as well as the world, has probably never been as polarized as it is now about so many issues... not in my lifetime, anyway. Kryon even gave us some of the reasons why this might be, and you can find it very well explained in chapter 12 of this book.

Even within our work, a few former Kryon supporters did an about face. It seems that they had waited and waited over the years for Kryon to do something that never happened: They were steeped in an old energy concept—of a future on the planet that just had to contain fear, conspiracy, and the instructions from Kryon on how to organize into groups to fight it. Kryon never gave that information, and since the message they expected wasn't forthcoming, they began to believe that my work wasn't accurate.

So even though the much-prophecied Armageddon didn't happen, and whereas the future of Earth—as told by both the Jewish and Christian scriptures—and Nostradamus, didn't happen, somehow the things they carried in their "fear bag" were still supposed to manifest anyway. Kryon also presented a history of Earth that wasn't as dark as they'd been told, either. When the conspiracies weren't taught, and the dark players weren't itemized, and the actual history of the planet that Kryon gave didn't coincide with what they were given in the old energy, there was disappointment that somehow Kryon had "tricked us with the light."

In an e-mail exchange, a so-called special galactic group felt strongly that I was masquerading, and that I wasn't channelling Kryon. They wrote to warn those around me, since these few were allowed to "see" things that the rest of the world could not. Who I was masquerading or why I would do it was never mentioned. Even though I present to very spiritually sophisticated audiences all over the planet—many who come to discern this very thing—this special galactic group was beyond everyone else (according to them), and their specialty was in their discernment abilities.

My take on this is that their specialty is fear and conspiratorial consciousness. I openly stand on stages all over the Earth and let everyone see and discern. But almost without exception, those who would discredit my integrity are in selective dark corners, out of the eye of the general public. They pop into Internet chat rooms, or send e-mails, then they disappear.

So for some, Kryon (or Lee Carroll) simply becomes one more dark entity to fear on their growing list of conspiracies. In all cases, I bless them and send them on their way, but I'm sad, knowing that by hanging on to the drama, they'll go to their graves looking over their shoulders, waiting for this or that to "get them," not understanding that it already has! What a waste of Human resources (my opinion). Their energy could have been used so much better by sending light to those in the dark, rather than hovering in the dark and hunting for dark things. Humanity has changed the actual history of this planet, and with it, we have changed the past... all of it. Now that's drama!

Fakes: The Kryon work is now published in 18 languages representing more than 100 actual separate Kryon books. We also draw large crowds when we travel to some of these worldwide areas. The crowds are there to feel the energy, and to glean new information.

I guess I shouldn't be surprised, but I'm disappointed with those in certain countries who have taken the Kryon name, (there is no law against this) and who are frightening people with fear-based information! So if you're one of those in another country pretending to channel, and are reading this, I hope that my frankness doesn't startle you, but this book *will* be translated into your language, and people should know the truth.

Anyone can channel Kryon, and the invitation is open. It's not an exclusive club, and God isn't proprietary. However, a "real" Kryon channel—and there are many valid ones all over the earth—will have the same attributes of love and integrity that people have seen exemplified for 15 years in these books. We set the standard for the behavior and energy of this loving angel (Kryon) for all to see, yet there are those who hope people on a different continent don't find it. Even if they do, it's in English... a different language for them.

So these fakes feel safe at such a distance, and have jumped on the Kryon-name popularity wagon and have decided to be a guru, or collect large amounts of money and scare people by saying they must go this way or that... paying for this lesson and that lesson... in order to be "clear." One group has even mounted a campaign to "beware of the dangerous Indigo Children!" (Country to go unmentioned). It sounds absolutely silly to most of us, but not to the police in those countries! The unfortunate part of this scenario is that when these fakes get in trouble for their obvious scams (and they eventually do), the Kryon name is right there with them for their governments to see.

If you're one of the many who have wondered if some of these other Kryon channels are real, don't write and ask me. We're not the authorities on this—*you are*! Not only do you have the power of discernment to "feel" if it's true, but you also have thousands of pages of Kryon writings for comparison. The Kryon messages have been coming since 1989. They contain no conflicting information, and have a loving energy that's unmistakable and very consistent.

Kryon never asks us to do anything but find our spiritual core and enable ourselves. So, use these resources, including your own spiritual power, and get an internal answer that will be from your own spiritual core. Don't ever depend on any other Human to tell you what is, or what is not, spiritually true. This includes the material in this book.

Dumb things that people love to believe: Okay, I know that even includes Kryon in some circles, but I'm talking about real bad science that's taken as spiritual fact, frightening thousands of people. Remember Planet X? It was supposed to hit us in May 2003. The author of a popular book about it was featured on the Art Bell show many times in less than one year! (Let's hear it for doom and gloom!) His interviews made it sound like the event was a certainty. Supposedly there were many scientists who agreed, the Vatican knew about it but was keeping it a secret, and even NASA was supposed to be "in on it." Dozens of Websites were created around it, satellites were supposedly observing it, and many were very concerned. We got lots of letters.

Well, it didn't happen. (Surprise!) There was no event, and nothing, not even a big rock, "sneaked out from behind the sun" at velocities that were impossible (if you did the math) and got us! The sad part about this little circus is that anyone who did an once of research on this subject knew that Zecharia Sitchin (author of *The Twelfth Planet*, and discoverer of the *Berlin Seal*) didn't think so either, and he was the quoted source! He knew that the ancient Sumerian calendar he had discovered was base 6. So if there is a Planet X, we have about 3,000 years to go before it returns.

Please forgive me a harsh opinion, but I feel that The Art Bell show is often one of the worst sources of real information that exists today, often doing a horrible injustice to those on the planet who are trying their best to send light to dark places and create peace on Earth. There are occasional notable exceptions, and I'll give him that, but most of the interviews are dark and fear-based. After all, that sells soap.

Even now, there are psychics with more demonic "end of the world" information, being interviewed often. So I ask you readers... how many times do we have to void the end of the world before we believe we're actually changing the earth's future? So far we've done it twice... perhaps even more when you take into consideration all the things the Art Bell show has brought us. Isn't it time for some spiritual logic?

The death of friends: Although not an actual death, many metaphysical publishing people mourned the demise of *Book-people* in Oakland, California, in 2004. This company was a major New Age book distributor, and had distributed the Kryon books since Book One. They bowed out gracefully and with integrity, but under circumstances that were unfortunate. They represented a team which we came to depend on for publishing expertise and help. Thank you, Bookpeople, for all the years of great service!

No matter how much Kryon speaks about how death isn't really the end, it's still painful and sad for the Humans left to live out their lives without that specific person. This year we lost *Roger LaChance*, healer and Lightworker. Roger and his wife, Karen, presented seminars with us many times in the early days of Kryon, and his death was a shock. So Roger, we know you're here, but we miss your large physical body and your large laugh.

Our hearts go out to Karen, who's working through a new life without him.

We also lost *Halé (Harry) Makua*, our spiritual leader on the big island of Hawaii. Makua was an Indigenous Grandfather, mentor, and wise man for so many of us! He was pure Hawaiian, but included us all in his lineage of Lemurian ancestors. We will never forget this man, and how he taught us love, patience, and understanding. Makua, we miss you!

Let our sorrows for these men be transmuted to wisdom, and our loneliness be manifested into truth. We don't understand the timing of death on Earth, but we understand the love of God that allows us to have peace with these things.

Joys:

My joys are my friends! This is always first. So I have a lot more joys than disappointments. I can't list them all (of course), but the ones who have made such a difference in these last years are those who have meant so much to Jan Tober and myself through our growing years, right up to the present. I know it's dangerous to list just a few, since I may accidentally be leaving out some that I didn't think of, but there are some that need to be thanked publicly for perhaps the first time. I know that Jan has her own list, too, but many of those on the next three pages are included, also. (I won't list business partners or my family or pets... that's too obvious.)

Okay? So this is where we thank our friends. Most of you readers may wish to skip right to the good parts, but why don't you pause anyway and read these names just once? They really are the ones who help "make" the Kryon work what it is.

Thanks! We wish to honor the Kryon team: *Dr. Todd Ovokaitys, Peggy Phoenix Dubro, Robert Coxon,* and *Maria*

George. These folks have been with me all over the world and continue to be my friends on or off the road. You can read all about who they are in the *Kryon Family* section of the Kryon Website.

We also wish to honor those who are "out there" channelling and making a difference in the world, whom I consider to be good, lasting friends. *Steve and Barbara Rother* (Planet Lightworker), *Ronna Herman* (Archangel Michael channel), *Fred Sterling* (Kirael—The Great Shift) to name just a few. We don't compete with each other. In fact, we have the same message and have even channelled side-by-side on occasions. We honor *Melody O'Ryin Swanson,* editor of the *Sedona Journal of Emergence,* for her continuing support of the Kryon work, and her great efforts for years in publishing one of the only New Age magazine sources of its kind on Earth!

We honor those who work within the periphery of my publishing: *Joe Moriarty* and *Morgan Ki'ilehua* of Awakenings Bookstore in Laguna Hills. These folks are the people you talk to when you purchase a Kryon book by calling our 800 number. They also have represented the home-room of Kryon in Southern California for 10 years. We honor *Kimberly Lockwood,* our e-mail specialist, who plows through hundreds of e-mails about specific body-part enlargements, 4 percent mortgage rates, porn sites, and Viagra ads to find the real e-mails from people like you. Also *Connie Okelberry,* who's the e-mail contact for active pages on two of our Websites, plus she's a regular helper on seminars and cruises, too. *Emily Green, Sharyl Jackson,* and *Bonnie Capelle,* thank you for your friendship! We also thank our office helpers of many years, *Valerie Alean* and *Cookie Perrin.*

We honor and thank *Barbara and Rob Harris* for the great graphics and planning they continually provide for our Website,

E-magazine, and all our Kryon seminar flyers over the years. We also thank them for giving so much away of their fine talents to the Kryon work.

We honor *Drs. Sid and Amber Wolf* for their great work on our new, yearly *Journey Home Experience* retreats, given on a mountaintops in beautiful places. Jan and I honor *Sandie Sedgbeer* for starting a national magazine called *Children of the New Earth*, which includes resources for parents and teachers on the Indigo Children, Crystal Children, and others.

We honor our French-language sponsors, publishers, and good friends *Marc and Martine Vallée*, who have been with us since the very beginning of the Kryon work and who took us to Europe for the first time years ago. We also wish to give a nod to our German and Swiss connections, *Jürgen Lipp*, *Konrad Halbig*, *Steve and Petra Ostergaard*, and *Elisabeth Conrad*, who, by the end of 2004, will have helped bring Kryon to German-language audiences over six times within three years. Some of them have also published all the Kryon books in the German language (plus other Kryon material only available in Germany). We honor *Louise Hay* for letting us be part of the "Hay House" family, and we honor *Barbra Dillenger* and *Michael MaKay*, names you may have heard before from the very first Kryon book, for their encouragement in the very beginning, and the ones we feature on each Kryon cruise every year. We also honor *Luise Hansen*, *Joanie Jiannine* and *Janie Emerson* for their financial support when we have needed it, to print more books just like this one!

We wish to thank the Kryon hosts who have been with us for many years, organized Kryon seminars more than seven or eight times, and in some cases were the very first to do a Kryon meeting in their area. Names like *Gary and Jan Liljegren* (also

Web managers for Kryon), *Les Mound, Terri and Jim Coddington, Rebecca Evans, Geoff and Linda Hoppe* (promoters and meeting planners for Kryon for seven years) *Beth Iris, Ruth Dingwall, Trisha and Winston Ellis, Sandi Malagara, Ryan Maluski,* and *Virginia Slayton.* You other hosts know who you are, too... including the Kryon hosts of all the many "Kryon At Home" events (up to 50 a year organized by my wife, Patricia). Thank you!

We honor my editor of many years, *Jill Kramer,* who pores over words like other people vacuum floors! She's looking for every single thing that will make me look better. See, if you only knew how I really writed... wroted? Oh well. She is also careful to keep the editing correct on the channelled work, and knows all about the energy of Kryon. Editing is different for a live presentation, and Jill keeps it fresh and meaningful, sometimes leaving strange syntax alone, as part of the "Kryon experience."

Thanks also to *Mary Ellen* and *Len Delekta,* our Hawaiian-based cruise specialists, for delivering four wonderful Kryon Cruise events over the years, and working so hard on the one coming up (as I write this book) to the Greek Isles. Coordinating lots of people from thousands of miles away to one point, and then delivering them to a ship for a week is an amazing feat! (Not to be confused with amazing feet, which is a Hobbitt thing.)

We also wish to publicly thank *Zehra Boccia* again, for not only taking us to the United Nations in 1995, '96, and '98, but helping to stabilize the spiritual situation within the Society for Enlightenment and Transformation, and allowing for a 2004 invitation for Kryon to return! Someday, if you look up "warrior of the light" in a new-energy resource, you'll find her picture there!

Finally, there are good friends whom I personally just hang out with, and we throw food at each other. Some of those, I've already listed, but I wish to also honor *Russ and Lee LaHoud*, and *Karen Wolfer and Fred Ashman*, for their undying support.

Okay, if your name isn't here, yet you're a key player in my life, you've worked for the organization for years, or live in my house... what can I say? Like the famous line of comedian Steve Martin goes: "I forgot!"

Recognition! The New Age got noticed in 2003. The Vatican did a full report on it!* Here is perhaps the largest church on Earth doing a report on the New Age... a spiritual affiliation that isn't an organization, has no leader, no power, no prophet or main book, no membership, schools, pastors or priests, and no money! So why did the Vatican do a report on it?

The consensus is that we are indeed not only getting noticed, but actually gaining tremendously in popularity. How does a non-organization do this? The only reason we can think of is the principle that "truth seeks its highest level." Without any organized effort at all (impossible if there's no center), the New Age movement has gained such momentum that it's actually affecting some of the largest religions on Earth.

It's due to a combination of things, but among them is the disappointment in churches (not God), and a growing feeling that there might me "more than what they were told." So it includes many who are seeking something else, and may not actually call themselves New Age. To us, it doesn't matter, since we have no membership rolls or money to collect. But it's an indictment on those who would place God in a box, and tell people that it's the only box. Those who embrace the New Age don't embrace a doctrine of spirituality. Instead, they embrace the *"freedom to understand and study a God that may be bigger*

* The Vatican report on the New Age can be read in its entirely within the pages of the Sedona Journal of Emergence, March issue, 2003.

than they previously thought," and perhaps a plan of life on Earth that is grander and more profound than they were ever told. I think the beauty in all of this is that the love of God, which they found in their organized spiritual experiences, never changes, and they simply seek to expand it.

The Vatican would never have spent the resources on such a report if we were invisible. Some have indicated that priests all over the world are being asked about things like heaven, hell, the devil, sin, reincarnation, and meditation. Why? Because the energy of Earth has changed, and millions are starting to feel it. With that, comes an awakening.

Funny or Interesting Things That Happen

As you might imagine, there are myriad experiences that occur when we travel to so many places. Some are boring and some memorable. In France, the most memorable thing was the food. Same thing in the UK for different reasons! In one country (again, to go unmentioned), Jan and I walked for blocks to find a Burger King just so we could "recover" from the food of the area. (That's drastic action!) But there are a few things that I tend to remember about specific meetings, which oftentimes have to do with the technical issues involved in putting on large seminars.

Wireless microphones: I don't like them... never have, but they're needed by speakers who do a lot of walking onstage. I don't travel while I speak. I need to hide behind a lectern or podium so that nobody can tell how much weight I gained since lunch, and the thought of pacing around onstage, well... just too much exercise! I'll leave that for the younger guys like my friend Gregg Braden (who probably walks a couple of miles or so from one end of the stage to the other within a three-hour lecture!).

So part of our list of technical items we give to promoters and auditoriums is that we be supplied with "microphones with wires." We've had two notable situations that I'd like to tell you about, where we didn't get them.

Australia: I think I may have told this story before in another Kryon book, but it deserves to be told again. This story took place a few years ago in Australia when we were visiting a large conference complex under the auspices of our good friends Trisha and Winston Ellis. Jan and I were given wireless microphones, since that's all the conference center had. Wide-eyed, the sound technician reported to me right before the Kryon channelling, that he had just been informed that a famous rock group was rehearsing in a conference area in the same building as ours, and that (gulp) their guitar pickups were on the same frequency as *our* microphones! He apologized, but he couldn't get in to their closed rehearsal to change it, and he couldn't alter our microphone set-ups in time. So we went on anyway.

These are the times when I just have to trust Spirit. Having a raucous guitar solo coming in at full volume on our PA system in the middle of a channelling wasn't what I had in mind for the meditation time, yet it was a looming possibility. I put it out of my mind, and we did the channelling without any problems whatsoever. It was only later that we learned that in the middle of the band's rehearsal, out of their guitar amplifiers came a loud message: *"Greetings, dear ones, I am Kryon of Magnetic Service!"* I can only imagine what they thought! Perhaps band members are writing books right now about the "haunted" complex in some town in Australia!

France: Over the last years, I've realized that for whatever reason, I drain batteries when I channel! This, I've found out, is more common than I thought, and others who give spiritual meetings and healing sessions have reported the same thing.

Okay... it's weird and strange information, right? In addition, it makes me sound like I'm "really important" if I can drain a battery! So it also becomes a message that many might think has an egotistical intent. Like... *"Hey, here comes the weirdo who drains batteries! Yeah, sure."* So I don't tell anyone (except you, of course... shhhhh), and I just deal with it. No big deal. I take off my watch before I channel, and I locate the cassette recorder so it's not on my lap, or touching me. All is well... unless I'm grasping a wireless microphone with a battery or two inside of it! That simply doesn't work.

Lyon, France, 2002, brought up this exact scenario. I had asked the stage people to please give me a microphone with a wire... something that I knew they had. Typical of stage attitudes worldwide, these technicians, who were simply hired for the day, ignored my request and gave me what they wanted to give me, and what just happened to be the easiest... a wireless microphone. My requests for a change were met with the typical "we can't understand your language, look" then they went back stage and discussed (in good English) the funny American who thinks he's magnetic and can drain batteries. I think I actually heard them howling with laughter! This was so recent, that when this book is translated into French, there are many who were there who will remember this scenario, and can attest to what happened next.

A wireless microphone is a radio transmitter. It uses a "carrier" frequency that "carries the audio." This carrier must remain constant, since if it's broken, a very loud boom noise will be heard through the speakers when it's removed. This is exactly what happened. I was holding the microphone in my right hand, and started to channel. About ten minutes into the channelling, the microphone went dead and a loud boom was heard over the speakers (startling everyone in the auditorium).

I had indeed drained the battery contained in the tube-body of the microphone. I sat there and Kryon said nothing. Right away, a stage person came running out onto the stage and changed the battery in full view of the crowd. He handed the microphone back to me and moved off stage. Ten minutes later it happened again! Boom!

This time I sat there for a much longer duration. No stage person... no new battery. Time went on. Then I perceived that something was taking place to my right, and out came the stage man, unwrapping the coiled cord of a microphone with a wire! I almost laughed out loud, but didn't. We proceeded, and finished the day without any additional problems. Afterward, the technicians wouldn't come near me. They didn't seem to be sorry, but instead, they were afraid! Human nature is funny sometimes. So, to most, it was a technical difficulty, but now you know the rest of the story (especially for those who were there).

Canada: We've experienced our share of technical difficulties off the stage as well. On three separate occasions, in three different countries, Jan and I have been evacuated (or we tried to evacuate) from hotels due to fire alarms going off! We still don't know why we should have had such a disproportionate experience with fire alarms, but the experience in Toronto years ago has affected our policy of hotel-floor choices. We now ask to be placed in rooms that are lower than the tenth floor.

In Toronto, we were on the 26th floor. The alarms went off, and everyone scampered into the hallway. We waited, and fire engines showed up outside. (They look real small from 26 floors up.) An announcement came over the loudspeakers, which I'll never forget. Basically it told us that if we were below the tenth floor, to proceed down the staircases. Don't take the elevators. We waited and waited for instructions for those above the tenth floor. Instead, instructions came over the speakers that if you were above a certain floor, to stay put. We did.

Later, the "all clear" was given while we were still in our robes, gathered in the hallway. Then the little fire engines left, and we could go back to sleep as though nothing had happened (yeah, sure). It was only later that we learned that in this hotel their policy was that above a certain floor, there was little hope of escape, and they didn't want to clog the stairwells with too many people coming from the floors above. So basically they were saying, "Stay put... and good luck!" Perhaps only this hotel had this policy? But now we ask for lower floors.

The early days: In the early days of Kryon, we did a meeting in Vancouver, Canada, our first one in that area. I think this has actually happened to many stage personalities and lecturers, but we were about to be initiated into that special group who had to learn the hard way to remember to turn off a wireless lavaliere microphone when you are not onstage. There's a little switch to remember to turn off, on a small black box that you hook to your belt. If a woman doesn't have a belt, then the device goes wherever it can (who knows?) But in the case of Jan Tober, she forgot to turn off her microphone switch and went to the ladies' room. Much swishing and water flowing was heard by the crowd. I'm not going to say anymore. They applauded when she returned.

Interesting people and happenings: There are many reasons for coming to a Kryon event, and many kinds of expectations. Each life-path is different for each Human Being, so some come to be entertained, and some come to be healed. In between those extremes resides the attitudes of the bulk of the attendees, who come for the energy and the information. Overwhelmingly, they arrive with smiles and positive expectations.

In Australia, there was a man who called me in my hotel room after the seminar and wanted a full refund. He felt that Kryon never showed up! In Oregon, a woman told everyone that I had the devil talking to me in my ear as I channelled, and she had a tape to prove it! It turned out that she had a mass-produced Kryon cassette of a channelling where she could faintly hear the "bleed through" from the adjacent audio side... something very common in the high-speed duplication of cassettes. The faint voice she heard was of me channelling on the reverse *side* of the tape. It was playing backwards (of course), and sounded very sinister. Her conclusion was that as I sat there channelling, another entity could be heard whispering to me in *devil language*. [Sigh]

In California, a man traveled from Mexico with many others to attend a small Kryon seminar. He sat through all six hours, then decided he didn't like it (not dark enough—too much joy). He told the others (who he had brought in his car) that they shouldn't like it either! They all agreed (or they wouldn't get a ride home), and they collectively asked for a refund. I think to this day they expected my head to spin around and pea soup to come out... something like that.

I felt bad that they hadn't felt the energy of the day, which I thought was good. But then again, I'm the channel, right? Later on, we got an e-mail from a woman who was at the same gathering who had been healed of a lifelong health issue during the channelling! I got to thinking about it. It's so funny to think of opposite energies taking place between two people within the same meeting, sitting no more than ten feet apart. One was mad and judgmental, and the other was healed. That tells me a lot about the dynamics of the Kryon meetings... that it's the attitude of the people in the seats who drive the energy of what actually happens. Isn't that the Kryon message? We're all enabled to co-create whatever is appropriate in our lives. Some create fear, and others create divine healing.

One time, in the middle of my lecture, a man stood up and delivered a short political speech, then abruptly left. We all listened; I said nothing, and then just went on like nothing had happened. It was very funny, and everyone just "went with it" and nothing was ever said. I think we all knew at some level that the man did something that he needed to, and it was okay. Another time in California, a woman stood up and told us she was Jesus, and wanted to channel (basically, take over the meeting). I refused her, she got mad (Jesus is interesting when he's mad), and we all took a break. Then I started the whole meeting over. Those in attendance felt that my rebuke was appropriate, but I felt bad anyway, since I knew I had offended a person in the middle of a very personal, spiritual moment. These are sometimes the hardest decisions to make... for the one, or the many?

I also remember to this day, one of the first meetings with my now good friend Gary Liljegren. Gary, his wife, Jan, and I went into a restaurant. Gary had to use a cane because he had a knee that had bothered him on and off for several years. It was acting up in a major way, starting about two hours earlier, so the cane was needed. He limped in using the cane.

Gary told me that each time it became a problem, the only remedy was to remain horizontal for 10 to 24 hours. Nothing else worked.

We ate, spoke of spiritual and nonspiritual things, then left. The only thing was that Gary "forgot" that he had a problem with his knee, and when he was outside the restaurant, I asked him, "Did you forget something?" He looked around and realized that the cane was still on the seat where he had put it when he came in. Although he retrieved the cane, he has never used it since, and the leg problem disappeared and has never returned. (This was seven years ago.) What does that tell you? Some people (like the woman who heard the devil in my ear) might say: *"That means that God is in a booth at Waffle House!"*

To me, however, it says that you don't have to go to a meeting or read a book to accomplish the miraculous. It's all inside each of us, just waiting for the moment when we want it to change, anytime, anywhere.

Weather: Speaking of Florida, we were in Orlando some years ago giving a large Kryon seminar meeting. At the end of the day, during the channelling, Kryon was speaking about how some people believe that *"all things come from above."* Suddenly there was a downpour outside the hotel, and water started cascading into the middle of the audience from a leaking ceiling fixture about 15 feet above their heads! Typical of Floridians, they simply moved over and we continued!

That's not the only time we stopped for rain in Florida. Due to an overflow attendance in St. Pierce, Florida, I scheduled a return trip a month or two later. I had no idea it was in their rainy season. (Actually I thought Florida's rainy season was "when the sun was up.") Right at the end of the channelling, it rained so hard that nobody could hear anything! It lasted and lasted and lasted. I couldn't believe how much water was coming from the clouds! Many had to go to the Kryon Website weeks later to read what Kryon had to say that day. It was so loud that even *I* was having trouble hearing what Kryon had to say!

Weather hasn't really played much of a role in our travels. We travel wherever we need to, and the weather seems to cooperate wherever we go. However, it's often the people's reaction to weather (or nonreaction) that has often amused or terrified me.

Canada is one of my favorite places. It's beautiful, pristine, and filled with amazing citizens. When I landed in Nova Scotia during the winter some years ago, my flight was the last one to land, due to a white-out condition that was developing. My Southern California experience with a white-out problem was limited to what happens when the little bottle of white fluid next to the typewriter leaks all over your desk. So I really didn't understand what it meant. Obviously, neither did my Canadian Lightworker driver!

She picked me up and drove right through it! She was talking to me, turning her head to meet my eyes (which were very wide), and was seemingly impervious to the fact that there simply was no road visible! Later I found out that Canadians can all do this. It's kind of a *Canadian thing*—automatic driving in whatever weather! Meanwhile, my *Southern Californian thing* was to scream a lot and pray loudly.

Manifested matter: Speaking again of Canada, we were in Toronto in 2003 for a very unusual Kryon meeting. The six-member Kryon team had been reduced to two! Schedule conflicts and sickness had eliminated everyone but Robert Coxon and myself. So we did the "Robert and Lee show."

Robert Coxon is one of the most amazing New Age recording artists on the planet. Every time we go to Europe, he gets standing ovations, and his music is transcendent. This is the real difference between plain o' music, and music that moves you to anther energy state. If you have Robert's *The Silent Path*, you know what I mean. Every time we can, we try to give Robert a chance to shine by creating either mini-concerts of about 45 minutes, or a full concert lasting up to two hours after an event. There have been some validated healings that have taken place in these moments. It's funny: The Kryon channelling can take place, moving meditations can be given, but there's nothing quite like Spirit-filled music to pull you away from the problems of the world, and allow you to soar into areas you never would go otherwise. We've had deaf ears open, and nerve endings heal up. Again, we don't speak about these things that much, since they're very personal, and we don't want people to expect that coming to these meetings will heal them. Instead, we find that these healings often occur spontaneously when we least expect them.

It was during the mini-concert in Toronto that it happened: A woman who was visiting from India manifested flower petals in her lap during one of the meditation musical selections that Robert was channelling. It was a divine moment, and we quietly celebrated this small miracle of manifestation. In retrospect (and my skeptical evaluation of such things), we all believe that this occurrence was real. The petals were pristine and aromatic... fresh off the flower. None of them were smashed or wrinkled, as they might have been had they traveled and been taken out of a pocket or small bag. They also lasted and lasted and lasted... far longer than normal petals would. We had a nice little "gift" from Spirit that day, and we will remember it for a long time. Thank you, Robert, for your awesome contribution to our work!

The most profound moment: I'm going to finish with something that meant a great deal to me, revealed a lot about Human nature, and was profoundly sad, all at the same time. I'm telling you this since I've wanted to put this into words for some time. It's very personal, but needs to be shared.

I'm not a guru, and I feel that I'm a very average kind of guy. I just happen to also be a channel. To some, this places me in the *lunatic fringe* category... "over the edge and gone!" (Just ask my former friends, who still really don't understand what actually happened to me.) But to others, especially those who come from a different culture, I'm often seen as *close to God!*

I was in France, presenting before a large crowd, and the break for lunch was at hand. During this time I often stay in the dressing room behind the stage, rather than trying to fight the crowd at the sandwich bar. It's a relaxing time, and many times I don't even eat. My host came to me with a message that there was a man from central Africa who desperately needed to see me. I agreed, although it's very unusual for me to meet with anyone in an unscheduled manner. I waited for him to be ushered to the back room by the security people.

Indeed, he was a simple, gentle black man—carrying a dress! He was accompanied by an interpreter (perhaps his brother) who translated from his African language into good French. Then my interpreter translated the French to English. He came into the room, handed me the dress, and immediately prostrated himself and began sobbing and crying out. The interpreters spoke to me as fast as they could, through three language barriers, trying to keep up with his story.

The man had heard about Kryon and was here to ask him to heal his wife. Back in Africa his wife was dying, and he had brought her dress along for me to bless, so that when she put it on, she would be healed. There I stood, holding the dress, and watching him beg on the floor for the life of his wife.

As long as I live, I will remember this moment. Here was a man very much in love with the woman he shared his life with. He was desperate, and also under the impression that somehow I carried the "magic" to make it all better. The four of us stood there while I decided how to handle all this. I felt small and unprepared. I don't have any magic, and was sorry he felt that I did. But what do you say to a person who has come such a long way? I asked him to get up and to understand that Kryon or Lee Carroll does not heal by themselves, but that perhaps all of us together could make a difference. We took the dress and held it up, then we hugged each other in a standing position, pressing the dress between us. We prayed and cried. My heart was in Africa, and I felt his pain.

About six months later I heard that the man's wife had died. I wept. I wanted so much for his trip to be successful. It brings up the big question about the appropriateness of death, and why some are healed and some are not. It exemplifies the fact that we don't know everything, and we can't always second-guess why things are the way they are. All we can do is to "stay the course" and create joy wherever we walk using the love of God... even in the midst of challenge. I heard that the man is doing okay, and is dealing with all of it. Perhaps this event will create a difference in his life that nothing else would have ever done. Perhaps his wife is standing next to him in some way, celebrating his change. But as I said earlier about death, nothing is quite the same in 4-D, is it?

Dear ones, as you read the loving words in this book from the angel-entity we call Kryon, understand that this isn't spooky, weird, and esoteric information just for the elite few. It's about real-life experience and everyday living. It's about life, death, and dealing with the unexpected. It's about a God who knows who we are and what we're going through, since this God sees us as part of the God-family. It's also about a changing and evolving Earth, and about how we all fit into a grand plan that somehow is appropriate for the Universe.

It's also not the first or only time that angels have spoken to Humans. History rings with these occurrences. When it happens in modern days, however, some react negatively and feel it can't be so. Again I'll say that my God didn't go behind a curtain thousands of years ago so that I could only get messages from certain Humans ordained to do so by other Humans. I feel that spiritual information is always updated, and that we're part of God and can communicate.

There will come a day when I present myself to the other side of the veil, looking backwards at everything that used to be Lee Carroll. I will slowly walk away from this life and all its flight schedules and clocks and books to write. I can't remember what it's like on the other side, but I'm told by Kryon that I will then take back my "real name."

Kryon says that part of me will remain on earth to help the ones left behind, and part of me goes to a place where I begin to arrange to come back yet again, leaning against the "wind of birth," as Kryon calls it. It's part of my God-self that is able to split and be many places at the same time. Kryon says we all do that, since we're all part of a complex system that loves the earth, and loves the potentials of what it might be.

I believe that we can create peace on Earth, and I believe that it's going to happen. But it won't be as we watch. It will be as we work the puzzle of life and death, sorrow and joy, and one-by-one, claim the wisdom of the ages that is our legacy. We're being asked to understand the energy of how it works, and to roll up our sleeves and manifest it. So it sounds like we have work to do.

Let's get to it.

Lee Carroll

You sit in a time that no entity, anywhere, predicted. Yet here you are. Almost 13 years ago, we told you of the changes that were your potential. Now you've manifested it. The earth is doing a housecleaning, and it's about integrity and wisdom: what is, and is not, appropriate for the planet. Not for a country, but for individuals... for civilization. You're now deciding the value of humanity—the rules of how it's to be seen and treated. You're making the difficult decisions we told you would never have to be made unless you made the switch to a new reality... and you made that switch.

From the Writer
"Channelling"
A Message from

Lee Carroll

Channelling

Channelling
by Lee Carroll

Despite all the real-world evidence to the contrary, there are many who still believe that channelling is a tool of the devil, an occult experience, and inappropriate in a spiritual setting. This, of course, is information given to us (almost from birth) directly from the oldest and most established religious organizations on the planet.

I believe that the truth is far different, though, and if you've gotten this far in this book, I congratulate you for your open mind. Some say that simply reading material like this is an affront to God! Most of the Christian doctrines of the planet agree (something they don't normally do) that channelling is bad stuff! They also intimate that if you somehow look at these words long enough, your intelligence will slowly be sapped from you, your logic will go down the tubes, and the entities involved in these messages will take you over (sigh).

Channelling, by its basic definition, is actually the way that all scriptures on Earth were written, the Holy Bible among them. Think about it. When you stop to consider who wrote the Bible, you begin to realize that Humans did. When you then further examine how that all came to be, you begin to understand how channelling worked to bring us spiritual energies back then and perhaps continues to fit into ongoing spiritual information today.

After the death of Christ, the man called Saul became the apostle Paul and a follower. After he had his spiritual experience on the road to Damascus with an angel (who some say was Christ), he was a changed man. With his newfound excitement—and while in prison for his beliefs—he then wrote letters to friends in Ephesia, to his friend Timothy, to the Galactians, and Corinthians, among others. He was a highly spiritual man, one who founded many Christian churches and helped guide the doctrine, but when he was writing letters to friends, he probably had no idea that his words would be seen someday as the holy word of God.

Long after Paul's death, his letters were discovered and slowly became scripture. So, you might ask, what was it that made simple letters to friends become holy scripture? The answer is that it was the energy of the words and the profundity of the information, as seen and examined by other Humans of his faith. This is channelling at its best!

About 1,400 years ago, the prophet Muhammad had a similar experience. He received information directly from an angel, and it spawned the nation of Islam, a huge spiritual belief system on the planet today. By the way, before you go to the next thought, I'd like to remind you of the prophet's basic message: unity! On the record is the fact that this great prophet was to unify the tribes of the Arabs and give them one God, the God of Israel! I tell you this to remind you that in only 1,400 years, you get to see what men of power have done to a divine message that you might not be as familiar with as you are with our Western religions.

The Pope, representing more than one billion Catholics on the planet (almost a sixth of the world's population), also channels (but don't tell *him* that). The church authorizes a system where he sits in the "Chair of St. Peter" (a Vatican relic) and gives spiritual information. This information, according to ancient church doctrine, is absolutely infallible at the moment the Pope gives it (not later after processing), and comes directly from God. The process is called *Excathedra* (Latin for "from the chair") and it's the Pope... channelling!

Charismatic Christians have a real-time information system called *Glossolalia*, or "speaking in tongues," whereby one person gives a message in a worship service in a strange language that they don't know, and another will often stand and interpret it. When it's not a show (sometimes it is), these messages are uplifting, and are accepted as messages from God—channelling, once again.

The actual definition of *channelling* is "the word of Spirit (or God) as given to a Human or Humans for their enlightenment and information." In recorded history, it was often given by a messenger-angel who started the conversation with "Fear not." (I always wondered about that until I realized that having an interdimensional creature unexpectedly show up, walking through walls, might be a very frightening experience!) Those two words also carry a larger message: An angel of God will never give you a message of fear. It's often one of liberation, escape, fulfillment, action instructions, or just plain joy! Today's channelling messages haven't changed in this respect, in that they're still often given by an angelic entity who first speaks of the love of God.

If I'm allowed some "plain talk" here, let me speak about something else. First of all, "plain talk" is what normal folks do, and it's not often reflected by politicians, ministers, priests, or anyone else in the public eye. Today's climate of "correct speech" assures that absolutely the fewest people possible will be offended. That also results in a climate where nothing is explained well or gets done, and where honest feelings and opinions are never really known.

So if I offend you, just sit there a moment and breathe... you need to know that my truth is my truth. If your truth is different, know that I respect and honor your intelligence and also your right to voice it, as I do mine. I don't know if that will help, but perhaps your reading experience will be a better one if you know that I'm not presenting my thoughts as anything but thoughts. I'm not evangelistic. This discussion isn't given in order to provide anyone with still another spiritual box that they're supposed to climb into, throwing away everything they believed.

True New Age thought isn't evangelistic. It's a philosophy, not a religion, which explains to some degree why the New Age has no organization, church, or written doctrine. Instead, it encompasses all faiths and invites them to receive updated information, allowing them to potentially become stronger in their spiritual experience because of it. It doesn't tear down anything or become empirical in presenting new sets of spiritual rules. If my discussion ever sounds that way, then forgive me, but I'm excited to share my truth... just like Paul was, except I don't want you do join anything.

***

If there was ever an outcast group within Christianity, it's the *Church of Latter Day Saints* (LDS). Now that's not a negative statement, it's just the truth. Ask any Mormon about this. It's unfortunate, but the LDS church isn't even considered a Christian church in some circles (but it obviously is). Now before you write me another letter (I get lots, so it probably won't make a difference), understand that I'm very familiar with the Mormon faith. My sister's family is Mormon, and I have very good friends who are both active and formerly active members (elders) of the LDS church. Some regularly host me for meetings in Utah.

I refer to this group because the overview of its lineage is actually quite ironic in this discussion. The Mormon church is considered negatively by Christian organizations because its founder, Joseph Smith, had the audacity (I'm being cute here) to actually look around and decide that the Bible was outdated for his culture. The world had changed, he felt, and through his writings, he gave additional information (given by an angel) to extend the Bible (*The Book of Mormon*) and give Humans updated information. Therefore, he's considered (by the LDS church) to be a modern-day prophet. Where did he get his information? He received it from angelic sources (channelling). He was also killed for it and never made it to Utah, yet the church survived and prospered. However, if you told Mormons that Joseph Smith was a channeller, they too might be offended.

It's also interesting that the LDS church is the only Christian doctrine that believes that your soul is "out there" waiting to be born into a spiritual family on Earth. Part of the seemingly odd and unusual ceremonies they do for the dead in their temples is simply an honoring of the family and a spiritual blessing (baptism) of souls they feel are very much still with us, or at least waiting for us somewhere. Although this isn't reincarnation, it gives credibility to a soul that is eternal in both directions (Kryon's way of saying that the soul always was and always will be). Most of the rest of Christianity's doctrine has the soul created (or completed) at birth somehow, then it becomes eternal after you die. (This never made spiritual sense to me, even as a child in Sunday school.)

The past: Here's where Human nature takes over. Every single one of the faiths I've mentioned above considers new spiritual information from outside their own sources to be inappropriate and not permissible. Many have considered this attribute of religion to be a struggle between men for control and power rather than a real article of faith.

The clerics of Islam walk a tightrope as they dispense the prophet's words, too. They'd better not add to it or have original, modern thinking or they'll lose out on their power (or more). Their task is to only reflect or interpret what the prophet taught. Even so, like all the other religions, over time many kinds of Islamic teachings emerged with differing views of what the prophet's words really meant.

In Saudi Arabia, Mohammed ibn Abd Wahhab founded *Wahhabism,* which is still the major (and official) Islamic religion for that country. In Wahhabism, not only can't they add to what the prophet said, but there's no provision for tolerance or any Human rights. If you disagree and are a Muslim, you could be a target for *fatwa* (on a list to be killed). This is all sanctioned by their belief in a prophet who taught unity! Not all Islam is this way, but it's still amazing to many of us raised in the West that so many disciples of a modern religion (less than 1,500 years old) don't recognize the tolerance of God, and at least allow others to have their own faith. Instead, nonbelievers are infidels and therefore deserving of elimination *(jihad)*. All this is to say that here is one huge, modern religion that's absolutely anchored in the past.

Most of the largest religions on Earth want you to adhere to what was said by their originators, and nothing else. It has to come from history to be valid, even if it was just normal spiritual people writing to friends long ago. So new information is not usually allowable, and the prevailing thought is that there's plenty in all the writings of the past to keep you on track in your faith. Here is where I, and many others, depart from that traditional thought.

Does it make spiritual sense that all communication with Spirit (God) stopped more than a thousand years ago, and that we're supposed to believe that God went behind a curtain and stayed there? No more updates? No more messages from angels or prophets? For some reason known only to the highest spiritual leaders, God stopped talking, so we have to search the scriptures for answers to today's situations, or go find a priest or minister to explain it all. Some solve this problem by asking the Holy Spirit to give them answers, but these are only for the moment and do not represent new scriptures or new paradigms.

Our current "situation," by the way, is way past any prophecy in any scripture, anywhere. The Armageddon didn't happen (if you noticed), and even the book The Late Great Planet Earth, a full explanation of the Holy Bible's Book of Revelation referring to current times, is "past its 'sell by' date" (a joke referring to products that spoil), according to an article in Time magazine in July of 2002. In other words, the prophecy didn't happen, so the book that explained it can no longer be considered relevant. We're in a New Age, navigating new spiritual paths with very old spiritual information.

This process of only trusting what "was said," unfortunately, has us searching very old history books, written by the spiritual leaders and prophets of very old cultures, in order to help us with our current-day struggles. And here's the rub: If you truly believe that you can only use past spiritual writings to judge what you're supposed to do today, then you're not going to be very popular! Slavery is still fine (according to the prophet Muhammad), and if you're a Christian, you'll find that it's okay to kill your neighbor if you find him working on the Sabbath (Exodus 35:2), and you can sell your own daughter into slavery (Exodus 21). Also, eating shellfish is an abomination to God (Leviticus 10:10).

See where this is going? In other words, these things that are obviously way out of touch with today's consciousness are soft-peddled in the largest doctrines, promoting a system where you get to "pick and choose" which scripture is relevant and which is not. That alone might indicate that perhaps some are outdated. So, should there be updates? We think so.

So who's qualified? I guess this is another big question. Even if mainstream religion allowed channelling, there would be tremendous argument over who could do it. First, you'd probably have to be dead, and then someone would have to find your writings in a cave. And it would help if the writings were found in an exotic place such as a long-lost library in Tibet instead of an abandoned mine in Arkansas. Again, this is Human nature... to honor only those who are gone who wrote something profound in the past... which was found in a significant place.

There is also the argument that if God is the same yesterday, today, and forever, then sacred writings of the past should carry us through. That sounds logical, since there would be no need for an update. All that's written should be a complete enough explanation of an unchanging God. This is fine for God, but what about us? We change, and our cultures change. Humanity also has a dynamic ability to change the planet's path (according to the Old Testament prophet Isaiah) and when that happens, doesn't it beg the question for new information about our relationship to God? When the prophecies of Revelation didn't happen, did anyone think that perhaps humanity changed something? If so, then what's next? God may stay the same, but we don't. If we were static in our spiritual evolution, never changing and always the same, it might be different.

Some have indicated that the study of their spirituality is the "water of life." If this is so, then most of the planet is drinking from a very old, stagnant well, with no inflow of fresh water.

The channellers of today don't believe the old paradigm of having to be "dead to be read." They also don't believe they're the apostle Paul—or the Pope—either. What many of us believe is that channelling is a blessed, authorized, informal, and personal link between God and humanity. We believe that we receive updated information about a changing earth, ourselves, and about new communications with God. We also believe that it's for everyone, and that anyone can channel. Much channelling is personal, just for the individual.

Also, you don't normally find us trying to create a new Bible (there are exceptions) or new empirical truths for anyone to cling to, throwing away their former beliefs. We don't want to be gurus, start a cult, have followers, be worshiped, or start new churches either. (Again, as in anything involving people, there are noted exceptions.) It's about information that would personally enable another person. It's information without the paradigm of a structured church, given in love for anyone to ponder, consider, and act upon.

The Kryon books are presented in this way, as "loving information to enhance the Human Being." All the books combined try to help explain the relationship of God-to-Human, and not much more. In the process, people get to "see" their spirituality better, make better choices for themselves, and come into a loving partnership with others and the planet. They make better partners in love and in business. They make better parents and teachers, and are more likely to see compromises in difficulty and solutions in drama. They are the ones we often look toward to solve problems between countries, and to avoid war. They are the ones we wish were our politicians! Isn't it nice to meet a balanced person who radiates tolerance and love, yet doesn't spout doctrine at you or want you to sign up for some organization or give them money? It's a person who listens to you and whom you feel safe with. That's what we're talking about.

Perhaps this is just a bit different from the idea of an evil entity who will capture your soul if you're not careful, taking you to dark places. Maybe it's time to update the perception of channelling as something honored as much as going to church. Okay... maybe that's a dream, but hey, I'm one of those who believes in the Human Being's ability to cut through some of the old ways and come out with a better balance of thought. I want to be considered one of those authors who speaks to the smarter parts of people, and not one who talks down to the lowest common denominator (as in advertising or politics). I guess you could say that I believe in humanity and the changes in Human nature that I'm seeing. I'm also an optimist who believes that we're actually built for peace on Earth, and that we're beginning to understand this. Our commercial news reflects the pain of a changing consciousness on Earth—a pruning of an old paradigm and the beginning of another—not the end of everything.

For me, I believe that God is alive and well within the Human spirit... able and willing to have a divine conversation with ordinary Human Beings. My God is not behind a curtain. My God celebrates me as part of the "whole of God," and therefore I'm part of God. My God lives through me every day and creates joy in my life, since I'm part of all creation. Kryon is an angel. He/she gives me information about the planet that's uplifting, current, often validated, and always loving. I appreciate being in a place where I can share the love of God with humanity. I appreciate being in a place where your eyes can meet my words, and a kind of author-reader friendship can be kindled between us as members of the same spiritual family.

Reader, I honor you.

Lee Carroll

"Our commercial news reflects the pain of a changing consciousness on Earth—a pruning of an old paradigm and the beginning of another—not the end of everything.

For me, I believe that God is alive and well within the Human spirit... able and willing to have a divine conversation with ordinary Human Beings. My God is not behind a curtain. My God celebrates me as part of the "whole of God," and therefore I'm part of God. My God lives through me every day and creates joy in my life, since I'm part of all creation."

Lee Carroll

Live Channelling

"Ascension and the Power of Human Consciousness"

Channelled in Philadelphia, Pennsylvania
June 2002

Chapter One

Attributes of Ascension and the Power of Human Consciousness
Philadelphia – June 2002
Chapter One

Greetings, dear ones, I am Kryon of Magnetic Service. Here is a familiar voice that is accompanied by those flowing with me through a crack in the veil. It is a flow from our side of interdimensionality to the side you call four dimensions. This is a voice that brings with it an energy—one that may be confusing to some. It's difficult to explain how such a thing can be. I don't know how many times we've started this message with, "Today we explain the unexplainable." Suffice it to say that out of time and space, this room fills itself with an interdimensional family... some of whom you might even recognize.

If Human consciousness really has power [as was explained in the seminar before the channelling], then can you imagine the power of Human consciousness intermingled with those from my side of the veil who have decided to come in for a few moments and sit with you and surround you?

This evening is already different from the others [speaking of other channelling sessions]. It seems like each time we come before you, there's an enhancement caused from the acceptance—from the understanding—from the core of those who sit in the chairs. Some are beginning to "recognize" family. It's more than just energy, you know. You're starting to recognize the personalities of those who stand around you, pieces and parts of who you've called the guides. Pieces and parts of what we call *you*.

So here you are, dear Human Being, brother and sister. It has been so long since we've seen you! Do you realize that you all have something in common? You have all emanated from where I stand [speaking of Kryon's interdimensional position on the other side of the veil]. There is so much respect on the other side for you who come into this planet! Yet in your reality, you dilute all the things that you are. You do not see your magnificence, and you think of yourself in a singular way. You walk around in a linear reality with no seeming evidence of what's actually taking place at the moment.

So we say to you, let the evidence that this is real be in the emotions that touch you, the pressures that you feel, and the colors that you see during these moments as we explain some things to you.

Did you ever ask why we arrive like this? Why would Spirit have such a process as this? Perhaps you're beginning to understand that regardless of what is said today, and regardless of the teachings that are presented here today, something is going on for you that is completely apart from all of it. Reader, what are you feeling at this moment? Is it a casual read, or do you understand that it's no accident that your eyes are on the page at the same moment that we're saying these words?

There is something happening that is out of the 4D reality that you have here, and I'll tell you what it is: Each one of you has a group around you—a group that you know. You know them as well as you know yourself! You may say, *"Well, there's really not room for that, Kryon"* [speaking of the fact that the crowd is tight with the chairs in the room]. Oh, yes, there is! Into this room pours those whom you've known and lost even in your lifetime. Some of you may smell them! You'll know they're here. They'll touch you if you want. It's all part of the teaching tonight. They must be here for this.

So what do they want? you might ask. *Why are they looking so expectant?* you might ask. It is the intent of one Lightworker who indicates, *"I'm ready"* that suddenly changes everything. Those around you come into your auric energy and you have a party! And in this party, you have a smiling group of entities—more than you can count. These are pieces and parts of a puzzle that you've been asking yourself about all of your life. Is there more than meets the eye? The answer is yes. There's more of you to be discovered. There's more love here than you can see or feel. There is compassion, which creates the energy of solution, stability, and joy. There are answers to questions around you that you've been asking for a long time: *"How can I go through this? What's next? Please, God, I can't do this alone."* We're saying that it was never intended that you do anything alone! Isn't it about time you let us in? Isn't it about time you let the family in? When you do, you create the definition of what we brought you in 1989: It's the definition of *implant*—implanting yourself with the pieces of you that have been standing on the outside patiently waiting for your intent. It's implanting yourself with the pieces and the parts of family that have been standing on the outside longing to come in.

This energy around you has been seen and identified for ages! Many have actually seen it and believe it is angelic energy... guide energy... or perhaps even those from the past. Who ever thought it might be divine parts of you? Who ever thought it might be part of a grand completion [more about that in future channellings]? This energy has been called everything from evil to mysterious, and many have feared it. All along, it has been about love.

Blessed is the Human Being who understands this premise—looking to Spirit through the mechanism of a divine self, for good things. It's about taking your power—a power that does not equate with the word *force*. Instead, it's a power that equates with love. The more powerful you are, sometimes the quieter you are. Did you know that? The more powerful you are, the more you sit with yourself in full awareness that you are a group! That's what we want, dear Human Being... for you to begin to understand that much of your help is from a personality who understands you better than anyone, anywhere... you.

You sit in a time that no entity, anywhere, predicted. Yet here you are. Almost 13 years ago, we told you of the changes that were your potential. Now you've manifested it. The earth is doing a housecleaning, and it's about integrity and wisdom: what is, and is not, appropriate for the planet. Not for a country, but for individuals... for civilization. You're now deciding the value of humanity—the rules of how it's to be seen and treated. You're making the difficult decisions we told you would never have to be made unless you made the switch to a new reality... and you made that switch.

You're on another track now... firmly. You have to identify and define *civilization*. What is the appropriateness of one helping another? How far does it go? What should you demand from your leaders in government, business, and religion? Seen any changes in these areas lately? Have you equated it with what we told you two years ago? We indicated that your highest institutions would have to reevaluate themselves and restructure because of integrity reasons. We told you that they would break apart due to a new energy of integrity. We told you that gone were the days when your spiritual leaders could claim the love of God, yet not live it. Now you sit in this very energy. How many of you remember that this was what we said?

In addition, now you know all about the power of Human consciousness [speaking of the scientific validation that was presented at the seminar]. When you sit in a group and visualize peace for another area, do some of you walk away thinking, *"I don't know whether that did any good or not?"* I'll tell you what you're doing, Human Being. You're visualizing light in places that are dark. There is spiritual integrity in this! Visualize light in places that are dark, and leave it to Spirit to do the rest. As you visualize light in the dark places, it provides a better view for Human Beings who are struggling to find answers and solutions in those places. Because of you, they're able to see better. There you are, sitting in a remote place—without any specific answers—without any specific solutions, ready to help. Take the piece of divinity that you are, and project light into their area so they can use their own free choice while sitting in a place that has more light. And that's the process. Blessed is the Human Being who understands how this works... that the power of Human consciousness works! It works from anyplace to anyplace. Do you have any concept of how interdimensional this energy is? You can't see it work, so you often don't believe it. Yet it is so, more today than at any other time in Human history.

Knowing this, how would you like to project your light today to the darkest places on the planet? How about the Oval Office? Let me tell you something: There is family there, too—a family that, inside their divine part, is saying, *"We can use all that you can send!"* The willingness is there to receive light. Another place: Send it into the heart of Africa. See smiling faces of those cured of disease. See families united, knowing that they'll live a long time. Do you understand what we're saying? All over this planet, humanity is coming to the realization that completion is the energy at hand. Final solutions that really work are needed. In the Middle East, they long for it. There is the feeling that "this is it." Whatever happens next must create a lasting and wise solution to thousand-year-old problems [more on this solution energy is coming in future channellings].

Meanwhile, here you are, going through a process you've called "ascension." Here is the definition of *ascension*: a new spiritual overlay that's so profoundly different from the energy you were born into this planet with, that it feels like, and often is, another life. Ascension is moving into the next life without dying. You don't "go" anywhere. You stay right where you are [speaking of Earth]. However, everything else changes around you. Your passions change—who you are changes. The dimensional reality that your DNA works within, changes. It changes so much that some of you even look different! Many will measure their entire lives as "before and after" this change, being very aware of who they are now, compared to who they were before.

The ascended Human is willing to take on the new interdimensional energies and the new powers—willing to take the gifts of Spirit—willing to do the work. Now, finally, you may understand what we mean when we say, "warriors of the light." The word *warrior* indicates a battle, does it not? We told you the battle was in front of you, and now you are in it. The battle is not between Human and Human, but is instead a battle between old and new consciousness. Both have power, but yours, my dear Human Being, is the only one that has the light of love connected to it. The more of you who decide to use it, the quicker the solutions will be found.

Let me tell you about ascension: There are still so many misunderstandings about what it is and what you are able to do with it. The last time we sat together, the question was asked, *"How many steps are there to ascension?"* I gave the answer: "One." The one step is the intent to start the process with purity. It's the intent of your "God-self" that says, *"I'm ready. I give intent to know more than I know. I give intent to sit quietly and let Spirit tell me what I need to know—without pretense—without ego—without agenda."* That's the one beginning step, and that's the only one. From there on, we call it ascension because you literally vibrate higher. Your biology and all that you feel is you, ascends in vibration.

There will come a day, dear Human, when your science will actually be able to measure the choir in your cells. We have spoken of this before within a biological and scientific channelling setting. Now we're going to mention it in an ascension setting. There will come a time when scientists can measure that choir in the cells, and they'll find out that those of you who are "youthing" and those of you who know about the core of Spirit inside have cells who are "singing" a different tune than others... a tune with a much higher vibration. The vibration is the metaphor of music—a higher note. So when you hear the phrase "vibrating higher," we are now telling you that it's not necessarily always metaphoric.

Here are some questions, concepts, and things you need to know about the subject of ascension. Some of them have never been broached before, but all of them have been asked. In addition to ascension, I'll also give you some information about enlightenment in general... and even about the way some things work that we haven't discussed before.

Emotional Habits

"Dear Spirit," you might say, *"I have some emotional habits I cannot get rid of. I split my time between certain kinds of things that I know intuitively are not right, since they are out of balance and I indulge them with excess. Emotionally, they lay upon me. I think about these things all the time, yet I want the ascension status. I want all that Spirit has for me. My habits don't seem to*

hurt anyone else, but they consume me. I've been told by some that I can never vibrate higher and also keep these excessive habits. What about it?"

I want you to listen carefully, for you're going to hear this over and over: God, Spirit, your family—are not in a vacuum considering these things. You think we don't know? We stand next to you wherever you go. We know of your trials, and we know of your habits. There is no judgment from any of us. You are the one directing the path... the one in charge of your own energy. All we see is a split of energy, by your own choice. This choice of yours is absolute.

If you've chosen to make these things part of your life, then you've decided to segment your time, spending only so much time with spiritual things and so much time on the other things of your choice. There's no judgment! You're a child of Spirit, loved as much as anyone on this planet, and you'll choose on your own how much of your time to dedicate to your ascension passion and how much to the emotional baggage that you choose to have. And that's the truth. You're all honored, each one.

The segment of effort and time that you dedicate to your ascension work, we will enhance as you're able to work it. We stand ready to fill the glass to whatever degree you allow.

"You mean I can start the process anyway?" you might ask? Yes. *"You mean there's no judgment around me?"* Yes. In this situation, you're not serving two masters, as some have told you. You're instead admitting that you wish to start a process... one that will proceed at your own pace. You're in charge of your cells and your body, and you may choose to divide it with an energy that belongs specifically to you. And in the process, dear one, the solution to your balance will be enhanced. Don't be surprised if those things that seemed out of balance become easier to deal with and solve.

Substance Abuse

Others go to the next step. They say, *"Kryon, I've got something even worse. I have substance abuse. I'm addicted to substances, and I'm aware of it. I'm aware of what it's doing to my body, but I have a very difficult time stopping. There have been those who have told me the two don't mix. I cannot choose a spiritual path and then go and abuse my body at the same time. What about that?"*

Oh, a very good question! Are you listening? There's a family around you that loves you unconditionally and eternally. They're supporting you—everything you do and everything you want to do. If you openly choose to abuse your own cellular structure with substances that are harmful, there's no judgment. You're the boss of your cells. They see this, however, as your telling your cellular structure that you're not going to be here as long as you might be. There's no judgment in this. It's literal and honored.

Some of you have wondered why you feel like you have an accelerated life... where time is sped up for you. I'll tell you why. It's often because Spirit looks at you and says, *"We couldn't help but notice that you've chosen not to live as long. So we're going to accelerate some spiritual things so that you'll get them done more quickly!"* This may explain some things that you never knew before. There's no judgment around what you do to your own body.

At the same time, however, we tell you this. Those things that you feel you have no control over, which your cells call out to have, and that you feel addicted to, can change! When you start the process of vibrating higher, the cells know it. There's a process that we're going to discuss soon [later this year] within your DNA that responds to these new interdimensional gifts. This process changes your cellular structure. You can drop habits you never thought you could drop. This is the new power of the cells we speak of. You are the boss of you. This new power is your consciousness finally talking to your cellular structure, taking charge and becoming part of you. Why do you question this, when the yogis showed it to you in 4D?

Dear ones, we need to say this again: How many of you sit in fear of your body? You've been told in the old energy that you can't control anything. Instead you sit and worry, hoping that the things called cells will behave themselves. You hope they won't allow a disease. You hope they don't grow inappropriately into a cancer. It's as though you had nothing whatsoever to say about it! Who taught you that? I tell you that this is an old energy concept. You actually have control over all of them! The process needs to be relearned, and with the new grid alignment, this invitation lies before you. It's time to talk to the cells! It's time to have a meeting.

Forgiveness

"Dear Spirit, I have areas in my life where I cannot forgive. I know the process, and I read the books. I've listened to your messages. You talked about forgiveness and compassion being the catalysts for enlightenment. I have areas where I'm having trouble forgiving others. These things stick with me, and I honestly want to take them away, but it's very hard. How 'clean' do I have to be in this area to start the process of ascension?"

Oh, Human, if you only knew about those who "stand on the outside." Some of those entities that surround you have your name on them! They have your face on them. This is hard to describe for you. How can I talk about the divine you... with you? You feature a linearity where there's only one you. How can I speak about that? Can you visualize part of you that's missing, wishing to come in? All the while, the singular, biological you beats itself up with doubt, saying, *"I'm not ready."* There's no limit to the love of Spirit. Why don't you see yourself as pure? Start the process and watch what happens to the forgiveness issue. What we're telling you is that maybe, just maybe, it's time for you to understand that you don't have to be one thing in order to start another. Stop that linear thinking. On the other side of the veil, you don't have to put on your socks before you put on your shoes! You can put them on in any order you wish. I know this is a difficult concept, but it is so! What is your greatest challenge? Is it in your way? No. The interdimensional Human proceeds anyway, knowing that out of linearity, it's gone!

Why don't you just surrender and let it happen? Understand this: There's no judgment about those areas you have. Don't be shocked and surprised if down the line you'll begin the forgiving process in a way that will make you weep with joy. You can't help but do that, because at the cellular level when you start letting Spirit in—peeling that onion of duality—you begin to understand where your power really is. You start to expand the "you with you," and something happens. Some of the hardest things in life drop away as frivolous. Some of the most compassionate things you never thought you'd be aware of start to become important. You begin to fall in love with Spirit. You begin to fall in love with you. You change.

Near-Death Experiences

"Kryon," some have asked, *"I wish to know about 'near-death experiences.' What are they, really? Do you almost die? I even have this question: Do I have to experience one in order to become a Lightworker?"*

I'm about to broach issues that I've never broached before. I'm about to tell you a truth that has not been mentioned before in any of my messages. What you call a near-death experience (NDE) is very different from what you think.

First, there's no such thing as an accidental near-death experience. Humans who have this experience give permission for it before they get here—to have this spiritual experience—one that may or may not (depending on their free choice), change their spiritual lives. With their permission, although they might not remember giving it, they experience an NDE.

Here's another fact: No one who experiences an NDE even gets close to actually dying! Oh, it may seem like it and it may feel like it, but they don't. They don't even leave the planet. I'm going to tell you what happens with an NDE, and it's going to be different from what some of you have heard or have imagined.

An NDE experience is set up by the preconception and energy of the Human who experiences it. Not all Humans have the same story when they "return." I remind you that some have come out of a near-death experience (so-called) to say it was awful. *"I saw hell,"* they might report. *"I'm now very afraid of dying,"* they tell you. Some have said just the opposite. *"I saw heaven; I saw the tunnel; I saw the Light; I felt the love; I saw the family!"* It's all there to "see." It's true. Every shade of energy is there to see, but there are such different reactions! The reason? It's all about what's at the core, or the essence of the individual who is experiencing it. Humans have free choice to choose their own core energy. Is it fear? Is it hope? Is it grand?

I will tell you what an NDE is, and it's spiritually logical: It's when you meet you. Yes, it's often the first part of the death experience, but an NDE just represents the first few seconds of death. You never actually broach the outside of the core energy that you've set up. Real death is very different. At the point of death, the first thing that happens to the Human Being is the marriage of self and remembrance and connection. After you meet yourself—which is a grand experience—one where you're meeting the "God energy," there's an alliance, then a three-day journey. It takes three Earth days before you ever leave Earth. And those days are spent collecting what we can only call—oh, this is so difficult—*information on the cosmic question.*

Listen to me, family member, because we haven't discussed this before. Every single one of you knows what the big issue is—the reason you're here—the reason you disguise yourselves as Humans and walk around on an even playing field called Earth—the reason you're going through what you're going through—the reason you come back and come back and come back. What's it all about? What's going on in the Universe that would create something like this? I'm telling you that not one of you here knows this, yet all of you do. It is the biggest question of all—the one you ask about before you arrive, and the one that you ask about when you exit.

The first thing you do when you have full awareness is to ask, *"How did we do?"* There's a reason why you're here, dear Human Being... a good, logical reason. Blessed are you who take it in faith that there's a loving reason why you're going through what you're going through. For what you're doing is helping trillions of life forms at another place—seemingly another Universe—even another reality. It's not about sacrifice! It is, instead, about work.

Therefore, an NDE is a manifested opportunity to change... something you gave yourself. It isn't about dying at all. It's about the potential of change. Those who come back having had a grand experience have made the choice to find out more about themselves, and they do. Those who come back frightened have made the choice not to seek more. And... need I say, there's no judgment of either. In each case, the Human's energy guided them to the experience they had.

Listen: The next time you think you're alone and suffering and you ask God, *"Why me?"* I have a suggestion. Instead of shouting *"Why me?,"* instead, why don't you feel our spiritual hands around you and our arms around you and the hugs around you? Why don't you take it, in faith, that there's an entourage around you saying, "Hang in there! Vibrate higher. You have no idea how you're helping the rest of us... no idea."

Your earth is called "the only planet of free choice." It is. Oh, are there other planets with life? Of course. We told you this before. You are the only one, however, that's going through this specific test for this specific reason, and the only one populated by what we call "pieces of God." We've hidden you all in an arm of your galaxy where you don't even have the two suns that most of the life planets do. We've indicated this before. It's not in your understanding to know why it normally takes two suns to create life, but someday, when you find the others, they will mostly have two suns! We have also explained how life got to Earth [a channelling last year]. The "free choice" is the choice to select your ascension!

So, many of you stood on-line [metaphorically] with other angels, waiting to get back here for this age. You said, *"I can hardly wait to get back!"* You knew what your potential future was. You were on the train of Armageddon, yet you wanted to come back! Why? Such is the mind of God when you are on the other side of the veil. It seems silly to some of you. Why would I come back? This would have been a good lifetime to skip! [Laughter] But here you are, sitting in the chair anyway.

Oh, powerful shaman—oh, monk—this earth needs you more now than at any time in the history of the Universe. Here you sit, thinking about ascension status. Do you have any idea why we love you so much? It's because you're actually thinking about ascension! It's so different from what you thought you would be doing here right now.

Talking to Loved Ones on the Other Side of the Veil

Some have asked: *"Dear Spirit, is it possible to talk to past loved ones on the other side of the veil?"* I almost didn't bring this subject up, because I can't answer it properly to your satisfaction. All I can give you are scenarios of difficulty. It's a 4D question with multiple-D answers.

You're in a linear reality with four dimensions. When you decide to involve those with the gifts [psychics], to move to the other side of the veil and communicate even briefly, they experience an interdimensionality that you can't understand. It's completely out of linearity. There's no time on the other side of the veil. All things are happening at once. Potentials are intermingled with the past, and, by the way, that's why your intent today can change your past. Did you know that? It has always been that way.

Can you speak to somebody on the other side of the veil? The answer is yes. It's done every day. But those who help you do it, who have the gift, are translators. They're interdimensional translators. They have to try to sort out what they see and feel in a very confusing place, bring it back to you in a very simple place, and present it in a succinct fashion that you'll understand. And they know this.

Let me give you an example of how difficult this is: Let's say that you wish to talk to your grandmother who has passed on, so you involve a translator with the gift. They go over to the other side to find and speak to the entity who used to be your grandmother. When they get there, what do they find? Instead of finding a little old lady called "Grandmother" somewhere in the ethers, they find a multiple-presence—a beautiful, grand, interdimensional one who is experiencing many lives at once—one life that used to be that of your grandmother's. Now, what part of this group are they going to talk to? It would be like finding a huge bowl of soup, where all you wanted to do was talk to the salt! Unfortunately, the salt is mixed in with everything else.

To make things even more complex, what if your grandmother had recently reincarnated as your neighbor's son? Wouldn't it save a lot of trouble to just go and talk to your neighbor's son? [Laughter] You laugh! Indeed, this is how it is. When you go to the other side, you touch only a fragment and a fiber of what used to be a Human Being called "Grandmother." This small inexplicable piece is what is often "brought back" with messages. It's disjointed and sometimes makes no sense. Often there are no validations of it either.

How do you know if it's real? Let me tell you, because real messages will always have a commonality if the translator is actually in touch. Here will be one message to look for: "I love you as I always have. Stay the path and love God." The message won't necessarily be where the treasure is buried! [Laughter] Human Being, it's tough for you to even touch the divinity in your own core, yet you expect so much of these translators that go to the other side of the veil and bring you back messages from beyond. As far as, "Is it possible?" what do you think this communication is?

Better Places on Earth to Be for Ascension and Enlightenment

"Kryon, you've said in the past that there are parts of Earth that are more conducive to enlightenment than other parts. Where are they?"

Yes, indeed there are. Fair or not, the magnetic grid of this planet postures itself with some very interesting phenomena. The grid talks to your cellular structure. Do you wish to know what the magnetic grid is really about? It's not about a language that speaks to the two strands of DNA you can see. Instead, it's about the ones you can't see. It's about your setups—the magnetic imprint from your solar system [astrology sign]—and about the predispositions that you bring in as a blueprint of potential. It's about all of the lives you're living at the same time right now as you pretend to live one. It's about phobias that cannot be explained... all within the 12 interdimensional layers of your DNA. Do you realize that there's no such thing as a "past life"? Go figure that one out! In your interdimensional DNA layers, modulated by the grid system, all your past lives and potential future ones are affecting you all at once... right now! It's active; it vibrates; it's part of you. It's the personal essence inside you that's timeless, but who pretends to be in a linear time frame on Earth in the year 2002. It's a cosmic joke. It's part of the revelation when you step away and remember what it's about. Therefore, the grid affects you greatly—especially the part that prods you to ask, *"Is there more?"*

The question would then be, *"If there are places on Earth that are better, which ones are they?"* Let me give you a generality: It isn't at the equator. There's a "zero point" there... a null. Take a look at the problems there—the consciousness there. Did you ever correlate this?

I'll tell you where the best places are: They are where the magnetic grid is the least effective but that are closer to the poles in very defined regions between enlightenment and imbalance. But you knew that, didn't you? Some of you have even been told by your friends that this phrase defines who you are! [Laughter]

Over 12 years ago, we said, "Go to where it's cold." Go to where it's cool. Go to places where you can still live, but that are closer to the poles. There is a greater chance in the cooler parts of the earth, toward the poles, for you to discover things you cannot find in places that are heavier or neutral, like the equator. The worst places of all to live? In fact, a place where no Human Being can ever live? It's the magnetic pole itself.

Now, remember, it moves, so that place isn't stable. But if you could live in that place, that would be the culmination of where the ley-lines attach and come together; you would find yourselves neutralized to a point at which disease is allowed to attach itself to you. For there would be no defense, and there would be no communication from the grid to the cells in your body. It would be very difficult to meditate, too.

Let me tell you, there will be a correlation someday with those who have made the trek to study certain polar aspects and found themselves in this very energy we speak of... only to have been brought back with a disease. Go check the correlations of how many researchers in those areas have developed the cancers, and you're going to be alarmed. You'll find that it does not correlate at all with the regular norm. The magnetic grid postures your enlightenment. This is our core information, and what we told you originally when the grid entourage arrived. When it moves, it's purposeful and is with your permission. It's part of the "free choice" engine.

We've repostured and repositioned it, and we're almost ready to tie a bow on it. Then we've told you that the grid group leaves at the end of 2002. What we mean by this is that this group is an "Earth-working group" who has focused on the grid for 12 years. We gave you a metaphor about it in the past: of a grid-entourage called "Excalibur." We used your own mythology in this metaphor about a magic sword, an emblem of battle, that could be pulled from a stone only at the right time and right place, by a Human who had the magic. That is you, dear Human Being. You were the ones that did it. It's alchemy—a metaphor not to be lost on any of you. This is what you have done as a Human race.

Listen: In a linear sense, the grid group leaves. But in actuality, that group is only reassigned. It does not go flying through space to some other planet to do something else. This group is here now, and it will always be here, but not as a grid group. Difficult to explain: "The soup will stay, but it will change its flavor and become a different size." It is a metaphor that says, yes... they are leaving. The "I AM" of who they were in the group will leave. But the parts are only leaving their positions of work as they flow into other places of the earth as the new guardians of the canyons. They'll be placed into the rocks and into the volcanoes, and into the places of the earth that need to remain steady, even when the geology says they shouldn't. There are other tasks at hand that we've never described to you. There are many new things in this message today. We will close with one more.

The Appropriateness of Worship

"Dear Spirit," some have asked, *"what is the relevance of worship on Earth? What is the appropriateness of worship? Whom should we worship? Where should we worship?"*

Why don't you try going inside first? Why don't you see if you can honor the core inside, and worship the angel with your face and your name? That's the truth. A grander truth there has never been! What men and women have made of it is what you see on the planet—in all degrees of light and dark—with many names and beliefs. When you are safe with yourself, you can love yourself. When you find God in your own essence, you can carry it to any church or building or temple, and it will always serve you. You can move from organization to organization, and even call yourself this or that, but as long as you are in love with "God in you," you will have a grandness that will shine through.

We're going to do something different. This is where we leave. We've always said that it's difficult to leave. Some of the hardest things we do in this new energy, after we've been accepted and hugged, is to move away and return through the crack in the veil that we came from. Today, however, it's different, for many Humans in this room are becoming interdimensional. Whereas there was a finite group of us who came in through the crack in the veil, not all of us are leaving! How about that? No. Instead, some of us are going home with you!

Reader, listen: Do you feel included? You are. As I give this message, you are seen in the place where you read. You are seen in all of this because it's no accident you picked up this book. Many of you gave permission for this moment, and you said, *"Yes, I wish to know more about these spiritual things. I wish to sit alone and know that I am surrounded by Spirit. I wish to be quiet and let God tell me what it is I need to know. I wish to start a path where for a short time each day, I visualize light in dark places. I wish to combine with others of like mind and send light into those places. I'm beginning to understand the power of Human consciousness. I'm beginning to believe that I am indeed eternal."*

And if that's you, dear one, I hope you have room in your house for the additional energy! Some of us are going to stay with you. Such is the love of God. You are family. I tell you that when I see you next time on my side of things, we will sing your name in light, just like so many who have recently come over en masse... all smiling... all remembering... all reconnecting.

Stay the path. Do the work. Then when you ask the big question, *"How did it go while I was gone?"* I will be able to stand in front of you and give you the good news... of miracles created by angels pretending to be Humans. And that's the truth.

And so it is.

Live Channelling

"And So It Begins"

Channelled in Santa Fe, New Mexico
Sixth Annual
Kryon Summer-Light Conference™
July 2002

Chapter Two

And So It Begins
Santa Fe, New Mexico - July, 2002
Kryon Summer-Light Conference™
Chapter Two

Greetings, dear ones, I am Kryon of Magnetic Service. The room is filled with love. Hearts are wide open, created by this sanctuary made from your own consciousness. You do that, you know? Wherever you sit, you create a sacred space. I know you've heard this before.

Into this place, where there are open hearts, pours a sacred family with open hearts. There's a radiant, beautiful cup of energy, overflowing with love and placed upon this group. All of you gave intent to sit in the chairs this evening, and we're here due to that. Entities that you've met and have not met are here—ones who are specific to the energies of your divinity are here. Entities whom you have known, and loved and lost, are here. The family is here. You have no idea who surrounds you. In the safety of your chair, with a heart that's beginning to prepare for messages, you're also getting ready for the hugs and the hand-holds and the foot washing you know will arrive.

As we've said before, it may give you pause to wonder who came to see whom. Indeed! There are so many of you here, and perhaps you expect something tonight? Perhaps your intuition will provide you with the solutions you came for. We invite you to smell the energies that are here. Some of you will know exactly what I mean. These are aromas that cannot be faked or duplicated—they are those of ones you've loved and lost. If you experience this, consider it a "tap on the shoulder," a "spiritual wink" that says, "Did you know that I am here?"

We're not making this up, dear Human Being. There is a consciousness of invitation in this place. That is not always the case. We have sat before family many times when family denied us access to the heart. When that happens, there is no judgment. But on this day, there is celebration and joy that so many would come with a like mind and sit prepared for messages that need to be heard. And what does that tell us about you? It tells us what we already know—that it is no accident that finds you here today sitting in your chair, or reading these words.

There is one common thing that brings you here together. It is your willingness to listen and be loved by Spirit—to understand fully what is happening on your planet—to take the information and "paste it" upon yourselves so that you will vibrate higher and create light.

Warriors of the light and Lightworkers are names you call yourselves. It's an indication within these very words that you are ready to roll up your sleeves to create something that has never been created before. There are many of you who would say, *"Well, what could Kryon say today that's different from yesterday or the day before?"* It has been more than a decade that you have continued to allow such a thing as this—for my partner [Lee] to come before you in large groups and small, to speak to open hearts. Some of you feel a presence of Spirit and know absolutely that this experience is real, that this thing called channelling is real. So to the degree that you will allow us in today, the results will be proportional to the energy that you allow to flow into you—all with your permission—all by choice—each one unique within your own intent. And yes... it will be a different message.

We speak of things this afternoon that are planetary and personal. It is the way of Kryon. We speak of things that you need to know. We have instructions; we have predictions and potentials, and we have information. And so it begins, for we're ready, and we're positioned in this place. There will be no more added or subtracted within the next few moments. This is a finite group—an energy that is developed uniquely for this message. The readers are ready, and so are you.

We speak now in an astral way... an interdimensional way. For the ones who have poured in here will not amplify or diminish this unique energy from my side of the veil until this message is finished in this special meeting of warriors. There's a reason why we've never given that statement before. It's so that nothing changes the energy of this message from its beginning to its end, as we deliver these words to you. [This message alone is different from what Kryon has ever said before. What we now understand it means is that it sets the potential of no interruptions from any entities or energies during the message.]

If we had to linearize this message any further than we already must [due to Human 4D], we would title it "And So It Begins." There are lots of beginnings and lots of endings going on right now. If you're sitting here with an open heart, without judgment this night, you're fully aware of the endings and the beginnings that have taken place in these last few years. So it is that the grid has moved and is almost finished. And so it is that it has moved more in a decade than it has moved in a hundred years... just as we told you it would back in 1989. Some of you must ask yourselves why such a thing would be. Indeed, it has even caught the attention of science. But even more, it has caught the attention of those who are spiritual. And when you see this kind of change, there is often fear. And so it begins.

Years ago we told you of the splits that would be potentially possible. Last year we told you of the fence-sitting—that there would be those who would be torn off the fence—ones who could not stay any longer in the new energy... and that is indeed happening. What is the battle at hand? I will tell you what the potentials have always been. It's a profound battle of light and dark. And lest you misname this, do not see it being between good and evil, for it is not. It is a battle, a seesaw battle of how far you wish to pull the light into this planet you call Earth. And so, there is no judgment about what shade you wish to pull forward, for this is why you exist at all! This is why you're here in this profound and different Earth energy.

I've got a small secret... and it's about me. I know all of you, even those of you who think you haven't met me. I know you in a way that warms my heart. Reader, are you getting this? Oh, I am the "magnetic master," but I'm also the one on the other side of the veil who greets you when you return. I'm the group in the Hall of Honor. You might say I wear many hats [cosmic humor as to what will take place the next day in the seminar]. Each one of you is a group, but you really don't know much about that either. You only know of the singular *you* and the linear *you* that sits here, pretending to be a Human on the planet Earth in four dimensions. Oh, if you only knew that you were each a group of divine angels... each one. I see you every time you go around, you know.

My little secret? I would like to tell you what you say when you see me... and many may not understand this. The energy that I have in the Hall of Honor when I see you prompts you to say to me: *"Hello, sister!"* Dichotomous? Perhaps. But it is so. My group is feminine, but my essence is masculine. I am a balanced group, just like you. Although genderless, the balance between what is absolute to you is variable with me. I am both, and I change to accommodate the circumstances. It's an honoring, and you can watch me do it.

Then the next thing that happens in that Hall of Honor, as we sing your name in light in a place that is filled with joy and amazing love, is when you ask, *"How's it going?"* You absolutely must know how you did while on Earth! It's part of "the big picture." It's the overwhelming knowledge known at the core level of every single Human on Earth, but which is hidden completely from you while here—about the balance of light on Earth. We've asked you to "hold your light," but you don't really know why. We've asked you to trust that what you're doing is something amazing and special, but you don't really know why. At the divine core level, you do, and intuitively you know that it's something far larger than any of you realize, but it's hidden... and it's the first question you wish to know about when you return. And that, my dear Human Being, is the crux of why some will pull away, and why some will be afraid of you. It's about a battle... one between those who are even in your own camps. We told you about this four years ago, and now it begins.

Let me identify the problem. Light often creates fear, and you're about to see this more than ever. You won't be able to walk from place to place without people looking at you. Even the most seemingly ordinary of you can't even go shopping without turning heads. When the Human consciousness field that you carry intersects another Human consciousness field, there is a message delivered. It's about light, dark, and a battle that is now before you.

Listen closely: There are those who are in your belief systems who would say that all of those gathered here today and reading this today are being "tricked by the light." There are those who study the ancient scripts, the histories of the Sumerians, and those who came before the Sumerians... who would tell you that it's written that in the last days, a battle would take place. They say that in order to delude you, in order to keep you from actually seeing what is taking place on Earth, there would be those such as Kryon and other Keepers of Light, who would assemble together and "distract you with light." That is the premise. And they'll pull up the ancient texts and show you the words. They'll even point to the prophecies, and even name the names at times. They'll say, *"See? It's taking place in these last days just as indicated." "Beware,"* they'll say, *"of those who will trick you with the light!"* And indeed, they say, here you are, sitting in the chairs... being tricked!

Perhaps you're wallowing in the joy and love that's being offered right now? Perhaps your heart is being opened? They'll tell you that you're being tricked. So I wish to address that. In this address, I want you to remember something: You're completely in charge of your own being. You're completely in charge of what's before you.

Is it possible that what is taking place on Earth at the moment is indeed the end? Is it a battle that you're truly unaware of... written by the ancients? Is it about final Human enslavement, as they indicate? Is it possible that all those conspiracies that you've heard of all your life, indeed are so? Could it be that there are those on other worlds, other times, other places, conspiring against you to enslave you as an entire race of humanity? And that this is all happening right now, except that here we are, blinding you with light? Is it possible?

There's something that's missing in the scenario, and we'll give you our side of the story, and then we'll give you the truth... a discernible one.

Indeed, on your reality track as humanity, there have been these potentials as described. As we've indicated many times, there are many reality tracks, and you've had the ability to choose which ones to select. It's called free choice. So, yes, these were potentials all through your recorded history. Even during the history before a hundred thousand years ago, some of your mythology wasn't mythology at all. Some of the things that you read about that you wouldn't understand, indeed happened. So many of the ancient texts have been written accurately. Yet some of you are in these "last days" wondering if what is before you could be a trick. Do the entities of love before you carry a hidden agenda? Well, you don't have to wonder. You don't have to fear. Here is what is missing—completely and totally from the formula others will give you about these end times.

You all think in a straight, linear fashion. You feel that what was uttered by wise prophets eons ago must be so, because the future is set. It's a straight line, the past leading to a set future. No one in those past histories, no intellectual spiritualist, ever expected humanity to change reality... to move out of the paradigm that it was ingrained within. Remember this statement we're going to give you now, and check it yourself, with your own discernment: "The prophets who give you predictions in one reality are clueless in another." The old energy of old predictions and old spiritual histories lay on an unused track of reality in a desolate wilderness with no Humans present. The train of current humanity will never roll over that track, yet there are still those stuck there in their expectations of what was predicted.

Even your modern physics now agrees that matter has a "choice" of realities. Think, therefore, of what your consciousness has created! You changed to a new reality paradigm, and we've told you this time and time again. It has been the staple of our teaching... that your planet would not go through what was predicted, and that all you had to do was look out the window to verify it for yourselves. But those whose consciousness is still on the old track, with the old prophecies, looking at what's happening on the planet, have no concept of what's really taking place. They take the same facts you can see, and instead fill their cups of fear with them. They give no credibility to the notion that Human reality can possibly be changed.

They see the church in trouble, business in trouble, and problems in the Middle East. They conclude that humanity is about to end, and that the very entities you've come to celebrate today are part of the conspiracy to make it so. They don't see an integrity battle, creating a new kind of humanity. Instead they see the beginnings of a fearful enslavement, control, and darkness for all.

[Pause]

Even though many of the ancients and the masters also wrote that humanity could change reality at any time, they still stick to the old fear—that what was written back then will indeed take place. And how can we come before you, dear Human Being, in all love, and prove to you that this is not the case? How can we prove to you that there's no trick? After all, we're supposed to be the tricksters! Here's where it gets good. We don't have to prove it, since you will.

There's a shift that will happen at the beginning of the year 2003. The magnetic grid will be finished moving and changing at that time. We call it a "hand-off." You'll be participating more than ever in every single thing on the planet. With an enhanced set of abilities, we say, "Let the Humans prove it for themselves, for it is well within their ability." We ask those on the other side of this argument if they would allow the same? Chances are they won't, for it disturbs a concept that says that you're a slave to others, in the dark.

Dear ones, do not build any walls around your belief. Open every single door and examine every book. Go to places where you would not normally go, and ask yourselves, your spiritual guides, and any angel anywhere... to give you the truth. Don't be judgmental. Don't draw lines between this and that. Unify your divinity, and discern without outside bias. Ask the question of everyone you can... in any dimension: *"Is this real or not? What's really taking place?"*

I'll tell you this. The Human Beings who do this will get truthful answers at the cellular level. They'll get them without being at a channelling and without anyone talking about love. They'll get them without the special music that you're hearing now [referring to live music being played by Robert Coxon on stage with the channelling]. They'll get them sitting alone in a room in an emotional way, and they'll feel the hug of Spirit that says that not only did you change reality, but this is not a trick. This is a new Earth, a new dispensation, with a new kind of Human.

The opposing force doesn't want you to do that. Instead, they want you to study an ancient text and submit to its validity. Now... who is enslaving whom? And so those who would say there's no changing the future won't give you that ability to look around for yourselves. They won't tell you to discern, or give you credit for that ability. They'll show you their texts and try to convince you that "it is what it is." Look carefully at this difference. We stand back and say, "Do it yourselves." The other is telling you that you should fear—that you have no power to do anything but listen to them. They will also tell you that emotion has no place in your discernment, and that it completely clouds your intellect. Kryon is emotional... always has been. I can't help it. I love humanity. Archangel Michael can't help it either. She loves humanity. All those who are before you today are emotional. But we say this: Go ahead and disengage your emotions, too. Go to the places and ask the questions, even with your best spiritual, intellectual mind. The answers will be there if you have pure intent.

Then when you're finished, come back and sit in the chair. We'll wait for you. Feel the hugs of Spirit, and know that what's happening is about a grand change for humanity, not about a trick to enslave. We told you that there would come a day when you would have to choose. It's here.

Your New Reality

So within this magnetic shift you gave permission for—a shift within your very DNA, your very reality—many of you are anxious (to say the least!). In this often unsettling energy, one where you're working so very hard, but one where you've had unexpected curves thrown at you, what is the advice of Spirit right now? What does Spirit say you're supposed to do with this enablement and change? Let me give you three or four points to ponder.

The first one is this: Claim your ascension status! How many times have you heard that from me? Many times! Now, there would be those who are critical of this, who would say, *"Well, there you go again, Kryon, giving them some generic message that has no rules to it. You're saying to 'go and do this, to feel it,' yet you do not give them any procedures. You don't give them any helpful manuscript. How are they supposed to do it?"*

I'm going to give you information that is 2,000 years old. I wish to take you to another place and paint a picture. We've told you in the past that the key to ascension status—moving into an interdimensional state, is called "The Third Language." We've discussed it for years. We've talked about "tuning your reality into a different station"—a reality that pulls upon The Cosmic Lattice. We've told you about creating energy that wasn't there before, instead of using what you feel exists. The instructions we've given are not linear, however, and they don't resound to those who wish to have a "by-the-number" explanation. We gave you a channelling not too long ago called "Trying to Explain the Unexplainable." How do you explain multiple dimensions to a four-dimensional Human Being? Believe me, it's not "by the numbers" anymore. Let me ask you to do this: Explain the color red to a person who has been sightless from birth, and do it by the numbers, procedurally. Difficult? Yes.

Let me give you information that's more than 2,000 years old. It's a story about a man named Peter. Some say this actually took place on the Sea of Galilee. It's written in the scripture of your own culture in three places. It's slightly different in two versions, so some say the story is actual and some say it's metaphoric. It doesn't matter, for it's the spiritual teaching that is profound and real, regardless of the accuracy of the event.

Peter had a master—a shaman. As the story goes, there's Peter with his friends in a boat, wishing he could join his master, who's on the shore. And he's disappointed, the disciple Peter. He wishes to have his master join him. We hear the master say, *"Peter, don't worry. Watch."* And the master begins to walk upon the water. Peter feels he can do this, too, but he needs permission. He asks the master to *"tell me to come to you."* The master looks Peter in the eye and says, *"Peter, you can do this, too. Come to me!"* And Peter does! He focuses upon his master and he takes the steps, according to the story, and he defies the reality of 4D and walks on the water, just like his master. Then something interesting happens. Peter looks down and starts to intellectualize. He says to himself, *"I shouldn't be able to do this!"* There were no rules given to me here. And so Peter starts to sink.

Let's back up this story for a moment and talk about Peter in general. There he is watching his master walk on the water, encouraging him to do the same. He trusts his master, so he feels that he can do it. But can you hear Peter's mind working? *"You know, I don't have a manual for this. Dear Master, how many steps are there in this process before I can transmute physics in this way? What am I going to have to do, spiritually? What are the rules behind it? I think I need to know this before I step out on the water."* Peter trusts, however, and when he takes his first step, he feels the tingle in his feet as one dimensionality meets the other—as the physics of one meets the physics of another through the spiritual creation of a Human... and his feet start to tingle.

Now, did you hear Peter say, *"Dear Master, I have to stop for a moment and ask you some questions. I want to know about the atomic phasic displacement of the time differential on my feet here. Is this normal or is it not normal to feel this tingling? Shouldn't I practice for a while on dirt? Should I back up, or should I go forward? Can you give me some information, please?"* No, you didn't hear that from Peter. He just *did* it.

Peter didn't need a manual. He didn't need to get the rules that day. It wasn't a procedural or linear event, because what he did was interdimensional. Peter was asked to do something that shamans do. Peter was told that all he had to do was focus on the divinity before him and within him. He didn't have to think about it, he just had to do it. And that's the truth.

So you have the instruction set, do you not, from the master himself? Within the actions of this parable are instructions to his Human disciple that says, "Just do it." No warm-up... no manual, no linear instructions. We're saying the same. Oh, don't take this out of context. Don't say that we've now compared ourselves to past masters, or even to Peter. Also, don't think that all you have to do is "nothing." Hardly!

What we're saying is that the process is the same as it was when it was first broached within the metaphors of the history of your current beliefs. It has always been this way. There will always be those who will intellectualize it all away, and who will say, *"Because we don't give linear rules and because there hasn't been a lineage of intricate training, it isn't valid."* And we say this: How can you argue with what you feel in yourselves? How can you argue with a life turned around with a healing? How can you argue with a Human Being who stands there, perhaps in an old contract—one who should have been dead in the old reality? You can't. How can you argue when you're walking on the water? You can't. It's about light.

Number one: Claim your ascension status. How? Not by doing nothing, but instead by beginning to write your own book of personal, intricate rules—interdimensional and profoundly personal. Start by verbalizing this to every cell in your body: *"I am changed. I am leaving a four-dimensional reality behind me, and I know that you all understand. Cells, listen up! I choose ascension status. We're going to vibrate higher, and we're going to know how by creating our own book as we go... with the divinity inside... just like the shamans did."* And that was number one.

Number two: It's critical at this time to find a group of people of like mind and spend time with them regularly. Don't put structure around it. Don't make it a "have to." Don't put judgment over it; don't create rules; just meet. And when you do, tell each other how you feel about one another and how you feel about Earth. Discuss your lives, and then sit down and send your light to a challenging place on Earth, and do it often. There's far more power in the numbers than there are individuals. Then again we say, don't do this because I said to. Do it because you've gone inside and have asked the source of divinity, *"What should I do today?"* Then discern: Is this accurate? Is this not accurate? Use your own divine discernment engine, not one out of some history book.

Number three: Make friends with the new energy! Now, you may not understand these instructions. And you might say, *"Well, I'm doing that. I'm sitting here, aren't I? I'm in a channelling session, aren't I? So I'm very friendly with the new energy."* Oh, really? And every door you pushed on opened wide, right? Everything you ever prayed for in the last two years is in your lap, right? There are no frustrations or challenges in your life?

I would like to tell you, dear Lightworker, that there has never been a more difficult time for those who deal in light than in the last five years. The term *Light "worker"* takes on a whole new meaning. It hasn't gotten any easier, and there have been things put in your path that are challenging. I'll tell you why—because this grid is a moving reality-target that you've been chasing. It's something that is so profoundly different, that just when you get comfortable, off it whirls. Just when you're satisfied with the clarity of one thing, another scenario moves past you. In 1999 we told you this was coming.

The settling of the magnetic grid combines with the other two. When the magnetic grid is settled, the others will settle. It's all about what you gave permission for, and what you've created yourselves. In linearity, you see the group that is the Kryon entourage prepare to leave. It actually only leaves its current job! The old grid group transfers to a new one that will start instruction sets about what to do within the new grid energy. This "new Kryon group" will give you the meanings of the interdimensional DNA layers, the names, the numbers, the colors, the interactions of all of the 12 layers. Then you'll start to understand how they intertwine onto the two you can see within your linear dimension.

The new teaching will begin shortly. The new entourage comes in, and the name remains. "Making friends with the new energy" is this: It's that you're not afraid to admit it's changing, and you express willingness to change with it. Perhaps you push on a door, even a promised door, and it shuts in your face? Things aren't going as you were told they might by your visions, or by your psychic abilities, and you're puzzled and wish to know why. I'll tell you. Because it's a changing scenario. It's a moving target, and it's work to keep up with it. It's not to say that these things you've tried won't ever work, and we've given you this message before. It's so very linear of you to try something and then say to yourself, *"Well, I tried it, and that's it. I'll never try that again! I'm throwing it away."* You do that, don't you?

Never cast anything away that's been intuitive for you. Never cast a hope or a passion in the trash. The very passion that you cast away in your "today" may be the contract that you promised yourself for "tomorrow." I'm going to ask you this: Does the artist paint all the colors at once? No. He can't! He's linear! Instead, he can only paint one color at a time. He has the vision of the painting in his head, and his limited 4D actions can only achieve his vision by combining the colors one at a time. What if he looked at his work after the first color and said, *"Boy, is that ugly! I think I'll stop now"*?

So, does that mean you'll never accomplish anything? That the doors will continue to slam shut on your linear plans? No. I'll give you a time line, but first, some potentials.

Potentials:

With the snapshot of the energy the way it is right now on the planet, these things are possible in the next few years:

(1) The discovery of interdimensional life, both in water and in air, in this decade. There will be an acknowledgment that life

is not what you thought. As Human Beings, you may be forced to redefine what "life" is. We've spoken of interdimensional life in the past. Now here's your opportunity to discover it. There is life in ordinary water. Not the kind of water that you're going to create with intent or alter magnetically—I'm talking about water that's normal on the planet, which bubbles out of the ground. Interdimensional life is everywhere. This is the force that receives the intent that changes the water as it's ingested, and works with your DNA. Did you ever wonder what it is in water that can do so much? Do you think it's within the simple few molecules of water? It's more than that, dear Human Beings. There has to be another force on the planet in order to cooperate with you and the field that you put out. Interdimensional life is the answer. How are you going to discover it? Well, let me give you a hint. It will be in a magnetic experiment! It's going to show up through experiments with intersecting magnet fields. It's not quite that simple, but the potential is there. You'll see the shadows of it. The scientists will be aware of the life force, because it will move away when stimulated. It will act in intelligent ways. It will respond to light. That will be the giveaway.

(2) Here's another. We've broached this oh-so-gently in the past because there's so much teaching around this, but it's something that hasn't been taught or completely acknowledged. You have a consciousness field. This day's instructions and validation presentation by my partner begin to show you how this consciousness field can even be activated in ways without your intent! That's because it's so strong within the Human, becoming stronger with the grid completion. My partner led you into the proof that even the scientists now say is valid, in this field. Nobody's talking about what might be "on" that consciousness field. Is it simply a field of your energy? What's in it? Let's begin here.

All of the four-dimensional health aspects of your body read like a book, presented on your consciousness field. Did you ever wonder how a medical intuitive could look at you and tell you about your health? Did this ever occur to you? What is this person doing who can "read" you? What does it look like? They're looking at the consciousness field around you, Human Being, and they're reading the physical book! The prediction? That there's going to be technology that will read you as well—technology that uses an interdimensional process when it gets close to you without ever touching you. The technology will be able to read a complete health scan of your body. And it's not anything that's probing within you. All it does is "listen," and that's the key word. And that was number two.

(3) Here's a prediction you've heard before from others. In two places, you'll discover life in your solar system, potentially by 2010. And what this is going to do is start to turn around how those in science, and Humans in general, feel about life. Here will be the acknowledgment that life is a naturally occurring event all over the Universe. Given that there is similarity throughout the Universe in which the elements come together over time, the creation of life must be present from one end of the Universe to the other. You never expected to find it in your backyard, however, but it's there. That is the potential.

(4) Here is another potential. There's going to be a war over ethics. Oh, not a big one, but a profound one. Lives will be lost—another argument about life. It's not what you think, as you'll see. Do you, or do you not, have permission to create it? And if you do, will there be consequences? For your technology is racing forward to a degree where what the Universe can do naturally, you can also do with synthesis. Will it be too sacred to try, or just simply a copy of common cosmic principles that occur naturally?

(5) One of the most beautiful predictions has to do with you and water. Water will be developed where intuition alone can posture it for healing. It will occur with water that's ripe and ready, beyond normal water, for the receiving of a Human consciousness "imprint" for the programming of healing. And that's all we can say at this time about that.

(6) Finally, we bring it up again: There are some artifacts just lying around waiting to be discovered that are going to give you some profound hints that cultures existed long before you thought. These are artifacts, not body parts! These artifacts won't be from Humans like you, but indeed from Humans. Way before the hundred thousand years we told you about, there was Humanlike activity and culture. In review, we told you not to look back any more than 100,000 years to find other Humans like you. Were there other Humans before that time? Yes, but not like *you*. And that's what this statement has always meant.

Something took place that we've discussed before. It was an energy interception that created the very Human setup that you walk around with today—the one that has allowed you to do what you've done with your reality. So again, what we tell you is this: Pay attention to YOU! If you wish to find other energies, other predictions, and a system of fear around it, then go ahead and immerse yourself on the old track where nobody lives anymore. All of the conspiracies of the ages will be there for you to wallow in. It's all there for you to choose... dark and light. But some of you are becoming spiritually astute enough to "see in the dark," so to speak, and are beginning to recognize an old reality from the one that's now outside your own front door. Don't take my word for it. Go through that door and check it out.

Here's a final instruction. It's the revelation of a time line that we've given before, but which some of you need to hear again. It's a time line within the scope of this teaching.

Whatever you're doing today, consider it temporary. For the actual grid settling will not be stable until March of 2003. Even though the actual change will be complete in December of 2002, the residual will last for another three months. So it is with spiritual things... God is slow! This is why there seems to be so much "not happening" for you at this particular point in your lives.

And so we say from now to then, "Have a nice vacation." Be circumspect, be alert, and celebrate your light. But it might serve you far better if you shelve some of the plans you thought you were supposed to do "now." It would better suit your magnificence, and a cosmic time line. You're all on separate paths, and many are in a time line even beyond that of regular humanity. So, if you've metaphorically pushed on doors that have indeed all flown open, don't stop! But all of you should be aware of the fact that this "moving spiritual target" is coming to a stop soon, and will stabilize.

Dear Human Being, this family of whom you are a part loves you so deeply! We give information that will enhance you, and promote you to graduate status. We give you information that you need to hear and which puts you in a place where you'll be able to enhance it yourself, validate it yourself, and continue the learning yourself. And that is enablement!

It doesn't subject you to sets of rules that would enslave you, put you in boxes, or ask you not to look around. It's just the opposite. It's about release, and it honors both the emotional body and the intellect. It honors spiritual logic and intelligence.

And so it is, dear Human Beings, that another time has passed when you let us hug you. There's such a difference between when we first started and now. For this day we can actually feel the hugs in return. We feel open hearts... open minds... family hugs. And we are so looking forward to doing this for a very, very long time.

And so it is.

Kryon

*Reference in the channelling about Peter walking on water:

Kryon has also told this story in the opposite way, where Peter is on the shore and Christ is in the boat. That's contrary to recorded scripture. In scripture, however, only Matthew's version had Peter walking on the water at all. Mark and John's didn't. So there may be the possibility that the whole story was a spiritual metaphoric teaching. I have changed this account to reflect Matthew's version, which is the more accepted one for many who might compare them and wonder about the difference.

Lee Carroll

We told you the battle was in front of you, and now you are in it. The battle is not between Human and Human, but is instead a battle between old and new consciousness. Both have power, but yours, my dear Human Being, is the only one that has the light of love connected to it. The more of you who decide to use it, the quicker the solutions will be found.

Kryon

Live Channelling

"A New Dispensation"

Channelled in the Caribbean
on the Third Annual Kryon Cruise
September 2002

Chapter Three

A New Dispensation
The Carabbean - September, 2002
The Third Annual Kryon Cruise
Chapter Three

This live channelling was given on the Royal Caribbean ship *Voyager of the Seas* on the way to the Caribbean on the first day of the third annual Kryon cruise. This is the first time we've presented a cruise channelling. It has a different energy due to the fact that it's given with the audience in motion, traveling over the open sea.

*****

Greetings, dear ones, I am Kryon of Magnetic Service. And so it is again that we fill a room—one that is in motion and does not "touch" the earth [speaking of being on the ship on the open sea]. Seemingly, it's not grounded and is in transit. It actually represents the "now" better than any other time we have come to you. The "now" is always in motion in a nonlinear way. It never rests and is always part of the circle of reality—always moving, and creating many things at the same time. Let it not be lost upon you that the entire vessel that you are riding within—this very room—is in motion. And so all of this enhances the message.

Here you are in a specific part of your planet with the intent to enjoy yourselves—to see the beauty of Earth—and at the same time to enrich your spirituality by having Spirit with you 100 percent of the time.

And so the marker is set—one that will be with you for these few days—one that is pasted upon you for a small duration of time during what you call the "Kryon cruise," a journey of the three [speaking of the third Kryon cruise]. It is a catalytic number. The "three" represents a resting energy, waiting for action. It's a number that often sits there with no action, waiting for another energy to manifest with it. We'll speak more about this in a while, for it represents much of our teaching tonight.

Today's catalytic energy may be upon you with your requested permission until the last day of this journey—until the closing message with the last words. During this window of opportunity, which some of you have given permission for, and which some were aware of before you ever arrived in this room, you will create an opening. Let us call it a "moving portal" of intent, one that marries well with the "now," and is responsible for personally lifting the veil.

Each individual is asked to be aware of only themselves. It's a time of pondering, a time of rest, a "time-out" to be with yourself. Some of you need an excuse like this trip to do that! It's time to ask the question, *"Who am I, really?"* Could it be that you are actually eternal? Could it be that you will never die? As you pass from one energy to another in transition—and as you pass to places that you cannot even conceive of while you're here, but which you call "home," is it possible that you will live forever? Will you continue to go on and on? Is it possible that the essence that is "you" will never die?

Could it be that those who surround you, whom you pretend not to know, even those from other countries [here on the ship], are actually family? Could it be that when you look in their eyes, there is grand familiarity? Could it be that although you pretend that you've never met them, you can celebrate personal victories together?

Let me tell you, dear Human, that if you can say yes to these concepts and conceive them as actual, you're far closer to reality than many others. Indeed, it is so. A much larger picture is at hand, and a few days together to ponder what that might mean is yours.

We pour into this place, invited by all of you. It is a unique and special energy today, one that you have invited in here—to sit next to you, to be with you, to hold your hand. It's an energy that's not in judgment. It's one that knows you personally and celebrates your joy. And whereas in the past this energy would leave at the end of the message, today that won't happen. This energy is being dispensed to you personally, one-by-one, not as a group. The energy is one that asks, *"Do we have your permission to join you for a few days? Can we leave this room with you upon dismissal and go up the elevator? May we sit with you during your meals? Will you let us in for just a week? Can we be next to you as you enjoy the beauty that you may see within these days? Will you let us hold your hand as you walk the path this week? May we speak to you in your sleep? Do we have permission to wake you up? May we show ourselves to you in your dreams? May we give you messages about you? If you will allow us to do that, we won't retreat at the end of this message. We're not going anywhere but with you."*

It will be only within the final words of this conference at the end of the week that we will consider a retreat to the other side of the veil. Some of us will then wait for your return. And when we see you again, we will speak of this time where you gave permission to be with us in an interdimensional way for a whole week! Call this a personal lifting of the veil. And speaking of that, we must remind you of the new dispensation you've created.

The Dispensation of Revelation

Let's describe what *lifting the veil* actually means: For many of you, "lifting the veil" means the reduction (lessening) of the barrier between humanity and Spirit—in other words, a reduction of the "duality" energy. For eons in your spiritual development, this is what these words have always meant—a closer walk with Spirit. But now there's more than this.

We're going to give you a linear definition of "lifting the veil." It means "turning on the light." And in that illumination, humanity has a choice it didn't have otherwise, since it reveals what has been hiding. Call this a "dispensation of illumination" that is upon you. Individuals may now make choices within their own lives that reflect the revelation of what they now can observe firsthand.

Suppose you were in a darkened room your entire life [a metaphor]. This is your seeming reality, and you go from place to place, mostly in the dark. Much like a sightless individual, let's also say that you've grown accustomed to finding objects in your path that you can't see, and with years of going from here to there, you've learned to dodge or avoid the obstacles fairly well. It has become intuitive over the years. It is normal for you. You go around this or that, somehow knowing that an object is there. Without stumbling over things, your life is better and you're used to where all the pitfalls and bumps are. And of course, within this metaphor of your reality, you're never aware that you're in the dark. Your reality has been this way for so long that it's normal—just the way things are.

Suddenly a light becomes available—oh, not a bright one, but one that allows you to see everything in the room dimly. You're amazed by what you see, and your first reaction is to laugh! You say to yourself, *"I've been going around the wrong objects! The room isn't laid out at all like I thought! Look! There was always a pathway through this way or that way that I never saw. What a funny person I've become, moving, dodging, going this way and that way, while all along, a pathway existed that was far more direct. What a revelation—the biggest of which is that I now clearly understand that I was not seeing properly. I was in the dark!"*

So what do you do with this information? You might think that this is an obvious question. What do you do with your newfound sight? *"Well, Kryon,"* you might say, *"only a fool would continue in the same routine as before."* Indeed! So you rearrange your life, do you not? You arrange your life to take advantage of the newfound sight that you gained through the light that arrived and illuminated the room of your reality. This process is called revelation.

This is what is happening with the *lifting of the veil* at this time on the planet—something that was actually foretold by your ancients.* Note that this is not something necessarily designed to increase your walk with God, although it will do that as well. Instead, it's about your walk with each other, and about your understanding of the energy of Earth.

Twelve years ago, Kryon began the teachings for you, and we spoke of the revelation. We spoke of the slight lifting of the veil, and how it would be manifested. We told you that this was a major step for humanity, and that it could only happen through a total realignment of many of the elements and attributes of your planet. Twelve years ago, we spoke of this clearly. We told you that the major change in Earth's attributes would be those that support Human consciousness.

We spoke of the "triad of the grid," and the one that we would be working with—the magnetics. And although some have seen the Kryon group as spiritual mechanics, our job has always been

* The word *apocalypse* is derived from a Greek word that actually means "lifting of the veil."

to alter the light. Our purpose has always been to stand by to allow for revelation through a grid shift, one that has always been possible, manifested by what the Humans on the planet could do with their own power. And now you sit within this revelation—a dispensation of light. This is not a return to any energy that Earth has ever seen. Instead, it is a new energy, posturing the light to reveal things never before sensed or seen.

With this light, new Human life-colors began developing. It was inevitable, was it not, that this would be so? With a planetary change of this magnitude, the very essence of Human consciousness would have to change. And when any of you hear the word *Indigo* when referring to a Human, it's time to understand what it means. There will come a time when you stop relating it to children. Instead, you will relate it to the new life-color that arrived with the changing of the grid. It refers to the only new life-color that was created by this shift, and represents a change at birth, which Human consciousness takes. It is an enhancement—an evolution in the spacial thought processes of the Human Being. All of this is possible due to the new alignment of the grid, and you're seeing it in your reality through the changing of your own children.

Several years ago, we also mentioned this: That even with these revelations on the planet, not all would see the light. We told you that the reality of one would be very different from the other, and that there would be divisions... personal battles fought over spiritual matters. It would be the battle of the old versus the new—a battle fought from those who were entrenched with a reality of ancient information and spiritual research. It was one that said, "God is the same, yesterday, today, and forever. Therefore, you cannot simply move the grid and change God!" What they haven't wished to see is that the changing energy is not God, but Human. Therefore, the change is within the relationship with God. Indeed, Spirit never changes, but the relationship with humanity does, and it does so with your free choice and your intent to know more about what is real and what is not.

Would any Human Being decide to ignore the newfound light in the room? Yes. Even more than that, they would say, *"It is not from God; therefore, I will not see it. It is so powerful that it must be wrong to use it. There is no ancient prophecy that tells of this enhancement; therefore, it should be ignored."* And this is their truth, and so it is also honored as one that comes from free choice. But the division begins even between those who call themselves spiritual workers.

Within this new energy, many have also become aware of what we will call "significant exits." There are lots of "ones" and "nines" happening [this is a reference to modern numerology and the meanings of the numbers]. This refers to many beginnings and ending, ones that are not expected, and which create an energy of change. Many are exiting by choice, even during this time that we're together.

Many are aware that right now the challenges are seeming to grow! This may seem counterintuitive to what we've just told you... where you can now see more clearly to avoid obstacles. Here you are, wondering what you've done incorrectly to manifest this! Here you are, confused by a seemingly increased load. Dear Human, this is why we love you so much! The duality is still significant, so you don't understand the overview. With increased light comes increased responsibility and also an increase in your power to deal with it. With this new energy also come new tools to deal with solutions to the unsolvable... a revelation of the puzzles of life.

However, it still looks as though the challenges are personally getting bigger. Many have thrown up their hands in surrender. *"It just isn't working!"* they say. *"There are too many surprises in my life. It doesn't seem like the one I expected or that Spirit told me I might have. Things that were stable are now failing."* Then the Humans often fall on their faces and pray to God, asking, *"What did I do wrong?"*

The Way Manifested Energy Is Created

Dear Human, I'm going to give you a postulate—a spiritual physical rule—one we've given before, but one you can never hear enough. It's about the creation of energy: Lightworker, every single time fear starts to well up within you and you successfully void it due to the wisdom and knowledge you carry, you have just won a battle. More than that, within the process of voiding this fear, you've created a third energy. Seemingly out of nothingness, you've created what we call a third energy. It's a "third" energy, for it responds to two others. The others are: (1) the energy of your consciousness [Human energy], and (2) the challenge before you [energy of the situation]. When you're able to use the (1) to void or change the (2), counterintuitive to what you might expect, a (3) occurs, which is a "manifested new energy." This is placed at the top of this situational pyramid [interdimensionally]. Call it the "challenge triad." Although the newly created energy is at the top, it is called the "anchoring" energy.

This third energy melds to the grid of the planet and increases the storehouse of something we wish to discuss in a moment. It's the actual creation of energy from the Human Being that affects the physical earth. Before we continue, note this: We didn't have you walk through a horrible experience! Void that thought. Instead, we had you void the fear of the situation with understanding. Within the voiding of the fear is the manifestation of the solution, and the help for the planet... a real win-win.

In other words, by looking into the eyes of the tiger with grace, wisdom, and love, it has made the tiger lie down and roll over. Do you understand the difference between an old battle concept of "search and destroy," against a new concept of "search and harmonize"? Who said the enemy had to be eliminated? What if, instead, the enemy gains understanding? Too strange, you say? Against Human nature, you say? What if this new kind of battle has both sides changing? What if, instead of simply destroying what is not wanted and continuing as before, both sides gain something and change? You'd better get used to this concept, since the new "indigo" consciousness is based on it!

How does this work within a personal battle? Let me explain something that is interactive and interdimensional, but which we will endeavor to give to you in a linear way: Within the above example, did you eliminate fear in your life? No. It will be back, you know. What happened instead is that you faced it, understood the specific energy it had, and let it go. That changed the Human [part one]. Getting out of fear creates cellular change. Did the situation [part two] change? Not by itself it didn't, but yes, it changed. What happened was that the situation changed with the addition of the new manifested energy [part three]. This was created through the Human's new understanding. So indeed both (part 1 - Human) and (part 2 - situation) changed with the creation of (part 3 - manifested energy of solution). The pyramid is complete. The triad is one with completion. Also, look at the triad in numerological terms: When you add the 1+2+3, you get 6. The simple energy of 6 is balance.

Therefore, every single time your challenge is met with the lack of fear and eventual solution, you're adding to the planet's core energy. Where in the planet's life-core? Although it might not make sense to you, it goes to the grid triad, which is above and below. We've spoken before of the complexity here. What it means is that often your challenges are given specifically to you to generate an energy that this planet desperately needs. And who better than those who love Spirit? Who better can generate this energy than those who have signed on for it? But we know that this seems confusing right now.

There has never been a more confusing time for Lightworkers. Can you imagine being in a stable home for 20 or 30 years, perhaps? You're comfortable and have everything figured out. Now we tell you that the house must change. It has to come down. The foundation must be scraped clean. New mortar will not stick to it unless it has integrity. A new house must be rebuilt. It has a metaphoric name, and we've continued to call this new house "The New Jerusalem"—the beginning of a new era, of solution and peace on Earth.

So, dear Human, as you sit there in the chair, we're telling you that the most insignificant problems in your lives, when compared to others, are jewels of discovery. They're invitations to help the planet. They're not given in reaction to something you did wrong, but rather they're given as work... something you gave permission for when you said, *"I want to come to Earth at the point of transition. I want to be part of the new paradigm change. I want to work and be part of a new dispensation for humanity."* And, indeed, here you are.

We've told you before that Lightworkers are different. Their power is tremendous. They are dynamos of light, cloaked in ordinary appearance, walking the earth with purpose and love. They generate energy you cannot see, which many do not even believe in, and which others are afraid of. Such are the makings of the battle at hand. And you wonder why we love you so?

Resonance—New Information

Here is something else that the new grid system is doing for you... and this is new information, given easily during this time, since we're moving [speaking of the ship]. There's no energy around us that's static or that's of the land. There's no root energy here created by a land-based grounding. As we said before, we're all in a unique situation at the moment, one that's clearer due to the motion you're in.

Let us speak of *resonance*. This is a key word relating to what is happening vibrationally on the planet. There's a basic resonance to the planet and all life on the planet. This may seem scientific, but it's also spiritual. A very low resonance frequency has surrounded all of humanity, and the ground it walks on, for eons. This resonance is a result of a reaction to other energies around it. [See the definition of resonance below]* The resonance of the life force of planet Earth and all that is around it is used for communication, something that we will discuss at a later time. This very low resonance has always been from seven to nine vibrations per second. This has been a staple of humanity since the beginning of time.

It responds to the "tonality" of the Human brain as well as the geology of the earth. It allows for energy symmetry within the plants and animals of the earth as well. It is pervasive, an anchor fundamental for all life, and an important foundation for attributes that you've yet to discover. As we've discussed many times, there are ultrahigh frequencies within the "choir" of the cells and other systems, but the fundamental anchor is the key

* The increase in amplitude of oscillation of one system exposed to a force whose frequency is equal or very close to the natural undamped frequency of another system.

to all of them. Although there are many "frequencies" to be dealt with, we're now speaking of something else—resonances and energies that vibrate with more intensity, and change frequency more, due to what's around them.

Think of it this way: Resonance is about harmony. When something resonates, it's due to another source around it that has a similar but more powerful harmonious frequency or set of frequencies.

So what we're telling you now is that part of what the new grid alignment is doing is to reset the resonance of planet Earth. The new fundamentals will be based on the number 11 and beyond. We cannot tell you where this will end, since it's modified by the Humans who will decide this as they solve the planet's many problems. This also means that the harmonics will change, too, and that even biology, and the "choir of instructions," will change.

When Human cellular structure begins to resonate with frequencies that it was not born with, with energies that shake it in a new way, it reacts! This can create anxiety, being uncomfortable, and yes... waking up at 3 A.M. every night. You lie there saying, *"Is everything okay? This somehow feels different."* That's because it is!

DNA

We've spoken so little of the new DNA—one that is responding to the new resonances of the planet—but there will come a time when we will. There's so much hiding beyond the 4D that you're used to. Much is only sensed that is actually part of the DNA engine. There's a creative engine inside you that's a storehouse of information about you, your past, your present, and your potentials. It's all in the DNA.

We've said in the past that there are twelve layers. You are aware of only one layer, the 4D layer set that you can see. We will call this layer "the root set." All DNA information starts there. It is the base, since it's within your main reality. There's no hierarchy of DNA layer importance. This root layer set is, therefore, not number one. Out of linearity, you must think differently, and the root layer is in the middle of the circle of DNA. It's difficult for us to tell you about the interactions to the other layers from the *root set.* There are no "strands." Instead, there are layers. Think of the unseen interdimensional ones as lying on the ones you *can* see. If it makes you feel better to count them, you may. But we remind you that once you pass four-dimensionality, time is no longer linear. Therefore, there is no such thing as a fifth dimension either, but it makes you feel better to say it is. [Kryon says it has to be four plus one, or better still, four plus *all.*] We've discussed this before. Therefore, we tell you that the other layers don't have numbers, but rather, they have names and energies, all in the circle of the 12.

There are 30 specific interactions between the other layers of DNA and the root layer. Someday we'll tell you what they are, and also what is specifically on those other pairs. We will even name them. But for now, let me give you a hint: Have any of you wondered where you're really from? If you're eternal, where is home? If you're eternal, where were you before you came here? The earth didn't have that many people until recently, so where did you arrive from? Did you ever wonder about the process when you were metaphorically tapped on the shoulder and asked, "Want to go to Earth?" What were you doing? Where were you? In the spectrum of the interdimensional existence of Spirit, where were you working when you got the call? Were you on another planet, another dimension, another time frame? What was your name? What was your purpose? Do you think you just floated around as some angelic form in a circle of eternal blissful infinity, then suddenly arrived on Earth for a while? Could it be that the plan of the Universe is far more complex than that? Could it be that you're called to come and go often as a spiritual being who works within a family called God?

Well, there's a blueprint within the unseen layers of DNA that tells that very story! It also affects who you are right now, and what you expect to accomplish from your brief stay here. How many times have you been on Earth? Who were you and what did you do? How does this affect you now? There are layers of DNA that contain your complete history here, too. What energies were developed? How do they apply to what brings you to this room now (or this page)? It's all in the blueprint of the layers of DNA you can't see.

Today the teacher Barbra [Barbra Dillenger] indicated that in an interdimensional reality, all things happen at the same time. This also brings up our response that if you consider this out of your linearity, this means that all your "past" lives are happening right now! We've told you this before, but perhaps you never considered what that might mean as far as how you're feeling in a new energy while the "lights are being turned on." Anxious? Waiting for the other shoe to drop? Fearful? Perhaps all those lives that you thought were "past lives" are starting to become more present? If so, then we congratulate you and give you the energy to match this new awareness so that you may celebrate it instead of fear it. You see, the root set knows it is in 4D. That's why it's in the middle of the circle. Everything else modifies, or modulates... yes, even resonates, the root set.

We told you recently that no matter what your 4D genetic setup is, the predisposition you think is there can be changed. This is profound information. It means that you have the ability to change your own genetics! We told you that the most powerful force on Earth is the consciousness of the Human Being, and now you know what we mean. Can your thoughts change your biology? Yes, yes, and yes. It has always been this way. Like a cocoon, the interdimensional layers of DNA wrap themselves around the root set and wait for a resonance of intent and compassion and love... all of which are the catalysts of Human change.

The root layer is actually just an engine. Think of the root layer as a dynamic biological engine that comes with a set of instructions that it follows biologically from birth, until other instructions give it new direction. Think of it as the ship blindly plowing through the waves without knowing anything about where it's going. But it knows how to drive the body through life. It knows how to speed up and slow down and how to sustain itself, repair itself, and exist. But the captain of the root set is the interdimensional set around it. The other layers modify the root layer set and tell it to change direction, steering it to safe harbors. However, these other layers have not always been actively accessible to a 4D perception... not until the light came on.

This interdimensional set of DNA layers, therefore, is the one that's awakening now. This is what is meant by "activating your DNA." It's a statement that tells you that the reposturing of the grid, and the other adjustments being accomplished, are speaking directly to the interdimensional parts of the Human DNA. This is the change that's going to make the difference between the Human Being of another dispensation and the ones who are here today—and those who sit here and read about this bridge between the old and the new paradigms.

Numerology

We promised to speak of numerology, one of the oldest sciences on the planet. We'll make this brief. Even the most complex numerology tends to center around the numbers in your linearity, which you can see in 4D. You tend to work with the ones (1's) through the nines (9's) and the systems around them. It's time to include the three "numbers" you cannot see. Just like the DNA, there are others that modify or resonate to the ones you can see.

Now, it may seem very strange to tell you that there are three more numbers in your system that don't have numerical value, but that's the way of it. For clarity, it's no different from asking someone, *"Which number is the color blue?"* You would be met with a curious response that says, *"What do you mean? Colors don't have an order. They're just colors. Instead, they have names."* This is so, yet they have energy, and they combine, and they are part of a system. So think of the new numbers in this way. We wish to expose the three interdimensional numbers that modify the ones you currently use.

There are three more that exist past the nine, and they're not zeros. Each has a symbol [sacred geometry] and a name. If you really want to accelerate your understanding, you should be including them with the other nine. They modify the first nine, so they change the energy of the system.

Let me give you an example. If you see the number one (1), you might associate it with "new beginnings" [the most simple interpretation]. It would simply lie there and say, "I represent new beginnings, a starting point." However, now if you take one of the three that's beyond the nine and place it next to the number one, it modifies the one into something else.

In order to clarify further, I will tell you what the other three non-numbers are in their simplest form: In linearity, they represent the energy of past, present, and future. These will be the names we give them for now, but they are in no order. Therefore, they're conceptual numbers, not absolute numbers.

The first nine are valued numbers [with absolute linear value]. The next three are conceptual, which have no value, but which modify the others.

These interdimensional three have no energy of their own. They must have the other numbers to function. This also makes them catalytic. It also places them in a circle with the others instead of a line or a column. Some will understand this, and some will not. If you had the numbers one to nine in a column going down a page that you were looking at, think of the other three as hovering above the column. This is the best we can do to explain something that's out of your normal 4D conception.

So, back to our example. What would happen to the interpretation of the number one, if the interdimensional number of "past" were next to it? The answer? It gives you extra personal information about the energy of the number. It greatly enhances the overview. In this case, it tells you that there's a new beginning energy around your past. What could that mean? Isn't that dichotomous? It doesn't make sense to many of you. What it might mean is that the energy of your past, which modifies your present, is realigning. *"What?"* you ask. *"How does my past affect my present?"* This isn't complex, dear one. What do you carry around that makes you angry? What happened in your past that gives you sorrow or grief? A number one in a reading, combined with this new modifier, would tell the numerological reader that there are new beginning energies around those things that have tempered your feelings and your reactions for years and years. Do you understand this?

What if the "present" modifier number occurred with the number one? It would indicate that there was a new beginning energy hovering around you that would tend to present itself in the 4D linear time of right now! It would indicate a "real time" change and help you understand an action you might take to modify your life this very day!

The "future" energy number placed with the number one would indicate a new beginning that was a potential—not now, not in the past, but a potential that you were seeing—one that might help you to plan—one that might alter your thinking about what to do next. Do you see how these new conceptual numbers might interact with your existing systems? It creates, however, much complexity. It adds three layers above the ones that are known.

Finally, to add to an already interesting complexity, what would happen if more than one conceptual number occurred with the number one? What would it mean to have present and future numbers next to the number one? It's going to create a puzzle—a new system—which we will call "interdimensional numerology." It's a brand-new tool. Of course the question is, *"Who can see those new conceptual numbers?"* The answer? "All of you, if you wish to." It's part of the new light. It's part of "seeing in the dark." It's all part of what is being given to you that will rewrite the spiritual textbooks and all the ancient writings that were so very valuable to you before the lights were turned on.

So what does this have to do with you as you sit here on this ship, or read this information? It is thus: Every single Human Being who is reading or hearing this knows all of it! This Kryon message is redundant. It's just a validation of what your "core" already knows. If I could, for a moment, strip back the duality and the linearity of your lives—if we could have a true family meeting for a moment, we would talk about high physics. We would talk about high spirituality. We would talk about the incredible healing power of compassion and love. We would discuss Human history—the millenniums that have come and gone. We could discuss the history and lineage of the Universe, and everyone would know where everyone was from. We would discuss an earth that at one point in your existence was only a plan. We would talk about your part in placing the solar system where it is, and how the grids were put together. And all of you would remember... and remember.

We would celebrate how much has been accomplished so far. We would celebrate the grandness of what you've done, and the potentials of what could happen. We would speak of the big picture—that what you do here on Earth affects another part of the Universe itself—the largest secret that remains unrevealed to humanity. It has the potential to change the balance of light and dark, perhaps even within the family of God.

And... we would celebrate your free choice to create whatever you wish on this, the only planet of free choice [meaning the only planet that has the ability to change its reality and its spiritual vibration].

Look up tonight at the sky. Count the stars. You can't. There are too many, and those are just the ones you can see! There is a vastness that is beyond your night sight. Yet your Earth is the only planet anywhere that has been slated for the specific task you came here for. You don't know how special this is. You still don't wish to believe that you're more than a grain of sand on a giant beach. Instead, we say to you that you're the jewel, hiding in a vast expanse of creation—a jewel waiting to be mounted in the necklace of universal change and appropriateness.

There will come a day when the lights are turned on fully. You will know your real names—and mine, too. Kryon is simply the name you can say in 4D. Then we'll talk about the journey to Earth and what it meant to the Universe. We'll laugh together and experience the joy of what has been accomplished. We'll talk about lives lived in 2002... the beginning of the end of the beginning. All that has gone before has the potential of only being the start of the real purpose of Earth and the humanity upon it.

Some of you waited to come in just for this time. You held back a natural process of returning in a normal cycle in order to target this very dispensation. You knew of the challenges. You knew of the potential Armageddon, yet you held back to be here when all this happened. Seven of you in this very group tonight are "holdovers." That is to say that purposely, with design and intent, you interrupted a planetary life cycle to create your life today, and it shows in your determination. You spent an extra amount of time on the other side of the veil, poised, waiting for this moment.

And you wonder why we love you the way we do. You wonder why we celebrate your lives and wash your feet. You wonder why we wish to walk with you all week long on this journey that you call the Kryon cruise.

You wonder why the mantle of challenge is upon you, don't you? Perhaps the warrior is awakening? Perhaps you now understand more fully who is really reading this page? Well, wonder no more. For the light is being turned on.

We go in love.

Look up tonight at the sky. Count the stars. You can't. There are too many, and those are just the ones you can see! There is a vastness that is beyond your night sight. Yet your Earth is the only planet anywhere that has been slated for the specific task you came here for. You don't know how special this is. You still don't wish to believe that you're more than a grain of sand on a giant beach. Instead, we say to you that you're the jewel, hiding in a vast expanse of creation—a jewel waiting to be mounted in the necklace of universal change and appropriateness.

Live Channelling

"Co-Creation Explained"
(Singing in the Choir)
Channelled in Toronto, Ontario, Canada
September 2002

Chapter Four

Co-Creation Explained
"Singing in the Choir"
Toronto, Ontario, Canada - September, 2002
Chapter Four

Greetings, dear ones, I am Kryon of Magnetic Service. This is a sacred place, a safe place, a sweet place. For a few moments, it's a place that suspends reality for even the busiest of you. It's a joy to say this as the entourage wishing to take you to safety pours into this place. Oh, that seems like only words, doesn't it? There will be those in the room who would say, *"It's impossible. Spirit doesn't speak to humanity in this fashion. There should be thunder and lightning, physical profundity of a magnitude that's enormous. Clouds have to part; seas must roll."* If you believe that, then you're denying the fact that there's a core inside you that knows everything I know... a core that is a part of the family of God.

It's a safe spot here... right now. And when we say "safe for even the busiest of you," we mean this. We invite you to take all the things right now that would interfere with a heartfelt message, and in all safety, put them away for 20 or 30 minutes. Put them away in a place that's so safe that you may even wonder later if you want to get them out again! This is the invitation right now. Reader, why are your eyes on this page? Are you serious? Then put yourself in a place of neutrality—one where communication is possible without the mind wandering to the worries of the day.

For those who would doubt that such a thing is possible—speaking to the other side of the veil—we say this to you: Do not listen to or read the words as you normally do. Instead, perhaps it's time to feel the entourage that brushes against you, which takes a seat behind you. Some of you know that this is happening here. If you do, then celebrate it right now... in safety.

The humanity that sits in front of me now is one that begins to understand a new reality. They're enabled to know and learn—to have wisdom. And they're enabled to become interdimensional. What a concept! It requires that a four-dimensional creature goes beyond the four and completely out of linearity. The invitation has always been open—one that asked you to understand the things that can't be understood—to grasp the ungraspable, and to conceptualize that which can't be conceived. It's going into a dimensionality that's not yours or the one you were born with. Instead, it's the one that you're beginning to absorb, the one that you've been given permission for, and the one that you're learning about this year.

Do you know what happens to beings who move into new dimensionalities? They attract attention! Has anyone told you lately that you "can't" do what you're obviously doing? Has anyone told you that if you really are doing it, then you must be evil or demented? These are the ones who cannot see anything but the old reality, old prophecies, and they make their judgments from a limited view... an old book that they continue to read. Let's sit a moment while the entourage takes its place. Let's celebrate the love of God.

[Pause]

Dear one, could it be that there's more to your reality than you can see? Just for a moment, suspend your disbelief. It won't hurt you, since you can always come back. Could it be that the words you hear and read are directly from Spirit—a family member Whom you know well when you're not here? Could it be? What is it that keeps you from knowing? Is it the fact that a Human Being is delivering the message? If so, then let me remind you: Humans always did! Human beings have been used since time began to deliver the most divine messages. It is the way of it, you know. The most profound scripture in every culture of the planet was given by Humans... ones who perhaps had seen something interdimensionally. Each time an angel from the other side of the veil would appear before men and women, they would have a brief message. It wouldn't last long, and the angels wouldn't stay. They would tell you not to be afraid, for their very visit broached Human reality... yet almost every religion on the planet was based on this premise. They would endeavor to place you in a safe spot, just for a moment, so that you'd have understanding, not fear. They even asked you to "fear not."

So perhaps this is broaching your reality? Perhaps it's time for you to feel what's happening here in order to validate this for your whole body? Did you know that you have an entourage of your own? We're going to discuss that today. It's a group who's sitting next to you, before you, around you, and above you. Some of you will feel it as it presses upon you in different ways, as if to say, *"We're here, you know?"* You think you're sitting in some chair, someplace in some meeting room somewhere? You think you've decided to read an article or a book? How many of you are aware of the appointment you made, through intent, to sit here all day long [speaking to the seminar attendees]? You gave intent to be touched by the music, by the meditation, and by the humor. You walked in with others whom you pretended not to know when you sat in your chair by appointment. It is not frivolous, you know... this synchronicity. It's not accidental that you're hearing and reading this. It's more than synchronistic that you sit before us. When you made the appointment, you made an alignment. It was an energy alignment—a triad alignment to sit there and create something.

The last time the Kryon came before Humans and gave a message, we spoke of a triad creation. We spoke about some of the puzzles that are before you, and mentioned that when you solve them, it creates a third-dimensional energy that forms a triad in The Cosmic Lattice. We're not here to teach that again, but we must review it, because what we're going to teach today is about Human creation and co-creation. You have to remember the concept that sometimes when two things come together, a third is created. Seemingly out of nothing, Human endeavor actually creates solution energy. We must also review two other concepts that we've spoken of before, but which you must understand in order to continue. So let the teaching begin.

[Pause]

Dear Human, as you sit there in your chair, convinced that you're singular, you really are not. Way beyond what you wish to accept, there's an interdimensional physical fact. A known fact. How many of you are aware that the Kryon is a group? Yet you hear one Human voice while he channels. You might ask, *"Well, then, who is everyone in this group today?"* [Laughter] And if you do, you'd be asking a good question! For the "group that is Kryon" indeed alters itself. It postures itself in response to the humanity that sits in front of it. The Kryon is a group—and always has been. That's why in your English language, we often say, "the Kryon." We would not do that unless it denoted a group. We are plural, yet you consider yourselves singular... one Human Being.

You see yourselves as one Human Being born into the world, and that's all you ever see from then on. When you look in the mirror, there seems to be only one of you. What a cosmic joke this is! You should see what's around you! Oh, this is not new information. We've told you time after time about the personal entourage "with your name on it" that's always around you. It's a recurring Kryon theme. We've told you that if you choose to ignore them all your life, there will be no judgment from them or God. We also told you that they'll never tap you on the shoulder—never interfere. It's like carrying a toolbox around that you never use. It's your own free choice to do as you wish. But let me tell you: I sit before an entire room of awakened Human beings who are starting to understand that they're a group. They're starting to understand that although the Humans may look singular, there's real activity that goes beyond singularity. It's "you and you."

We've even described how many "you's" there are, and what they/you all do. It has to be this way, you know, for this metaphysical puzzle to work. You cannot be singular, walking around in four dimensions co-creating, and not have interdimensional help from a very personal source. How does God work, if not in this way? Did you ever consider it? This spiritual part of yourself is what has always been known as "the Higher-Self." So consider this: the Higher-Self, and the Human-self together, are not singular, are they? The Higher-Self is the name for a group! That's two... so how about stretching your concepts a bit and begin to consider that there could be more? Do you see your Higher-Self in the mirror in the morning? Most of you don't. Could the group be bigger?

Let's talk about that group. That particular group interfaces with energy that's all through the veil. It's plural. There are many of you with you. The person next to you has the same attributes that you do. Two of you in a room who believe that there are only two in a room have no concept of the interchange of energies that goes on. Oh, perhaps you do if there is a conflict between you, or challenges or love! Some of you are very aware of the other energies that are created sometimes in these situations.

You have even described the energy as being thick, saying that you could "cut it"! What do you really think that is? What is the energy when you say "I love you" to an entourage with your name, that's never heard that from you before? Have you ever heard of being able to "love yourself"? Perhaps now you understand that it's not ego-driven, but rather it's about loving the parts that make up your reality, and by that act, creating energy that feeds you.

How can a Human Being co-create reality... by changing the one you live in? There are so many things that you say you need to do in order to walk a spiritual life. You sit before God and you ask for this and that. Yet the information you've received from Spirit for years has asked, "Why don't you co-create it?"

The definition of *co-creation*: That creation of altering Human reality using the core of Spirit that dwells within—creating situations and synchronicities that allow Humans into areas that they would never have been in otherwise. Some pray to God: *"Dear Spirit, I wish to co-create in my life something that I've had visions of before. I've had dreams that show me doing this and that. I wish to co-create it. Dear Spirit, I don't belong in my current job. Oh, I'll stay here as long as I'm supposed to, but I know I don't belong there. I wish to co-create another way of making a living—something that helps people, perhaps."* You think we haven't heard this? *"Dear Spirit, my financial situation isn't commensurate with my magnificence!"* You think we haven't heard that? And you think we're not listening, don't you? The struggles may continue as the months go by... so you continue to ask the same things over and over.

The changes to the grid of Earth are coming to a close. Many of you are aware of the feeling of "chasing a moving target," spiritually, and are finding it almost impossible to do. You try to co-create abundance in your life, only to find things changing daily that seem to thwart your efforts. The grid is about to stabilize, spiritually. We've given you information that the stabilization shift will have a residue of change that will last through March of 2003. We've even told you that it would be wise not to start anything new for a while unless you want an uphill climb. Then we've told you this, that the promised energy you've created for yourself will stick upon you and will start to make sense. Co-creation will begin to be more effective if you understand how to do it.

Some have said, *"Dear Spirit, you've told me that I'm a unique individual, known by God. Is this really so?"*

It is.

"Dear Spirit, you've told me that I can do anything. I have a vision for myself. I have a stewardship of my life like no other. Is it appropriate that I should follow this seemingly God-given vision?"

Indeed, it is.

"Then do I really have the ability to co-create for myself these things that I believe are appropriate and true?"

Yes, you do.

"Then I wish to get to it!"

And so it shall be.

In order for us to explain what we need to, we must tell you about the orchestra. We have to give you a word that we're going to be using more and more of. We brought you the concept years ago of The Cosmic Lattice. I want you to take a look at The Lattice for a moment. Gaze into that vast area of strings connected to strings. The Lattice is profound in its shape. Energy is connected to energy—everyone to everyone—everything to everything—every planet to every planet—every solar body to every solar body. It's a giant puzzle that moves with purpose, but which always changes. And if you look at The Lattice as a giant musical stringed instrument—a lute of Spirit—you will see that the strings can be plucked in many ways. When they're plucked, they make harmonious spiritual music, and that harmony creates overtones that resonate and create still other strings. Those new strings are called... job, abundance, solution, and peaceful purpose.

If you understand this metaphor, you might ask, *"Which string shall I pluck? Which is mine? For I wish to find my energy and create a uniqueness so I'll have the abundance, so I'll have the job, so I'll have my life's purpose complete. I wish to move forward. Which string should I pluck?"*

So what you might do is look for the string with your name on it. Doesn't that make sense? If you're unique in the universe, certainly it's there, correct? Perhaps not. I'm going to give you some information that you might be missing: Don't look for your personal string. What if you looked, found it, and plucked it? What good would a one-stringed instrument be when you know that energy is created by one string resounding against the other? No. Instead you should be looking at all the strings and saying, *"They're playing a tune. What tune is it? What note can I pluck or sing where I will create resonance with the tune that's being played? If I can find that, then all will vibrate and resound in harmony... and the energy of co-creation will be accomplished. If I can vibrate with them, I will have my own unique co-creation."*

This is a difficult concept. It's the concept of spiritual resonance. Co-creation is spiritual resonance. The definition of *spiritual resonance* is this: It is an energy which, when harmonized with, will amplify and create another unique energy that vibrates in synchronization with the original energy, but which has its own uniqueness. In music, these new energies are often called "overtones." You get them by beating one frequency against another. Sometimes the newly created tones are strong. Their addition increases the amplitude of the whole. But sometimes they actually reduce the whole, diminishing the entire thing. The metaphor is a good one, but metaphors and analogies only go so far. However, even in music you realize that not all the strings or notes in the scale are alike. When the tune is unique, so must your ability to decipher which note to pluck or sing in order to resonate, or not. Note that we haven't asked you to match the energy... but to harmonize with it. There's a big difference.

You can't just jump on the lute and play any note! You must discern and search for the string that will harmonize and resonate. Don't worry... we know that many of you aren't musical. However, all of you have the spiritual tools to sing in "The Lattice Choir." It's intuitive and beautiful. This tool is what we wish to speak of today.

In order to explain this information in a more profound way, we will bring you a parable. We're going to present this parable so that you might see this new concept in a practical way. This parable has been presented once before to a group of Humans in a small room, a room that belonged to no country, a room that was not on land [speaking of the Kryon cruise].

I'm going to give you another parable of Wo. For almost 12 years, we've told you about a creature, a Human, named Wo. We've used Wo to give you spiritual examples, and we've told you that Wo is an average Human Being just like you. But, like you, Wo also has extraordinary power. We've also told you that Wo, although we call him a "he," is not a man. Wo is just like you—genderless.

"What?" you ask. That's right. When you're not here, you have no gender. I wish you could understand that the real you

is a magnificent creature of God, shaped in the image of light energy, and not biologically biased. But you don't understand that, for there's tremendous polarization when you're a Human Being. You're either one or the other, you know. Biologically, you're one or the other. And although you may feel very happy with the gender you are at the moment, pieces and parts of you are both. Wo is not a man. Wo is a "wo-man." And so Wo is both genders. But because of the language limitations in your culture, we will call Wo a "he."

The Parable of Wo and the Magic Glasses

Wo is just like you. He's a spiritual being, and he feels the new energy. Wo is walking the earth at a challenging time, watching things develop in front of him that had never been prophesied, just like you. Waking up at three in the morning with questions in his soul, Wo hears that small, still voice within asking, *"Is there something I should worry about?"* See... he's just like you. He's part of a new Earth that changed directions—one that's on a virgin track or reality that's never been traveled before. Just like you.

Let me tell you specifically about Wo's life. If you could ask Wo about his life, he would say that there are three challenges that he's faced with constantly, in this order: (1) His life's purpose. Wo would tell you he knows he's a healer. He has wisdom, and he knows he can teach. Perhaps he's not a healer in the classic sense, but perhaps a healer through wisdom and teaching. He has wise and good things to offer if only people would listen. (2) Wo also feels that his abundance is lacking. He wishes to create a situation where he has that storehouse that Kryon has talked about. He wants to see that storehouse, and he wants to claim it and use it. (3) Third, Wo would tell you that there's something going on where he works. They don't know who he is. He comes and goes, and it just seems like he walks through life with people he would never have chosen to be with. They don't know him. They don't know that Wo is a leader. He's actually good management material, but oddly enough, they never ask him for help. They don't pay any attention to him. He's never noticed or promoted. He just "is." He comes and goes every day. Nothing ever changes.

Now, this is a metaphor. These metaphors or allegories we present are "things that mean other things." They consist of a message within a story, or a story within a story. The deeper you look, the more you'll see. Many of the things are given in a subtle way today, but they'll seem more dramatic later. They will only reveal themselves to those who look harder and study this parable. There are layers of truth here, not all of them obvious.

Wo had something happen to him. He sat before Spirit as he normally did and said this: *"Dear God, show me what it is I need to know. I don't know where to begin. You know about the three areas in my life where I wish to co-create miracles, but I don't know where to begin."* In the days after his meditation, an energy appeared to Wo. It happened during one of those mysterious times when he wasn't really doing much of anything. Actually, he was singing and playing. Suddenly, an angel appeared to Wo and said, *"Wo, fear not! I'm here because you asked me to be."* And Wo was overjoyed. He spoke to the angel and said, *"Oh, I think I know what you're here for. You know about the three areas of my life that I'm having trouble with. I need your help. I would like to co-create my way through these. I want it to be appropriate, and I want it to be correct. I wish it to honor my spirituality and my uniqueness in the universe. I'm ready!"* Wo's heart was in the right place, and he really was ready.

The angel replied, *"Yes, that's why I'm here. Wo, I have a tool for you here. It's a new tool of co-creation. I have a hammer,* a chisel, and there's even a saw. And you're going to be able to hammer, chisel, and saw-out the pieces that you need to fit in the puzzle of life. It will co-create the things that you need to fulfill your vision."

"These are my new gifts!" he exclaimed. "Three of them. I am so thankful. Thank you, angel."

And the angel said, "That's not all, Wo. I'm going to be back later—after you have fashioned your pieces—with one more gift."

"I'll look forward to that," Wo said, and the angel vanished.

Can you imagine the euphoria of actually having that kind of an answer during a challenging time? Wo was excited! He began the process of creating the pieces of the puzzle he needed. He was going to create three pieces. Each piece would be fashioned uniquely, for he was a unique creature of the universe, fitting into a complex interdimensional puzzle. He would need to have a unique feeling of what he would do. So Wo sat down and stated: "The first piece I wish to fashion is that of my life's purpose—what I see myself as—a healer, a teacher. It's going to be a beautiful piece. Here's how I see it: It's going to be square here, round here... it's going to have some protrusions right here. It will be beautiful. There will be symmetry, and it's going to be a lovely piece of the puzzle. God will be pleased!" And he began.

And so Wo carved and he chiseled, and when he was done, it was indeed beautiful. Wo knew that it was a spiritual piece that belonged just to him. He had used his wisdom and his imagination and all the things he felt were unique to him. He carefully sanded the piece, and then he oiled it so that it would shine and be unique so that others would notice it. Then he did something he knew he had to do. He put a rope on the piece and hung it around his neck. It was a statement that said, "I am

Wo, the teacher. I am Wo, the wise. This is my co-created piece. It is done in all appropriateness and love. It is who I am."

Wo sent out advertisements, knowing full well that the energy of everything he was doing regarding his talents for wise teaching and healing would pay off because he was wearing his piece. Wo waited and waited... and nothing happened. Nobody came. There was no change. Wo thought to himself, *Well, maybe I'm doing something wrong. I'll just wait. Maybe the grid has to change a little more. Maybe the energy is not right for me and the unique piece I have. I'll work on the second one. Perhaps two are needed for one to work?*

So Wo began his abundance piece. *"Well, now, what does that piece of abundance look like?"* Wo asked himself. *"I know what I need, and I know where the storehouse is, so I'll just put this here and that there. I know it will relate to the first piece. Yes, that's it! The pieces must fit together with themselves."* He thought he had it. *"I will make all three pieces fit with all the others in order to have a trilogy of pieces, creating energy for the things I'm trying to co-create."*

Wo went to work on the second piece. Oh, it fit great with the first piece! It was his abundance piece. It was beautiful and unique. It took him a long time, but when finished, he sanded it, took off the rough edges, oiled it, and wore both pieces around his neck. It was getting a little heavier now. And it made a statement that said, *"I am Wo the wise; I'm a teacher. And by the way, I'm also abundant. Take a look."* Well, the money didn't come in. Wo had to go to the bank and borrow again like he'd done many times... with his hat in his hand... and his spiritual pieces hanging there. Wo felt insulted.

Wo had an idea: *"If I'm a healer, then that will bring the abundance. I'll never have to go to work again."* He saw the trilogy completed, and he set out to make a third piece that when completed, would activate the other two. Wo knew it would work. *"The three together will be unique. It's going to represent my co-creative energy in the Universe."* And he made the third piece. Oh, it was gorgeous! It fit wonderfully into the first two. He had to make the rope bigger, however, since it was a bit heavy. He finished it and sanded it. He took the rough edges off and oiled it up. It shone in the light and was gorgeous.

So there he was for the entire Universe to see. Behold Wo, the co-creative. Wo, the wise, abundant teacher... and management material as well. Wo went to work that way. He knew everybody would see it. And they did. They fired him. It seems like a little bit of Wo goes a long way. [Laughter]

What did I do wrong? Wo wondered. He had followed the instructions of Spirit. He had the tools—divine tools, creating a divine part of who he was. They all fit, too. In three areas of his life where he was challenged, where he wanted changes, he tried to bring it about with appropriateness and love. It didn't hurt anybody. He didn't step on anybody. He loved everyone. Yet here he was, worse off than he had been before!

Wo spoke to Spirit in a meditative moment. *"Dear angel, I think I need you again. Dear Spirit, tell me what it is I need to know."* And the angel appeared!

"Well, Wo," the angel remarked, *"I couldn't help but notice that you've used the tools. My, those are beautiful pieces! However, I think what I have now is going to help you even more. Wo, I'm going to give you a set of interdimensional Lattice glasses. They will work only briefly, and when you put them on, you're going to be able to see yourself and The Lattice together. It's the first time that we've offered this to humanity. I'm going to give you the gift of using the glasses four times."*

Wo was so pleased to have this help. He took the glasses, thanked the angel, and said, *"I challenge the glasses to show me my piece in The Lattice regarding my life's purpose."* I wish to know what I did wrong. I wish to know if the piece was shaped incorrectly. Should it now be larger? Smaller? I wish to see all." So Wo created ceremony within the experience, and he put on the glasses.

Life's Purpose

Wo was instantly transported to a magnificent place in the Universe, a Lattice that sang to him—the most glorious music he'd ever heard! There, he saw pieces of the whole puzzle. He saw the strings of The Lattice. He saw and heard the orchestra and the choir. He recognized the resonance of what was missing... the missing piece of the tune he was experiencing. He heard and saw a hole in The Lattice music that indicated, *"Wo goes here."* Then the vision disappeared.

Wo had quickly memorized the energy shape of the new resonance piece. It didn't look anything like the one he had put together by himself. Instead, it was a piece that resonated with the rest of the energy around him. That was the key, he now realized. He had to take his place within a "whole reality." He had to play an instrument next to the other one who played an instrument. Together, the resonance, one with another, created still another energy... a larger one. Together they made what Wo would call his new reality. The secret? His piece didn't have to match Wo at all. It had to match what the others were doing, and theirs had to match his!

Wo went to work. He shaped the missing piece exactly as he had seen it in the vision. It resonated, and sang the note that the others wanted to hear—the note that was missing in the chord. And he sanded it and took the rough edges off, and it was beautiful. Then he hung it around his neck. Suddenly the phone started ringing. *"Wo, can we come over? We've got some problems to talk about. We know you're a wise man, and we'd like to talk to you about things."* And Wo said, *"Please come over."* Wo began his life's purpose. It began slowly, and there was much to learn, but Wo was helping people. Indeed he had wisdom. He resonated with them, and they were able to see his resonance because Wo was singing as part of the choir. The angelic song was complete, and all around him heard the tune at some level.

Oh, dear ones, are you beginning to understand? You can be as individualistic as you wish. You can be as unique as you actually are. But I will tell you that in your uniqueness, you must sing the resonant note. You have to understand the group around you! You are someone else's co-creation! Do you understand? The choir sings together. It resonates together, and it harmonizes together. What you're asking for is a piece and a part of what somebody else is asking for. Together, you make a complete energy, even though you can't see the whole puzzle. You wish to launch out on your own and leave the others behind? You better reconsider what you're doing, for frustration is the result, and Human drama is often the product. Instead, honor everything around you. See it as part of the puzzle, and listen. Be still, and hear the celestial choir. They sing in the "key of love."

Life's Abundance

Wo could hardly wait to see the storehouse piece. He again put on the glasses. Wo exclaimed, *"This is going to be my interdimensional piece. I always wanted this one. This is really going to be good!"* He put the glasses on and again was instantly transported to a special place in the Universe, with beautiful music and resonance. He saw his abundance, and it was astonishing! There it was, the storehouse that God had said was his, and it belonged to everyone. There was the missing piece! Then it vanished. But right before it vanished, Wo saw something really disturbing. Right before the vision left, when he was memorizing the shape, it changed! *Oh, dear. How am I supposed to make a new piece when it constantly changes?* Wo wondered.

What Wo saw wasn't really a changing shape, but rather a changing melody. The theme was always in motion. Every time it changed its melody, another piece was needed to fill in the harmony. Wo thought to himself that this was just too difficult. *Just when I finish one, I'll have to try to figure out what the next one should look like... and I won't even have the glasses!*

Then the wise Wo, the teacher Wo, the one who had learned to sing the note he needed for the first challenge, finally got the answer. This piece is not going to be a four-dimensional piece. It can't be. It's going to be an interdimensional piece that sings with a changing choir. Wo fashioned it in his own way—a piece that was variable. It could go many ways. It was unique, and he put it with the other one. This time he didn't put it around his neck, either. Instead, he put it on the altar of Wo—the place of honor and respect and of love of self. Then he saw the dynamics of the abundance that he was trying to create, and he laughed at his innocence!

Wo never got his storehouse. Instead, the wise Wo got something better: a sustenance, the actual knowledge, out of worry or concern, that every single day of his life would be taken care of somehow, in some way. The storehouse was so vast that it was the storehouse of the whole orchestra and the entire choir. It was like having a new sacred melody every single day. It was a sustenance that was so profound that Wo stopped worrying about money. Certainly there were times when he didn't seem to have the rent. In the past, he would worry, pray in an anxious manner, and prostrate himself before God on his knees and make a lot of noise until he felt he had somehow been heard. The difference now was that when the rent was due, he smiled before God and sang with the choir. His thoughts were positive. *"I'm going to create this specific amount. Oh, I may not have a large amount in reserve, but I have a storehouse of the orchestra, and my piece will fit when I need it to fit. I will celebrate the feeling when it arrives, even though I don't have any idea of the exact time or circumstance."* And the amount arrived... sometimes to the penny.

Listen, dear ones, we know that this process is out of the linearity that you are comfortable with. But the beauty of this? Interdimensionally, it's always there, unique and beautiful. No matter where you are or what situation you're in, the energy you create is the melody of the "now." In the past, you created a structure in your reality. Then you asked for abundance to be given to your structure. Now, let the structure be the choir, and let your needs be met out of the box, so to speak.

Fitting into the Human Culture

Finally, Wo put on the glasses for a third time. He saw and heard the missing piece that he called "his 4D work" and was astonished. It didn't look anything like he thought it would. As before, he shaped it in a unique way. He sanded and oiled it. It fit and sang beautifully with the choir. He didn't hang it around his neck either. Instead, he put it in his pocket, always available, but not seen by all. Wo received a job that didn't seem to be very important, at least not in the culture of his land. He was disappointed by this until the situation started to change. The "unimportant job" became important because those who saw Wo walking around in the hallway said, *"What are you doing here, Wo? We can see that you're wise and worry-free. Perhaps you can do something for this company. It's not an important company, but we need your help. Wo, we think because of your wisdom and attitude that you're management material!"* And so he was. And Wo started the process of fitting sweetly into an area of his life that he once hated. One note harmonized with the other, and the choir all sang in a way that made Wo peaceful. He was in a safe spot, kind of like you are right now, as you are being spoken to and loved.

Dear ones, do you just tolerate the job you "have to" go to? Did you ever wonder if there was anything there for you besides a cultural necessity for you to exist? What if someone else's synchronicity was waiting for you? What if they were praying daily for help in their lives, and you had answers? Did you ever think of that? What do you show them there? Do you show them a peaceful, joyful countenance? Do you celebrate an "unimportant" job? Do you emote a peaceful energy? Be aware—things are not always as they seem. Perhaps you are their solution—an angel of synchronicity? Did you ever stop and listen to the choir while you were there?

You might say, well, that's the end of the parable. The message is obvious—that you can be as unique as you wish, but every single Human creature on this earth fits with the other. The ones you least expect have a piece that's next to you, and in all of your uniqueness and in theirs, you resonate together to create a third energy that creates a co-creation for your life. In a four-dimensional aspect, you're doing it alone, but in an interdimensional aspect, you're doing it with everyone else. But we're not quite finished with Wo. There's a loose end.

The Big Picture

The angel had told Wo that he could wear the glasses four times. That was odd, since Wo only had three challenges he'd been praying about. The linear Human might have even thrown the glasses away, thinking that the energy was all used up. But Wo put the glasses on the fourth time. He said to the glasses, *"What is here for me to see, that the angel knew I should know?"* Wo then put on the glasses. That's when he saw the most profound thing in his life: Wo was given a glimpse of all the pieces together. He saw his pieces—the ones called Wo—the Higher-Self, and the others. He saw all of them.

There was no trip, taking Wo to parts of the Universe. Instead, right where Wo was, all standing side by side, Wo got to briefly see the group that was Wo. He saw something no Human had ever seen clearly. There were five giant blue forms, and we'll talk about those someday. But what Wo saw that tapped his heart was this: Metaphorically or not, making a circle around Wo was a family that Wo knew! His brothers were there, his sisters, his parents, and even his children! Understand for a moment that this Human family had not all passed over. No. Many were alive on the planet. Yet, here was a glimpse of them in an interdimensional way that indicated that they were part of him! What could that mean?

Listen: Dear ears and eyes of family before me, how can we tell you something out of the realm of understanding? How can we show you what you cannot see? You make arrangements with those around you before you ever arrive here. In this "soup" of Human energy that you call YOU, there are pieces and parts of this family that are also part of you. There is a support group here, and even after they're gone from your 4D experience on Earth, they remain as part of you. This goes way beyond the genetics and the biology and the one layer of DNA that you can see. It's far beyond that. Wo got a glimpse of the group that was Wo. To this day, he doesn't understand it all. How can they be here and also be part of Wo? What about his parents? He thought they were gone and by now, perhaps, had reincarnated into some other being on the earth and were working just like Wo. How could they still be with Wo? How could such a thing be?

Can you really be in two or three places at the same time? Yes, you can. You'd better get used to it. It's all part of the unthinkable—the unseeable. Perhaps the you in the mirror is also part of another's energy? If you understand that, then you're well on your way to understanding how you're all part of the orchestra on an interdimensional Lattice... yet all are unique pieces of God. The Lattice sings a beautiful tune—a tune of harmony—a tune of love. It's a tune with a message that tells all of you that you're eternal and interconnected.

Be as unique as you wish, but be quiet and listen to the song around you, because that's the musical key you're being asked to sing in. Metaphoric? Oh, yes. But you're going to get even more of that kind of teaching as we instruct four-dimensional creatures how to be in 23D.

So, whereas you thought you had the gifts of Spirit to make co-creation happen, and whereas you thought you had the unique pieces of the puzzle that would allow you to construct your own path, don't make too much noise as you hammer and chisel away, or you'll miss the key you're supposed to sing in! It's a key that represents the life next to you and the life next to that, and the life next to that. Then, dear Human Being, when enough of you sing in that key, there will no be more war on this planet!

It isn't just for a few, you know. It's an awakening that's taking place everywhere. It's represented in the wisdom of the indigo color, and new Humans [children] who see spatially—the whole puzzle first—before anyone teaches them about the pieces. That's the difference between you and them. It's about a consciousness shift—one that's aware of the orchestra as they walk from here to there, and that's the truth. It's the new key and a new tune for the planet. It's a tune that has a name, a potential, and a great solution. It's a tune we'll call "The New Jerusalem." Peace on the planet. Peace for your children. Hope.

You're in duality, dear ones, and always will be. There is old energy all around you, and the representatives of it will fight tooth and nail to keep the old prophecies alive. There are those who really do wish for the Armageddon. And what do you do in return? What do you do with those who wish for the doom and gloom—those convinced that you represent a farce? Love them and sing with the choir, for they are in it, too... they just don't have the song yet.

And so it is in this moment, normally a time when we would retreat from this place where you sit listening and reading that we will instead say to you that not all of us will go. For some of you really did receive this interdimensional message, and you really need somebody to sing with. So let the song begin, and celebrate the new voices in your choir.

Go in peace on this beautiful planet.

And so it is.

Kryon

Ten years ago if I had told you that the largest businesses in this great land of yours would fall over and expire due to "integrity issues," would you have believed me? If I had given you the prophecy that one of the largest religious organizations on Earth would be brought to its knees because of integrity, would you have believed me? The answer is no. Such things were not seen as possible. Big money and big religion were untouchable. Well, look out the window and read your news. It's called pruning. Country by country... belief system by belief system, the sparks will fly.

Live Channelling

"What's Happening?"

Channelled in Bedford, New Hampshire
November 2002

Chapter Five

What's Happening?
Bedford, New Hampshire - November, 2002
Chapter Five

G reetings, dear ones, I am Kryon of Magnetic Service. What a joy that you would allow something like this, dear Human! We understand your duality. We understand that many of you still question whether this could be real. So, some of you will be touched. Some of you will smell things that cannot exist where you sit. Some of you will see the colors in the room, and it's all for one reason: so that you will understand the validity of what you have created here today. This event and the message from this event are being created because you are here. This does not happen in a vacuum. If there were none of you sitting here, there would be no channelling, so it's a sweet place, one created by the humanity who sits in front of me, and by those thousands reading one at a time.

Each of you is eternal, and not all life in the Universe is. There is no test here on this planet, only challenges of energy. None of you are beyond the ability to receive and endure these challenges. All of you came in with that knowledge, and in order to make that operate in the correct fashion, we tell you this again: Each of you is plural! You think you're "one" thing? That's not accurate. You look in the mirror and see a four-dimensional creature with skin and a body, and a name you can say out loud. But you have no concept of whom you're looking at. Each of you is a group. Although this sounds odd, you are already acknowledging this when you say you have a higher part of you, and many of you design your lives to take advantage of those higher parts. But you still see and feel the separation. There is much of you that desires to be part of the other part, but you create the separation naturally within your reality, instead of seeing yourself as part of the great I AM.

The great prophets walked the earth as Humans. You saw them as different, however... unusual, sacred, divine, and powerful. They looked just like you—all of you. So what is it that made them different? I will tell you: These Humans were able to peel the duality away and create a miracle. They didn't participate in the separation of Human-Self and Higher-Self. Many followed these special ones because they saw joy in their lives; they saw the power. So you have to ask yourselves, what is the difference between an ordinary Human and the masters who were worshiped—whose lives were known to many, and still are through your history?

This is where it gets good. When the masters walked the earth with a lessened (lighter) duality, they did so to be able to see the bigger picture. They were not affected as you are. They had less darkness where they walked, and they could see more clearly. When you were born on this planet, a strong duality was in place. For the masters, it was spiritually lighter, and that made them "different." That's what you saw that was so abnormal. The prophets and masters of old were able to integrate the group!

Dear ones, you sit in an energy that we predicted 12 years ago. It's an energy that is going to become far more stable than it has been, but we'll get to that in a moment. What we want to tell you is this: The attributes of the masters are upon you. What is it all about, you ask? It is about a changing humanity and a changing spirituality. The veil is being slightly lifted! It is being lifted so that you can see dimly through it the things you never could see before. Some have asked, *"Could this really be? Can I really change my life?"* The answer is yes. You come into this experience with what is called a contract, and the compartmentalization in your brain says, *"This is my contract. It always will be."* So many never understand the truth around this. These contracts are what you agreed to as "starting energies." They get you going. No angel or prophet ever told anyone that it was forever! It just feels that way. You had to start somewhere, and your contract is a good place to begin. This beginning starts with where you left off, and is a simple agreement. It represents unfinished business; residues of past experience; choice of parents, race, place on the planet, fears, and joys. What is not seen is that it's the Human who has complete and total free choice to move in any direction he or she wishes... and yes, that means moving out of the starting contract!

Without an awakening to that fact, and without the ability of knowing of your enablement, that starting contract is often the one followed right to the end. How many of you have contracts that you wonder about? What about your biological contract? Does it include what happened to your sister and your brother and your parents? Genetically surging in your DNA, what are the "starting" patterns there? What are they going to "do" to you? Are you afraid that what your relatives received, you will, too? Do you feel predisposed to biologically follow that path? Well, dear Human Being, perhaps it's time to put on the mantle of the master—the master with your name, with the layers of who you are. If you do, the genetics in your body will all listen to the mantle of the master. And when you speak to yourselves and say, *"It is time for a change,"* the new contract is upon you. Your cells change! They say, *"We wish to be joyful and enjoy the love of Spirit. We wish to change our cellular structure, our genetic makeup. We wish to influence all that we have with our own intent, just like the masters did."* Do you understand what we are telling you? Do you understand how profound it is?

Take a moment, if you wish, and think about what the masters were able to do as they walked on this planet. They left many in their wake who were healed, sobbing and weeping in their joy and gratitude. They spouted profundities and wisdom, and they helped everyone they touched. They brought tribes together and affected nations. They unified the separated. They presented paradigms that were so different that they often lost their lives because of it. Now this same energy visits you! Why don't you take a moment and celebrate what you have created!

We're in place now, you know, and we're ready. And so it is that we take our places around you, above you, even below you. Interdimensionally, there is no limitation about where we can sit or stand or be. Each of you is surrounded by your own group—one that knows exactly what you've been through—that knows your weaknesses and your many questions. It is a group that is ready to take your hand and lead you one way or the other, if you ever come to that place where you would allow it... or recognize that you have the choice to ask for it.

Some of you are in touch with that group, and others are afraid of it. Being afraid of it is something that is absolutely natural at this particular time. Even this day there have been unverbalized questions asked, and we will deal with a couple of them. And then, of course, we're going to give you some science, too [something that the New Hampshire seminars are known for].

The question is asked, *"What is happening right now? Kryon, you've spoken about the grid, and you've also spoken about the fact that the adjustments to it are coming to a close. What will that mean to us?"* We just defined what the grid is really about. It's about the enabling of Human biology and consciousness. When we speak of biology, we also mean your spiritual biology, for it is all entangled in one. It all speaks to itself at the same time, and the "layers" sing to each other. Here is what is happening: As you know, and even with the proof of where your compasses now point, the grid has moved. It will continue to move for some time, but the spiritual alignment—the part of it that lifts the veil—will come to a close at the end of this year [2002]. There are some of you who have spent many years chasing this moving target—this changing grid. Now, here you are, facing still another attribute to deal with. For when it finally settles and the movement stops, there will be some stability, and in that there is also change.

There are those of you who might say, *"Well, it's about time!"* But do not be fooled for a moment. There are those of you who have become used to the motion, as in a moving deck on a ship. When it stops, you'll know it! Coming to a complete and seeming halt and stopping has its own attributes. Here is some advice: You don't have to chase it anymore. It's at your feet. You've gotten used to certain kinds of motion, and it's taken a decade for this. There are those of you who will feel it and be happy that it is being stabilized. But then there are those of you who also got used to the movement of it and who now have to get used to it being in one posture. Some of you will actually feel the motion even though it has stopped!

What does this mean to you? None of this is going to happen instantly or overnight. There is a residual we have spoken of before, information that is now one year old. The residual of grid alignment change will last at least three months. God does not do things quickly, if you've noticed. And therefore we say this: The stabilized grid will indeed come to its final position at the end of this year; it is a slow stop. But the residual is designed for your comfort so that there is no fast stop (and this is metaphoric). But what a joy it is to have the entourage almost finished with your gift.

Humanity is feeling this. We've told you before that this track you have produced for yourself is unique. It has never been traveled before, and therefore there's nothing in front of this new track. You are creating it as you go. This alone causes anxiety. There would be those who would sit in front of Spirit and plead to know the future. *"Where are we going? What are we doing? What's going to happen?"* And with joy we say this: Nobody knows! But we can tell the direction you're moving in. We can tell you the speed of the change, and it is profound... unexpected. You want proof of that? Go find any prophecy about what's happening today. All the ancients in their wisdoms—the master seers of their time—could not foretell what your ascending Earth is doing. That's what's happening now.

The part you play? It's your energy that did it. How many of you understand that you have a new contract in front of you? It's a contract that says we want you to stay longer. It opens up an entire new paradigm of life extension. And if you don't see it, your children will. It's not just medical science, and it's not just physics. It has to do with what the Human does for the Human. There will be those without any spiritual training whatsoever—those who carry the indigo color, who will understand totally and completely the overview of this. They will feel in control of their cellular structure, and there will be no surprises—you can see it in their eyes. They plan on being here a very long time, and they know how. It's intuitive. While you are sitting there wondering if it could be true that you can change your biology, they are already doing it. *"Doesn't everyone?"* they will say to you. Many will come in with the intuitive knowledge of what we are now teaching you. *"Of course we're in charge of matter,"* they will say to you someday. The things that you have questioned with your intellect and your logic will be second nature to humanity at some particular point in time. That's what's happening now.

Where Is the Grid Group Going?

And this grid group—where are they going? Should we be sad for them? Are they going home? Here is the answer: NO, and NO. This grid group that has been with us all of these years, that has moved the very magnetics of the planet to create your DNA, returns to what you would call other jobs. It stays and remains. It disseminates, but it is part of the earth itself. Some of you have recognized that Gaia has life. The indigenous believed that the dirt of the earth itself was part of an entity. They saw this in the elements, and in the east, the south, the west, and the north. And we are telling you this: that part of this magnetic grid group will continue to work with Gaia. This group has always been here and always will be. It has to do with the life-force of the planet. It has to do with the support of the Humans that are here. Where is the grid group going? They're staying right here. Consider it a job change, if you wish. That's what's happening.

There's another question that gets asked here, and it's one that we would like to endeavor to explain this very evening. Why is it with the grid shift lifting the veil, allowing for greater spirituality, insight, wisdom, and joy... why is it, then, that the dark side seems to be increasing so dramatically? Did you think we didn't notice? I'll give you information that seems unbelievable. I will say it again, and there will be those here who will not agree, but I will tell you the truth, dear Human Being: There is no such thing as the dark side.

Listen to this. Understand this. I am not tricking you when I tell you these things. I am giving you intuitive knowledge.

Check your Higher-Selves for the integrity of this answer. There is no group of entities who are part of your demise. There is no group that you would call "the dark side" that wishes to bring you into a place of darkness. There is no group of entities who are responsible for pulling you away from the light or taking your soul. And that is the truth. You might say, "Well, then, why does it seem like it?" This is difficult to grasp, perhaps, and not all will get it.

Let me tell you, oh powerful one: When you simply walk by water... and the molecular values within it change, what does that tell you about your influence [referring to the scientific validations that were shown earlier in the day]? Could it be that you are a lot more powerful as an "ordinary" Human Being than you ever thought? Could it be that you're not as ordinary as you thought? Indeed, this is the case. Listen: The Human Being who focuses on dark will get dark! And it will be *powerful* dark! The Human Being who focuses on light will bring in light. And it will be *powerful* light! Many times we've given you the difference between those attributes, for light is active and dark is passive. That's old information. But here is what it means: When there is darkness and you choose the light, a dark area exposed to light will become illuminated. The dark seems to vanish. It is literally not moving from dark to light, but instead it is an alchemy of "turning on the light." It happens all at once. It's not slow. And when the light is turned on, all of those things that were hidden in the dark are there for you to see.

The point is this: The Human Being who begins to move to the light is moving an energy framework. This framework is a finite area called Human consciousness. And when you move into the light, you're going to leave some of the dark behind. You can only hold so much energy in that Human framework. Therefore, if you choose a lighter energy for your system, there is going to be a piece of the darkness within your past duality that is going to be severed—lopped off—left behind. Think of it this way: Your personal jar of energy is always full. It's filled with a combination of dark and light. When you choose to add more light, the old dark part spills over the edge and goes away.

Now, what do you think that dark part is going to do to you? It's going to plead, *"Don't leave us behind! We've been part of you for a long time. Lifetime after lifetime you embraced us, and now you're throwing us away! Don't do it!"* And this severed part will come at you in *survival mode*, pleading not to be left behind. In this pleading, it will appear as though there's a legion—an army—pulling you away from the light. Much of it will be done with fear. Let me ask you this: Who knows *you* better than *you*? How does this "dark side" know about all of your weaknesses? How does it know about your habits? How does it know YOU so well? The answer? It's you, talking to you! It is the powerful part of you that you have chosen to lop off and leave behind. It's an actual interdimensional layer of your DNA, responsible for the balance between light and dark. Call it your duality engine. This is new information.

"Kryon," you might say, *"I still don't believe it."* All right, how about some intellectual proof? Let me ask you this. If it is true, dear Human Being, that there are legions of dark ones trying to trick you into submission—if there are armies led by entities with horns in dark places, trying to seduce you into the dark, then why are they so submissive? *"What does that mean?"* you might ask. Why is it that when you turn and face them and say no, they run the other way? What kind of an army of darkness is that? What kind of power is that? Did you ever think of this?

You are in control, and you always have been. The masters who walked the earth knew that. They faced the kind of energy balance you do, and they looked at it daily. The difference? Their enlightenment [less duality] showed them that they were in control, and the phantom legions of the dark armies shrank from them. You are no different! These dark parts will leave you alone, too... and that's the truth. It's you fighting you, and when you inform your cellular structure of your intent, it must obey.

This information is there for those reading this page. In a "now" that we see, we see the reader. We see your eyes and your mind. We see the joy in this information. So listen and read: There is no conspiracy to draw you backwards other than that which you create to survive in what you think is your reality. This is you with you. It is the giant *IT* presented in the parable of *The Journey Home* [Kryon Book Five]. Know yourself. It's time to look at this and say, *"I understand what is happening."* You can even say, *"I honor the darkest part of me that has been with me a very long time, and I release it."* And that is what's happening.

Oh, there will be those who disagree. As we've said before, they will tell you that Kryon is tricking you with the light. *"No dark side? That is preposterous,"* they will tell you. *"See, it's proof that Kryon is evil."* Really? Then don't believe me. Instead, activate your own light and order the darkness out. Then when it shrinks before you, celebrate the truth of God... that you are a part of the whole... holy, powerful, eternal, and in charge! Blessed are the Humans who take charge of themselves and pull upon the newly created divine power that is theirs!

These are challenging times, are they not? Perhaps you look at current events. *"Dear Kryon, what is happening on Earth?"* I'll tell you what's happening on Earth: It may not look like it, but you're solving the biggest issue we have. Collectively, I am here with you. Have you ever thought of that? I arrived to set the grid of the earth. I will not leave until the last Human takes his or her last breath. The entourage may come and go, the grids may be changed yet again someday, but Kryon remains. And so it is I am in this lifeboat with the Humans who are doing the work. So it is that I am in support of you, and I know what's happening. So it is that my teachings increase.

You have a word for what is happening, and it's called *pruning.* Sometimes it's not pleasant either. Perhaps you might question this? You might say, *"Kryon, everything I see around me is bad. There's darkness everywhere!"* Let's look at some changes: Ten years ago if I had told you that the largest businesses in this great land of yours would fall over and expire due to "integrity issues," would you have believed me? If I had given you the prophecy that one of the largest religious organizations on Earth would be brought to its knees because of integrity, would you have believed me? The answer is no. Such things were not seen as possible. Big money and big religion were untouchable. Well, look out the window and read your news. It's called pruning. Country by country... belief system by belief system, the sparks will fly. We told you that 12 years ago. We told you that many would have to leave the planet in this new arrangement. Oh, you may mourn those who are passing because you are part of humanity. It is normal and natural, for you love humanity. But there are those who decided to be part of this in a way that would help all of you. And that's what's happening.

So the earth prunes itself, and in the process, it creates something very slowly: It creates the beginning of The New Jerusalem. Now you know that this phrase is not a metaphor, don't you? It is what we have meant all along for all of these years. It really is Jerusalem. It is the pinnacle and apex of the problems—the thing that has brought Earth to its knees—the source, seemingly, of the strife of your time. The words *The New Jerusalem* also refer to a group of Humans—ones who represent a generation of Human Beings who decided to change reality, to skip the Armageddon and move forward. They are the ones who will solve the unsolvable, and begin a process of peace on this planet.

I am Kryon. I carry only a piece of the puzzle. You do not see what I see. I tell you this: Look around. There are many others who have many messages. Study them as well and "connect the dots." Listen to the channellings. Listen to the wise ones. Discern what resounds and what does not. Is the information fear based? Is it love based? Choose what resounds in your heart and also makes the most sense. It's called *free choice*. See the big picture by connecting the parts. Look around and see God in you!

It's a good time to see the colors—right now.

[Pause]

There's a great deal of honoring going on. *"Kryon, what's happening?"* God is loving you, that's what's happening.

Science

It might seem dichotomous to move from this message of love into physics, but I am the magnetic master, after all, and I love to talk about these things. Not all of you will understand what is coming next. In order for this channelling to be complete and for my partner, who does not understand these things, to have a clearer image, we will involve something we have only done two times in the past. We now invite the energy of **Metatron** to come forward!

Metatron and Kryon are of the same family... that of Archangel Michael. This is the same family of spiritual physics and is very entangled. And so it is that the energies of all three are here. One of them is my partner [Lee] who translates, and then also the meld between Kryon and Metatron, who speak of physics. We wish to talk about something dear to the hearts of the physicists. We're going to speak of free energy, and we can hardly wait. Not understandable by all of you, but some of the readership will know, and there will be those here who understand, also. So I ask of my partner that this be translated clearly and slowly if needed.

Before we begin, you must understand the premise. Humanity has been convinced for some time that there might be something called *free energy*. This might be manifested in a device that would be able to sustain itself seemingly without fuel. The question is, is it possible? The answer is yes, it always has been. Some will understand how this could work, for it profoundly involves magnetics. And indeed there will be some who will discover it at a macro level, but it won't be very efficient. What we wish to do is give you some answers that may surprise you, but which will allow you to achieve the goal of free energy far easier and quicker.

Let us review: Perhaps as children you were amazed at something—static magnets that when held in the hands, strongly repel similar poles of other magnets. You might have been amused at how much you had to push against the metal to try to get similar poles together. The magnetic material actually seemed to repel and push back! And the bigger the magnet, the greater the rebellion against coming together. Some of you children grew up to become scientists, and you asked questions about physics and nature: *"What is this force that pushes back? Why is it that Humans can throw their entire weight into this endeavor and end up with a piece of metal that pushes back? What is going on here? What is the engine of this? Can I get this to push when I want... in a direction I want?"*

The physicists, of course, developed answers about trapped energy and called it *kinetics*. There is actually all manner of verbiage that would try to describe to you why there would be a force trapped in metal that would push back. None of it is correct! There's something going on with magnetism that will indeed be discovered. It has a layer of interdimensionality that you are now just broaching; it is not definable in four dimensions [your reality]. The true reason why it pushes back is not even part of your four-dimensional physics. You named it, but you don't understand it.

Some scientists went on to postulate: *"What if we could get magnets to push against magnets? If we design something clever, perhaps the magnets could push against themselves and we could use this energy in a circle—in a machine—magnets with magnets. We could use this incredible natural pushing and pulling force to push and pull against itself. Then we would have an engine that fueled itself with nature's force!"* This, then, is the simplified way science first started to think about free energy. Today, if you talk to a physicist, you will discover that it isn't possible. This scientist will tell you that there's always what would be called the "trade-off," or what some may call "paying the piper." You can't get something for nothing. There is always something that's going to interfere with free energy, they say. Are they right? YES! But let me tell you what that "something" is: 4D physics! The restriction you find yourself in... the reason it doesn't work... is due to your own dimensional reality. That's the answer.

Now you know the puzzle, and hopefully we've explained it in a way that you understood it. The physicists are right when they tell you that you can't get something for nothing. Now we must tell you about true physics. With all this in mind, will this engine ever work? The answer: YES. This magnetic engine works very well! But not the way you think it might.

In order to broach the next issue, we have to tell you this: The physics that you are so fond of, and that you boast about, has consistency. That is when you find a postulate that proves itself 100 percent of the time in your real 4D world. When this happens, you have the propensity to feel good about it. Then you project whatever that rule is and apply it to the entire universe. Therefore, Newtonian, Einsteinian, and Euclidian physics—the rules that seem to govern everything at all levels—are absolute to you. As you discover them in your reality, you set them in cement for all realities. Well, that's not the case! Let me ask you this, scientist: Did you try this physics in all the forms it could exist? Or did you make some assumptions?

In the past, we gave you hints. Kryon gave you formulae that indicated that there were missing pieces in basic physics concepts that you still did not understand. You see, physics is variable... and to some this is not good news. What is the largest variable of physics? Size. The ratio of attributes between mass, magnetics, and gravity changes with size.

We're going to define this variable and call it "the quantum membrane." It's a membrane of attributes. It's one that you pass through at a certain quantum level, where physics changes. Now, these things have been seen, but up to this point those who have observed them have seen them as quaint. Some have argued about this and asked, could this membrane of attributes exist? Yes, it does. When you pass through this level, many odd, unusual things take place—things that might actually clear the way to free energy. Let me be more specific. It is actually a membrane of dimensionality—what you might call moving from four to five. Of course this is wrong to say, because when you move out of four dimensions, there is no more linearity, since your time changed. Without linearity you cannot count anymore, can you? [Laughter] So "five" really becomes an impossibility. So just say that you are "moving out of your dimension."

Listen. I'm going to give you information that your physicists will validate shortly. Let me ask you this: According to your physics, can two things exist in the same place at the same time? And you may say, positively no. That is impossible. Then let me change the question. What if the two things were really the same thing twice? You might say, *"Well, we've never heard that."* Indeed! It is what happens when matter passes through the quantum membrane! The same particle exists in two-dimensional attributes simultaneously.

[Pause]

Listen, my partner [Kryon speaking to Lee], this is important. It's important that you get this right. It's the first exposure that this topic has ever had, and Metatron and Kryon want to give it to you in a way that the readers will understand.

When matter passes through the membrane, there is an instant, infinitesimal portion of time where the matter actually contains both polarities, positive and negative. It actually seems as though the parts are in the same place at the same time. This is almost what you might call an anti-matter exchange. Through the membrane, there is a momentary, infinitesimal unbalancing of what we have called The Cosmic Lattice. And in that moment, there is energy created, seemingly from nothing. But it's not from nothing, but from everything! The Cosmic Lattice represents all energy of the Universe in a balanced, zero, "null" state, waiting to be tapped. We have described this before. What is the secret of tapping it?

The secret of free energy lies in becoming small... very small. The secret of free energy is very small magnetics going through the membrane—that is, an interdimensional force is at work. It is the quantum leap—the thing that seems to bridge the un-bridgeable, where particles can go from one place to another and yet seem never to traverse the path that must be traversed. What if the particles never actually "traveled" at all? What if they bounced to another dimension, since they were forced to due to a situation where they occupied the same space at the same time? What if they actually never *went* anywhere, but in your dimension (as the viewer), it just seemed like it?

The secret of free energy is very, very small machines... lots of them working together. If you can make the machines small enough and you can align them to a common purpose [common push], you could take advantage of what I have just given you. When you deal with magnetics at a molecular level, you're going to discover that it acts differently. Free energy is obtainable today through large arrays of very small engines. Think small... very small. Free energy is not only possible, it's there waiting. It's not free, either. It's not the creation of energy out of nothing. Instead, it is tapping the lattice where mountains of energy are available.

Here is something else you will discover, and something very fun for the mathematician: The large array of molecular engines will total a force that is beyond the sum of the parts! This alone should be the clue that there is unseen "hidden" energy at work.

The final new hint in this scenario of free energy advice that we will give you is this: Since it's going to take very small magnetics to do this, you may need some very small polarities to move around to accomplish this. How? Don't forget that you can magnetize certain gases.

Metatron and Kryon also want to give you this information about matter/anti-matter. There are those in physics who believe that the universe must contain the antithesis of itself, next to itself. That is to say that anti-matter and positive matter must exist somehow together for the balance to be there, which the math of physics demands. Yet the interesting thing is that although positive matter is all around you [the kind you are used to seeing], its counterpart [anti-matter] is elusive. There-fore, the question might be asked by the physicist: *"Where is anti-matter? Is there as much of it as there is positive matter?"* And the answer is yes.

Where is anti-matter? It's resting on the "attribute quantum membrane." It's also in a slightly different time frame. When you start to understand the ability within physics to change time-frame reality, all of the anti-matter will present itself. And the reason is this: It has to be there for balance! And there's a joke here, a very big cosmic joke. This phenomenon of anti-matter resting in a slightly different time frame is what is responsible for what you have mistakenly identified as the big bang.

Listen, scientist, and suspend your 4D bias for a moment. Matter showed up everywhere, all at once. There was no explo-sion. The membrane changed, and the universe was created. Oh, not the one that you see today, but a beginning universe. And the residual of that membrane shift is everywhere you look, and you'll never find a pinpoint source for any bang. You'll never find a center for any bang. That is because all reality became reality all at once. When you find these things to be true, you'll also find the secret of instant communication over long distances... through interdimensional attributes that suspend all the rules of time and location.

[Pause]

Metatron is leaving. Oh, he'll be back... there is so much honor in this!

We close with this. How many are afraid of this change? Are you afraid that a diminished duality will create the loss of friends and family? Perhaps you say, *"I'll be talking metaphysics, and they won't. Kryon, I don't want that, because I'm in love with my mate, and I appreciate my friends. I don't want to be an outcast;*

I don't want be a loner; I don't want to be ostracized. Is this what a changing grid is going to do to me?"

Oh, dear one, I don't think you've really thought this through. What happens when you take the mantle of the master... the master inside? What happens when you take the mantle of love? What happens when you take ascension status and you become wiser? What happens when you become more peaceful? What happens when you smile too much? I'll tell you: It is the opposite of what you're afraid of. People want to be with you because you've changed. You change into something that people admire and are attracted to. They see that somehow you have "put it together" and they haven't, and they want to be with you. It makes people fall in love with you again. It creates bonds that are permanent. It is the opposite of what you fear. Change? Yes. Did you ever think about that? Did you ever wonder why the masters who walked the earth were so loved... so desired... so peaceful? Claim this master-hood and watch those you love and admire become even closer!

And so the entourage that came in here willingly, wishing to hold your hand and be part of your experience, departs. But not with sadness. With joy! Because there are some here this very night who have made decisions to "turn on the light."

And so it is.

Live Channelling

"Plain Talk"

Channelled in Dallas, Texas
January 2003

Chapter Six

Plain Talk
Dallas, Texas - January, 2003
Chapter Six

Greetings, dear ones, I am Kryon of Magnetic Service. I was waiting, for there were some of you who needed to see the light change. I don't mean the lights in here. Some of you needed validation to see the color shift as we came in here, pouring into this place, which was already so expertly prepared by those who sit in these chairs.

My partner has decided to call these meetings "And So It Begins." This is channelled information, and some of you might say, *"Well, what is it that's new and different? What is it that's beginning?"* Well, for one thing, the grid is settled. Oh, the residual may take three more months to settle [until the end of March 2003]. Remember, things don't happen quickly with Spirit. But we can't even begin the teachings without going into a mode of celebration. It's a celebration that you've allowed such a thing to be—a new energy on the planet—that you've had the patience, some of you, to endure this moving target of spiritual consciousness, one that we've presented to you for a decade or more. You've moved in and out of purpose. Some of you have wanted to throw up your hands in the darkness and shout, *"Oh, God! I don't understand. I've tried, I've given intent; I've done this; I've done that!"* And we were there, and we heard you. We've been there every single time you cried out. We've been there for the words of celebration and joy, and for the words of sorrow. We've been there every single time, even when you wondered if anybody was listening. We've been there, too.

One of the reasons why there's so much celebration and foot-washing as this entourage pours in here has to do with your endurance. Lightworkers (you call yourselves), you are lighthouses anchoring energy, not afraid to walk from place to place, knowing that some of you will be ridiculed and scorned. Instead, you hold peace in your heart, believing that all is appropriate and that there are reasons for everything.

And so we celebrate you before we teach. The potential was always here that you'd sit in these chairs. Are you listening to this? Do you think it's an accident that you're here? Reader, do you think it's an accident that your eyes are on this page? I know you. Reader, I was there when you cried out to God, and so were those around me. There was an entourage that was next to you, holding your hand in your darkest moments. This is the way of it, you know. It isn't just about ascension, master-hood, or mystery. Oh, there's a lot of that, too. But what about right now?

We told you that the grid would shift, and it did. We told you that a grid group would be involved, and it was. Then we told you they would leave, and they have. We said that the teaching would begin in a stable environment of grid magnetics. The magnetics of the planet are always dynamic—that is, they'll always move around, but not nearly to the degree that you've experienced in these last 12 years. If I could give you one word or even perhaps a simple phrase that would explain what has happened in this last decade or so, I would say *lifting*. Lifting. We speak of a veil that creates your duality, and the energy of everything on this planet is lifting it slightly.

We speak in metaphors constantly, don't we? We speak in puzzles and parables. Some have asked, *"Kryon, why is that needed? Why is that necessary?"* It's because you can't pierce that veil. Metaphors are often the only way you can have interdimensional understanding while you sit in only four dimensions. So when you start examining the parables and the metaphors, that's when you get your own "aha" experience, and you know what we're trying to say. But in the new energy, this is becoming less used.

The new energy has been the lifting of the veil. Even when you look at this in physical form and not metaphoric form, you see a veil between you and something else. Through this veil, you're not seeing clearly, are you? If a portion of it lifts away to reveal what's on the other side, then you have clearer, plainer sight, don't you? So let's start this new energy in this new year [2003] with this group of readers and listeners, and call this particular message "Plain Talk."

It's about time, isn't it? Let's feature communication that may be clearer. Oh, there will still be parables, and along the way there will still be metaphors, since there must be. But one of the things that you're going to discover is that we, on the other side of this veil, are able to see you more clearly, too. Did you ever think of that? We stand next to you!

If you could define the veil, it wouldn't be "somewhere." It's not a place. Instead, it's a dynamic energy that surrounds your very consciousness—every cell of your body. It distances you... from *you*. Suddenly we're here to tell you that over these last years, this veil has been thinned, and now it's time for some plain talk.

Let's start by celebrating you! I can't pass over this lightly. Today we flood this place with the energy of "mother." It's unconditional love, which is feminine. We've described to you in the past—revealed, in fact, the last time we channelled—that the predominant energy of Kryon has always been feminine. That's plain talk, isn't it? You can add that up any way you wish to. But it explains a lot of what you've read and what you feel. The entourage I bring here washes your feet. Some stand beside you as you read and listen, some above you, and some are even below. Such is the way of an interdimensional visit.

What are you going through right now, dear Human Being? You sit in an energy that's anxious, right? What is taking place in the Middle East? Perhaps as you read this, there have been changes. But where's the appropriateness in all of this? Why did this happen? What is it going to mean? How does this fit in with anything that you've been taught might happen? The potentials we gave you all those years ago—how does it fit in with that? Not all is as it seems here. Historians will have something special to say about this time in history. Not all has been revealed—especially to you—about what's really going on. The wishes and the hopes of those even in the Oval Office have not been truly revealed to you either. But all will be, eventually. You see, it's impossible to carry these things as secrets from now on. Let me tell you what has happened.

We told you in 1989 that you had changed your reality. The good news was that the Armageddon you had expected wasn't going to happen. The challenging news was that you would fill it with a war. Oh, maybe not a physical one, although you've had two between then and now. No. It would be war between the old and new energies on the planet. We told you it could manifest itself in many different ways, but that *you* would fight it. Well, let me give you some plain talk—things that should be obvious to you, but aren't always.

The Human Social Effect

Even those who study society are not considering this yet. Consider these things: There are more Humans on Earth at this moment than there ever have been. In the last 50 years, Earth has tripled its population—more Humans reacting to more Humans. It's a more crowded place, isn't it? Adjustments have to be made in your society for this, and you know that. In fact, some of you have spent those 50 years here, noticing it... even complaining about it! Yet, what has the predominant social issue been? Wouldn't you think that with more and more Human Beings interfacing one with another, the social structure would eventually move toward a more socialist kind of existence? Doesn't it make sense to create a cooperative system that serves a more common interest in order to make things work? But that isn't what happened.

In fact, the systems that featured those elements fell apart! Governments that seemed to offer "the most good for the most people," fell apart. The consciousness of those systems wasn't supported by humanity. So what was created? Look around. You're left with systems on Earth where individuals are seen individually for what they contribute. These systems encourage participants to think for themselves, out of the group consciousness. Now isn't that counterintuitive for a population that's closing in on itself? Yes, it is, yet no one has really noticed that. Right now, the systems that promote self-worth and self-determination, even with worship, are the most prosperous on the planet.

Sweeping over the planet, even in the countries that don't wish to admit it, is a consciousness of individuality. Human Beings are awakening out of the darkness, and they're saying, *"I am special; I am unique; there is no one like me. I will think the way I wish."* It's everywhere. It has toppled governments and it will topple more... and that's the plain talk of it. It's universal on this planet, and that's just one of many phenomena that seem counter-intuitive to an increasing population. Yet it's a spiritual aspect, for we teach that you're an individual part of creation.

Conspiracy

Now let me give you some more plain talk. Let me take you back 15, 20 years. Here is something we recently spoke of in another venue: For a very long time, and we will speak of the entire civilized world, there have been many secrets about the way things work. Much has been hidden in the corners and the cracks regarding information available to the common citizens of Earth. Enemies can be behind rocks on your path and you'll never see them. They can clump in dark places, and they can conspire against your very life. They can conspire to make your economics, your elections, and even what you pay for everything, work in a certain way. They can conspire to make the earth work in a certain way. They're powerful and have a lot of influence. They're very Human, however, representing a controlling, greed consciousness.

The main attribute about them is that they're always in the dark. Rumors of their existence have leaked out enough so that they even had a name. They're the *Illuminati*. They're the secret group. They're the code-makers and the ones who pulled the strings of your very social situation. They made elections happen. They took your financial markets and controlled them. We've never spoken about this before in a live channelling, but this is plain talk. Many of you might say, *"Is this real? Could this be true?"* The answer is yes. Did you ever notice that there was a sameness about things—a stability about things in the past? You felt it was just a more solid situation... a good thing. Guess again. They controlled most of it. Like a large ship on a course that seldom moved, they steered your very existence into their pockets.

Where were they? I will even tell you that. You'll notice that I'm speaking in the past tense, don't you? They were in the country you call Greece. That's where it began, and that's where it fell apart. Much to their shock, an increasing vibrational consciousness of the planet, caused by a moving grid system, started to open a can called *integrity*. Then you developed technology, which allowed everyone to speak to everyone at almost no cost [the Internet]! They could no longer hide in the dark, and four years ago they began to fall. That's the plain talk of it. There can be no more conspiracies on this planet to that degree, and here's the reason: There are *Lighthouses* like you all over this planet who are dedicated to letting that light shine. There are lights being turned on everywhere!

There are far fewer dark places to scamper to or hide within. This didn't happen because there were some grand groups that rode in on white horses. You want to know who the grand ones who changed this were? They are the ones in the chairs who sit in front of me—the ones who read this right now, who, with the mind of Spirit many years ago, decided to come to Earth with the potential to make a difference!

You think this sounds like an allegory, a fairy tale? Well, go read your newspaper. Tell me about the largest corporations you have—falling over because an individual with integrity spoke up. When did that happen last? If we told you the potential of that happening ten years ago, you would have laughed! You might have said, *"Kryon, you must understand that nothing touches big money. It's one of those things that will never change. There are certain things on this earth that cannot be touched, and big money is one of them."* It just did.

What if I asked you, what is another one of those things that will never change? *"Well,"* you might say, *"big religion is another.*

It's a very large and old organization that cannot be moved easily." Really? Go read your newspaper. A very big religion is reevaluating itself, isn't it? An integrity factor is starting to show. There are those who are beginning to emerge within that belief system and are saying, *"Wait a minute! This isn't correct. The God that I worship would not have representatives that would do these things. My God is a loving God, and these individuals are not representing that."*

This organization you call the church is being reevaluated and pruned. And it's not just limited to the Western world, either. Watch for it worldwide. We told you about this almost three years ago when we said, "The greatest spiritual leaders you have who search for the divine on your planet are coming to a reckoning even as you sit here" [Kryon Book Eight, *Passing the Marker*]. Now the energy of what you've created has caught up with them! The result? There will be more integrity within the ranks of those who lead the planet on a spiritual level.

That's what a vibrational increase does. There are fewer dark places. And let me tell you what happens when those who would conspire against you have fewer places to hide. They show themselves. We're not in judgment, but we will tell you that it's a Human dramatic reaction to go find them and eliminate them! But there are other ways, dear ones. That's why you're almost at war. It's a different energy now... if you've noticed.

Many are in complete denial about all this. Even with your news, the weather changes, and the proof of the magnetics and crystalline energies changing, they stick to the old Earth energy. We also told you that a chasm would develop [Kryon Book 8], even within your own metaphysical beliefs. It begins. Many are looking at the new energy and feeling that it's false, and that you're somehow covering the truth of conspiracy with your light. Somehow they feel that your light is going to cover up the truth.

How can you know who's right? It's easy. Look at their lives. Are they comfortable, peaceful, and filled with the love of God? Are they tolerant with their lives and those around them? Would you like to have them around you? What is their "drama" factor? It speaks volumes of how their cells are doing, doesn't it? Blessed is the Human who lets in the truth of Spirit. For it will affect the very cellular structure of his blood. It will bring him peace in the face of war and give him tolerance when all around him there is none. It will produce ideas that were never thought of, and create a vibrational shift.

President Bush and the Election

We even told you about the man who's your president [January 2003]. We called him a "place-holder." This was not a criticism or a demeaning term. It's simply a definition of energy. It's one who holds energy while something else happens. In mathematics, a place-holder is used to hold the energy of a place while solutions are computed around it. It allows the columns to line up and the dots to be connected. It's a metaphor, isn't it? And that's what we told you about the man who's your president.

So what kind of a place is he holding? you might ask. Here is information you didn't expect. There are things around you, not in this country [USA], which need to be shifted and changed. There are those who need to move around so that the earth can be more even in its consciousness. And this is the man who's facilitating it. You may not like it, but it's what you planned. This place-holder is a catalyst for change.

Do you think it was an accident that he came into office? Go take a look at his election. First, was it a normal one? No. It was almost a forced election... one that seemed out of balance—not your standard election, was it? Here is a postulate of those who would control you: "Never create unusual circumstances that will beg investigation." Therefore, we tell you that this election was not something created by those in the dark. Instead, it was something you created within the new energy... to facilitate what you're seeing.

We ask you to look back on these kinds of things metaphysically. Suspend your political and humanitarian urges for just a moment and get above yourselves. Look instead into the future, and what all this might create. We told you about the potential of the energy on your planet more than a decade ago. That's why many of you feel anxious. We spoke of the battle to come, and we even told you that there were those who agreed to leave during these times [Kryon Book One, *The End Times*]. Now, here you sit within it, and it's not very comfortable, is it? Perhaps that's why it's called work? These changes are going to prune the planet. They're going to separate the old from the new. The old energy thinkers will have to change, for if they don't, they'll find themselves in an old consciousness within a new energy. Make no assumptions about who the old energy thinkers are! The result of living in one energy while in the posturing of another is dis-ease. It's appropriate that you have the leader you have, for much will be put forward that never would have happened otherwise. Perhaps what you do in reaction to him is the key? Perhaps it will cause more to be "torn off the fence"? Think about it. More plain talk. *(See more at the end of this chapter)*

God—Spirit—Source

Let's speak about God, or what many of you call Spirit or Source. Kryon comes from The Great Central Sun. Where do you suppose that is? Oh, there are those who say, *"Well, we know where that must be. It's up there—three stars to the left."* No, it isn't.

The Great Central Sun isn't a place. It's the best information we could give you to try to tell you where Spirit and family are—the pieces and parts of you. Where do they live? I'll tell you. I'll tell you where the great central sun is: It's in the space between your thoughts! The Great Central Sun is the distance between the nucleus and the electron haze in every atom in existence. It's great, it's central, for it's everywhere. It's the sun because it's the metaphor of light. It's where you emanate from when you're not here. It's not a place at all. It's a dimensional attribute that's everywhere all the time. It's difficult to explain to single-digit dimensional beings—difficult to explain. How can I prove this? I can't, but let me define *God* as "the missing piece."

I will challenge you. Scientists, are you listening and reading? Go find the missing piece. Did you know that there's a missing piece of your reality? It's everywhere. Here's something that doesn't make any sense. There's energy missing in the Universe. Where did it go? There's energy missing in mathematics. Where did it go? We ask you to start adding things up. Start looking at the truth—this is plain talk.

Why should the most profound and common mathematical formula in existence be an irrational number? Pi isn't complete. Does that make sense to you within the elegance of a universal system? That number goes on forever and has no solution! Does that make sense? You see, there's something missing. It wouldn't go on forever if there was just a little more of it. It would be a whole number. [Smile]

There are missing pieces in physics, and there's a missing piece in consciousness. Where is Spirit? It's everywhere. And that's why we tell you this—that if you wish to connect (and we'll get to that in a minute), you don't have to go anywhere! There are few procedures, and there are no books either. The most profound energy on Earth is the one you carry with you called

Human consciousness. This is plain talk. This consciousness will enable you, if you allow it. This will fill in the gaps, if you allow it. It will allow the visualization of what has been in the dark. The pieces that have been missing will start to appear. They will start to complement you. Your biology will shift, your consciousness will shift, and your vibration will begin to increase. Can it be that simple? We'll talk about that in a moment.

But where is God? It's so interesting to look at humanity, and the duality that's so rich. There are even those who don't believe that a higher power exists. Did you know that the search for God is intuitive within humanity? So let's talk about that.

Reincarnation

Some have asked, *"Dear Kryon, is reincarnation real?"* I don't even wish to use that word. I'd rather call it something better: *sacred creation*—a melding of an old soul in a new body for the purpose of a new experience on the planet—born in love with the equality of every other piece of God called Human. Doesn't that sound better? Yes, this system is real.

Humans think in very straight lines. Because of your linearity, almost every religion on your planet believes in the afterlife. Most religions profess that once you die, you keep going as an eternal being of some kind. Yet few of them believe in the forelife... an existence before you got here. And so we say again to you, is this spiritually logical? They teach that you arrive from nothing and nowhere, yet you're suddenly eternal—created out of nothing and becoming everything. Even physicists know better than that. There's always an energy exchange. Creation doesn't come from nothing.

There are those who've said that there's no proof whatsoever of reincarnation. No one has ever come back from across the veil and said, *"Yes, that's the way it works."* You're right! But let me remind you of something: No one has ever come across the veil from death and said that's not the way it works either. In other words, there's no proof either way. This is part of the way the veil works... that although there's some communication with those who have died, they don't come back and hold meetings. This is on purpose, dear ones.

Most of humanity doesn't believe in a forelife. And why is that? Because the major religions of the planet tell you that it's not so. What does that mean to you? Powerful spiritual leaders in strange outfits with lots of abundance in big buildings give you this information... and therefore it must be true? Where is *their* proof? Is it that they've been around a long time, so they must be correct? Well, so have you! Their answers are no better than yours. They're honored for their search and for their attempts, but so are you!

Here's an exercise: Wherever you are right now in consciousness, we want to bring you back for a moment and be alert. We'd like you to communicate in an energy that we've set up and allow you to communicate in a lifted-veil status. We'd like you to ask your Higher-Self a question, one question, then stand back and quietly listen to the answer in an alert state. Plain talk. Ask yourselves this: *"Am I eternal?"* You just got the answer. There was a piece of you that just wanted to leap out of its skin and say yes! Yes and yes!

This answer didn't come from any other source, and it didn't come from an Earthly organization. What better way to do this than to ask yourself, *"Am I eternal?"* The answer will be yes. Being an eternal being means that there's no beginning and no end. It's a circle, you know. In that circle you come and go and come and go and come and go. It's the way of it. It has always been the way of it. It's precise, and yet it's changeable.

Did you know that the very contract you agreed to arrive with can be changed today? How about right now? Who told you that the contract—the one to do with karmic experience—was set in stone? Let me tell you the truth. This is plain talk. That contract was a *starting energy*. It invited you to change it all along, but if you do nothing, that's the one you're living.

Considering God

Human Beings are so funny! You wish to put God in your own dimension, and then say, *"That's who God is."* You feel that there's a place where God must exist that is physical... and it looks a certain way—perhaps it's the third star to the left? [Laughter]

What if blood cells had consciousness? Ever thought about that? These are living things, aren't they? They reproduce; they go to work; they have purpose; they live a life; they're born; they die. It sounds like you! For the sake of this metaphor, let's say they have a consciousness in blood cell-dom. Then let's say they got together and decided that perhaps there was a higher purpose for why they were there. Racing around in the darkness in the veins of the body, whom do you suppose they might worship? The heart? Perhaps the kidneys? Maybe even the lungs? After all, that's where they stop and transfer energy. But how many of them do you think would be able to think outside the body "neighborhood" for answers? *"Maybe we're inside something that is bigger than we can imagine."* they might say. *"Maybe there's a consciousness that's above where we are. Maybe there is purpose here that we're not seeing."* Instead of worshiping the heart or the liver or the lungs, perhaps they might choose to think that there's something outside of all they know, something they've never seen yet, or can't. Would they do that? Not likely. Instead, they'd see God as a large blood cell with a light, perhaps?

Why do I bring this up? Because it's much like what Humans perform. They want to make God into an object and put Spirit in a physical place in the seeable Universe. Most Humans don't understand that God is not in Human reality. You may say you understand that, but then with angels... you have to put skin and wings on them, and even give each one a name just to talk to them! What if I told you that every entity was like a cloud of gas the size of Texas? Everywhere and nowhere... and that each cloud of gas was also with other clouds of gas. How could you name those? There's nothing to really see, and no form at all. Yet you want to bring them into your reality to deal with them. I have an idea. Why don't you be the one to turn into the cloud and join *them?*

Just like the blood cells carry oxygen, giving life to the Human Being, Humans carry the life of God. And that's the truth! You're actually a piece of the wholeness of what you call God. Spirit cannot exist without you. Every single one of you is an integral piece of divinity, and without you this beautiful tapestry called God wouldn't exist. Oh, it's true that you're here in duality and seemingly in the dark and you don't understand everything. But we're telling you that these last years, what has happened is that you've given permission to *turn on the light!* Much of what is happening now is due simply to that.

The gifts of Spirit and self-empowerment lay there waiting for your discovery in what used to be the darkness. They represent the new tools of life. They represent what you've called *ascension.* And what is this *ascension?* Did you know that this word doesn't mean "leaving the planet"? *Ascension* means moving to a higher vibration where you stay on the planet in an enhanced form and make a difference! How about that? How do you make this connection? How do you turn on the light? Now, this is plain talk.

How many steps are there to ascension? Only one. There has been great criticism in this statement. *"Kryon, you never give anybody any information that is specific in the way of procedure. How are we going to proceed with something like gaining a higher vibration when you never give us any steps?"* You're right—absolutely right. There's nothing you can grab ahold of because I'm not giving four-dimensional instructions anymore. Plain talk. It's about time you sat down and figured something out: Gone are the old ways of spiritual progress! You're being invited to a cooperative arrangement where you take the hand of your Higher-Self and move into areas that simply can't be delineated, measured, counted, or notated. There are no beads to count, no phrases to say, no meetings to attend, no altars to prepare, and no masters to beg forgiveness of.

The "one step" is a catalyst to a thousand personal ones. Say with pure intent: *"Dear God, tell me what I need to know to start this process of becoming interdimensional. What do I need to know in order to start vibrating higher?"* Then allow Spirit to slowly work with you. Don't expect a four-dimensional answer! You're using your own master-hood to create answers. Expect synchronicity. Expect passion to change in your life. Expect a different consciousness to develop. Then when each one begins, you'll work with it until the next begins. Each Human is different, and each path is unique. It's a work in progress for the rest of your life.

Create Out of Nothing

In the last few years, your science has proven that Human consciousness changes matter. If you believe this, do you think that it would be possible for Human consciousness to *create* matter? Well, the answer is yes, it always could! It can create something, seemingly out of nothing. Impossible, you say? The avatars did it. The masters of old did it. You can do it, too. So why don't you create something that's completely and totally apart from your four-dimensional existence? This is really alchemy, and we've told you before that it's simply changing energy. Here is how it's done.

Every day, create thought *engrams*. [Kryon's definition of *engrams* are thoughts that remain in your memory as energy.] These engrams are more than just idle visualizations. Engrams are sacred energy thought-groups. How do you create them? Use remembrance. Enhance what you've seen or experienced. All of you have experienced laughter. So emboss this joy into yourselves based on the model that's real that you remember. All of you have had youth. So emboss this remembered vitality into your mind.

These engrams will eventually create a new reality within you, which will slowly pull you out of 4D and into something higher. You may not understand what that means, but in 4D you're in a box. Use your 4D experience to climb the walls of the box and prepare to use what you're given... but not necessarily understand it. *"What?"* you might say. *"That makes no sense at all. We need to study a process and understand it in order to use it. That's just basic logic."* Really? Do you understand intuition? Can you define how to use it? No. But you use it, don't you? Do you understand gravity? No. But you work with it daily. Get used to concepts that you work with but cannot explain.

Predisposition

What is predisposed in your body? What disease are you going to get because your brother got one or your sister or your cousin? This is plain talk. Why don't you eliminate that? This information is about self-empowerment. It's about asking yourself, the Divine-Self, questions about God. Use the power of your own Human consciousness in what you've called intent, every day of your life. Talk to your cellular structure. Maybe it's time you stopped talking to Spirit for a while and instead talked to the Higher-Self within? Do you know that there are trillions of cells waiting for the boss to talk to them?

Some of you have never even addressed your cellular structure, and you wonder why it's out of balance! Have you ever sat down and had a meeting with your body? Perhaps this is something to do alone and not around your friends [good advice]. Then after you've healed yourself and balanced yourself and enabled yourself, they might notice. *"Whatever happened to that problem you used to have?"* they might ask. And you could say, *"Well, I had a meeting with my cells, and boy, were they glad to hear from me! Because I had never talked to them before. I've been alive all these years, and never knew I could. You won't believe what they were going to do on their own! So I rewrote their schedule. I created something—a longer life."* Now perhaps you'll also start understanding how peace is created in you and what happens when a number of people create peace in themselves. It's catchy, you know. [Smile]

If you could project yourselves 100 years from now, you might find that something has changed: It's a potential we always told you about. A hundred years from now when you look back, historians will talk about solving the unsolvable. They'll talk about the way things used to be and about the time when humanity turned it around. They'll speak of how a new consciousness on Earth prevailed, and how everyone had to agree on what civilization meant, and how there was an understanding that war would never be an option to problem solving again. They'll talk about Bush, and what happened. They'll talk about how he was a catalyst to the next step. Hindsight will be keen, and here you sit with a preview.

Oh, yes, there will be challenges, and yes, there will still be countries that don't agree with other countries—and cultures and religions will bicker. But the potential is for a higher vibration on this planet... believe it or not. That's the potential we see, and that's why we love you the way we do. And that's as plain as it gets. Now what are you going to do with this possibility? Do you understand the responsibility you have to examine that?

We pause right before we leave. There's never been a better time to turn on the light. You're going to hear this from us over and over—an expression that means: *Why don't you shift dimensionality and create those thought engrams that change reality in 4D and go beyond it?* How do you talk to 4D creatures in an interdimensional way? I just did. It's very difficult for me to explain to you what it's like out of the dimensionality you grew up in and live in.

We're in love with you, you know. The grid is settled. There is much teaching. Eventually, we'll begin, when it's appropriate, the teaching of the DNA. We'd like to tell you what the layers are all about, what the colors are, and what the numbers are. Before we do that, we'd like to tell you more about ascension—something we may call "Through the Eyes of Ascension." It's all part of a new teaching for Kryon, in a new energy of a new planet with the potential that's still remarkable.

In the face of war, in the face of anxiety, in the face of all the things that are your reality at the moment, there's a peaceful, sacred spot that you can be in—where you see the appropriateness, where you hold the light, where you send the light where it's needed most—to Africa, to the Oval Office, to Afghanistan, to Palestine, and to Israel. Send light, one family member to another. Don't send politics, and don't send your own ideas. Send light. Light will make a clearer path for those who make free choice decisions in partial darkness.

Does it make a difference? It already has, dear ones. It already has.

And so this entourage, which is the one that I came in with, pulls away from you—back through the crack in the veil until the next time. We're in love with you, dear family, dear sister, dear brother. When you're not here, and with us, we sing your name in light. Someday you'll stand next to us and all will be clear. The scheme of why you came will be clear. The big questions will have been answered. But until then, living in duality and in 4D is the hard part. That's why we stand next to you, willing and ready to take your hand anytime you ask it. And that's the truth.

[Pause]

It's hard to leave, and we don't want to... so we linger. It's because we feel we're being hugged back! That's what happens when the veil lifts a bit. It's not just one-way anymore. It's two ways. It's now a reunion where both sides express love to one another.

And so it is.

From Lee: Regarding the President Bush section.

At a time when political tempers are flaring, many are unable to think past the anger or the drama of world events. They might see Kryon's words as an endorsement for the American President. Kryon is not political, and never will be. In subsequent messages, Kryon even compared the situation to the attributes of allowing an abusive father to be part of your life. It's abhorrent to think that perhaps we would

plan something like abuse in our lives, but clearly this has been channelled over and over, so that it's exactly what we do in order to get the
"kick in the pants" that we need to move spiritually. There have been
many parables about this from Kryon within the last 12 years

So just as we allowed the 9/11 to be part of our reality in America,
so we also have allowed a leadership that will tweak the other world's
leaders, interrupt old alliances, and create a situation that will move
things off the peg of normalcy. It isn't an endorsement; but rather it's
an explanation of the energy of what's happening. You and I have allowed for the "pruning of Earth" that is taking place. Collectively, and
universally, we gave permission at the 11:11 window.

Lee Carroll

Live Channelling

"What's New and What's Not"

Channelled in Illinois, Wyoming, & Utah
May 2003

Chapter Seven

What's New and What's Not
Illinois, Wyoming, Utah - May, 2003
Chapter Seven

This message is a combination of the transcriptions of three live channellings in three different cities. It contains the concepts given in all three, packaged together into one message for clarity.

Greetings, dear ones, I am Kryon of Magnetic Service. There are those of you who are asking what the next step is. You feel the obvious energy pressing on you to expand yourself, or to ask the question, *"Is there more?"* There are those of you who should review the parable of the tar pit, given over a decade ago, yet still profoundly true. Many are still asking for outside help—not understanding at all why Spirit seems to have shut off the spiritual-communication spigot! So many of the facilitators who are here and reading this, so many of the meditators and the prayer warriors who are here and reading this are all asking much the same question. We're going to speak about that. Specifically, on this night we're going to give a message in the nines... in a moment.

Let me review something: No matter who you are here, or reading this—no matter what your belief or disbelief, there's energy being created here that can only be created from the other side of the veil. It will permeate the space where you are if you allow it. There are those, by your invitation, who are arriving here, who have begun to slowly fill this place in these last few moments. Those who arrived three days ago are now starting to walk the aisles. Some of the ones you will feel around you are here not for the message that's going to be given, but rather just to stand next to you. Some of you will feel them touch you.

Some may even smell them. There's nothing unusual about this, and nothing fearful. For this is the family. Some of these you *feel* have been with you all your life, yet many of you have never acknowledged them. They who are here are your family and your connection to the planet, ready and willing to help you understand the discussion that follows.

What's New and What's Not

There have been those who have asked about what's new on the planet at this very moment. When we communicate to you in channelling, we often use terms such as *new energy, New Age, new consciousness,* and *new reality.* There are those who would then believe that *new* is some kind of blanket on the planet that we throw over everything that exists, and that what was yesterday is old, and what is today is therefore fresh. That's not so. Naturally, it's far more complex than this.

Let's describe item by item, nine definitions of what's new and what's not. Perhaps it's time to qualify and verify some of the things that have slipped in between the many Kryon messages of the last years. Let's put them all in one message so you can understand more about the energy around you right now... an energy that's beginning to settle in exactly the way in which we said it might over a decade ago.

God

Let's start with the biggest concept of all, the concept of God. Some of you have studied the scripture of the ages—some of the oldest writings known to humanity—ones that are filled with spiritual history. Perhaps you studied civilizations way back then and have seen how God was represented in that history. In fact, you would have seen what God did, as reported by those who were there... such is the way of history.

Some have even labeled and compartmentalized God, due to the writings. Some have spoken of an old God, called the "God of Law." Many have reported, *"That was a very stern God back then. Look at what God did to humanity back then, when it misbehaved. There were many harsh punishments dealt out then."*

And they might go on to say, *"Well, I don't really recognize that God. I don't relate to Him."* Then there would be others who might say, *"There was another dispensation, the dispensation of love—that's where we saw the love of God. We saw healing—we saw compassion. That's more like it! That's the God I like. That's the One I relate to."* Then some of you are discovering yet another God—One that walks with you, but Who has your face! And you might say, *"That's the God that I claim, not the other two."*

By implication, many feel that perhaps God has changed over the millennium. Here's the answer: However you define God—whatever that means to you—if God means the collective that is you—if it means all of the spiritual energy in the Universe, filled with love—or even a God as an entity Who watches over everything, let me set something straight. God never changes! God is family, and this family is stable. There has never been a change in the energy of God.

"Well," you might say, *"then how can you explain the actions of an Old Testament God and a New Testament God? Or for that matter, a New Age God? They seem so different!"* Those who engage in this discussion have the entire concept backwards! What you're seeing is dramatic Human change! This has been our message since we began to give you the truth about the energy of Earth. Changes in the consciousness of humanity create profound changes in what's perceived as reality.

In an old consciousness, one that you called the dispensation of law, what was reported was how it was perceived through the "reality filter" of the times. What was written was what the Humans who were there thought about God as they wrote about the experience. In a dispensation of love, God didn't change. Instead, Humans did! Their consciousness brought in a brand-new energy of compassion within humanity. Humanity got to experience it, and that's how they saw it. That's how they reported it and *felt* it. Indeed, as the consciousness of the reporter changed, it would appear as though divinity itself had shifted. It was all in the eyes of the perceiver.

The ones who were in a dense energy didn't see the unseen. Therefore, they didn't understand the compassion and the love. All they saw and reported was to the best of their ability in a limited dimensional capacity. Now, here you are in a predicted energy where the gifts of divinity are being exposed in a stronger way than ever before. The veil lifts. Some of you are in discovery—some are even seeing interdimensional things! The magnetic grid of the planet has shifted, the crystalline grid is being rewritten, and the cetaceans of the earth are about to be engaged for their memory. It's an amazing time—one that brings humanity in line with what the masters told you was possible.

So, indeed, it is a new time, but God is not one of those new things. For the family has remained staid, and its energy is the same today as it was when Earth was created. That's number one.

Energy

What about energy? Has it shifted? The answer is yes! Grandly and greatly, the energy of this Earth, which therefore has given you new opportunities, has shifted.

Some might ask, *"Why are there so many on this planet who don't understand this—who don't feel it or don't see it?"* This, dear one, is called free choice. The ones who have not given intent to be part of this interdimensional shift will pay no attention to the things that are potent to those who are.

We've told you this before, and I don't think we have to explain to many of you about this energy shift. In 1989 we told you that this planet would shift so dramatically that there would be massive magnetic grid changes. Indeed, as you sit here now, that has happened. What does that mean to you? Did you have any concept that perhaps the earth was shifting dimensionally, or that it was speeding up in time? The now has changed—actual time has been altered, and the geology of the planet is responding to a faster time frame. You're seeing things geologically that perhaps you wouldn't have seen in your lifetime. But things are relative to your existence, so you didn't see them. But you *felt* them, and you watched the things we told you could take place. Meanwhile, the individual who's not aware of energy shifts simply sees them as part of life on a changing planet. This individual is not wrong and is not judged by Spirit. It's about the free choice of humanity, and how Humans will change energy on their own, without interference.

The energy of the planet has shifted dramatically and profoundly, posturing itself for something grand. The potential of solutions to the seemingly unsolvable is what some of you have prayed for since you got here. Indeed, within the scope of your lifetime, you're now looking at the potential for peace on Earth. Oh, there will be skirmishes, and there will be those who will be mad at others for centuries to come. That's part of Human nature. But we're talking about the overview—of nation with nation, a consensus on the planet that's evolving. Someday it will see trade and cultural compromise as far more acceptable than conquering war and religious intolerance. It's a profound shift in Human consciousness and even Human nature itself. This is why the Indigos are here, also! Did you consider that? Energy. That's what has shifted, and that's indeed new.

A Time Line for the Planet

What about the time line of the planet... the prophecies that have been given through the ages that all seem to validate each other? There are those who would say, *"These have always been the same and will never change. Certain things will take place because the prophecies all said they would."*

Let me give you some information that you won't understand. Part of this information is simplified and metaphoric in order for you to receive and understand it in a clearer way.

There's an Earth somewhere that's all by itself—you're not there. But it exists in another reality. Call it an alternate reality, if you wish, and this is actually true. To compound this vision, the actuality is that there are many Earths! But all are in another time frame, within something you and your science have called another dimension. This other Earth is one that you grew up within, but you moved out of that reality and changed the very matter under your feet. You changed the time frame, the biology, and the geology. Earth is now on another track... one that the prophets never foresaw.

Where is the proof of such an outlandish statement? It's all around you. Answer these questions seriously, and do your own evaluation of what you observe before you. How do you explain the fact that the Armageddon didn't happen? It was an event that seemed to triangulate and be consistently prophesied by many over the ages? Why wasn't the fall of the Soviet Union within any of the prophecies? Where was your 9/11 event in the scheme of prophecy? Have you seen any weather changes lately that might actually give you a hint that geological change has sped up in the past decade? How do you explain that the magnetic grid of the earth moved exactly as we told you it would over the past 12 years? Have there been any odd elections lately that were not foreseen... unusual leadership decisions that seemed out of the "norm"... old alliances broken? Have you personally felt that time has increased in the past three or four years?

You're in a different reality—one that has no prophecy around it, and one that's absolutely new. There's not one entity on the other side of the veil who knows what you're going to do tomorrow or what's going to happen to this planet. Instead, it's held in your hands. The days of turning to ancient prophecy for your guidance is over.

"But what about the ancient Mayans, who said that in 2012 we would see the end of time?" Think metaphorically, just like all messages are given from Spirit. First of all, this date is a marker and corresponds with one of the 25-year measurements of the planet (as we told you many years ago). The last important measurement was 1987, when the 11:11 took place. The Mayan message isn't a prophecy of the end of the earth, but rather a description of the end of an old paradigm. It's an energy marker, and not to be feared. It's just a date.

We will give you another potential around 2012: You have until the end of 2012 to set a standard for the energy of the next 25 years (to 2037). The end of time? No. The potential is that 2012 is the end of an old paradigm of time—a new Human consciousness that will bring great change.

Finally, does it now start to make sense that the new children of Earth that you call Indigo and Crystal have started to arrive at this new time? Why now? Perhaps you're beginning to see the correlation of events, both spiritual and physical, which all validate that something's happening? It's all around you to examine. Is it new? Yes.

Ancient Texts

What about the ancient texts? We've spoken of this before, but let's clarify. Are they all to be thrown on the floor and never used again? No, of course not. Let me differentiate their energies and tell you how this works.

If you have old texts and they give information about the healing of the Human body, of the processes, of the energies of discovery, these texts, if authentic, are revolutionary. They'll reveal much. There are still many of them that are hidden and yet to be discovered. When they're finally seen, they'll tie your own biology to the workings of the earth and even to the workings of the solar system! They'll expose ratios between your DNA and the geology of the planet... things that have yet to be discovered, hidden in the texts. Let's call them the energy texts.

Then there are the historical texts. Many of these have also been seen as spiritual texts, since they're a combination of history and spiritual reports. They're the ones that were created that told you about God—and about the how, when, and where. They were also part of the training of humanity, and they represent exposure of the divinity within.

Let me ask you this, dear Human Being: How many of you still have your first-grade primers? And if you do, how many of you refer to them daily? The answer is obvious. Why would you turn to a textbook that gave you elementary information, long after you graduated? You wouldn't.

Many of the ancient texts are exactly that way. They carry an energy just like I've given you regarding the dispensation of law. They're historic primers, and you're beyond them. These books are not for Humans who sit in an enlightened energy... a master energy.

You might ask, *"Well, how do I know the difference between the texts that still apply and the ones that don't?"* It's easy. Read them! How does the information resound with you? Does it feel fresh and accurate? You have a wonderful, divine "discernment engine" within you that knows what's new and what's not. You can never wave a hand and say that all of the ancient texts are wrong. This is a generalization and isn't valid. Use that discernment engine for yourself. How does it feel when you read something? Does it touch you, or does it seem like you're beyond what it says?

Then you might ask the question, *"Well, if that's the case, there may be no spiritual texts for us at all! We're moving into ascension status, so where are the texts for that?"* What a wonderful question! The new texts are in the pen being held in your hand... ready to be written. The ones in this room and rooms like this everywhere are writing them.

You are prophets each one—pieces of God each one—on the Earth—with purpose. Some of you carry the texts of the future within your consciousness. Historians, you are, of the now. If you understand the now, then you also have a conundrum, a puzzle before you... for the now also contains all time, both ancient and future. Therefore, as you pen these new texts, you draw upon the learning of the ancients as well. Such is the challenge of becoming interdimensional.

Here is the admonishment for those who have been waiting for this—do it! The wisdom will flow onto the page. Don't pay any attention to what others say; don't listen to your head when it says you're making it up. Let it flow. The words are already there; just trace them! And you know whom I'm talking to, don't you? Perhaps that's why you're reading this page, or why you came here? And that was number four.

Masters of the Planet

"Kryon, what about the ancient masters of the planet? Weren't they in the old energy?" Not the real masters, no. The true masters who walked this Earth are all one family, all of them. You can name them from the oldest lineage of Abraham, through Mohammed, to the cultures of the Far East, to the current messages of the avatars alive today. Take a look at their basic message.

Go back to the source. Don't depend on what people tell you they meant. Don't give away your power of discernment to someone who's going to interpret the words of a master for you. You're entitled and are as good as the best of the "trained" interpreters. Go back to the source and discover what they said! They spoke about compromise and unity. They unified tribes that were apart—they gave solutions to the unsolvable. Many stood on mountaintops for all to hear and spoke about Human enablement. They told those around them that Humans could be just like them! They gave all of you things to ponder for the ages... practical, spiritual, and historic.

The masters of the earth knew of the potentials—and they told you what you could do, all of them did. Ancient and recent, they all spoke about these things. Master after master told you that humanity was a part of all that is, some even inviting you to be "sons and daughters of God." Those masters were new then, and they're new now. They will always be fresh. They're profound pieces of God, unchangeable, for they represent the love of God that's the same forever. Not one of them desired to be worshiped. That was what men did, not what they asked for.

So all those masters represented new energy, and they knew all about the potentials of the New Age Human. They are, therefore, as new today as the day they came to Earth. Remember this: They're still here!

Guides

There has been so much information about guides! Some will tell you that there are no more. Others will tell you the opposite—that there are far more than ever! What's new and what's not? Let's begin by again asking you some 4D questions that will help you to understand multiple-D. Hold out your hands and ask someone, *"How many hands do I have?"* The person will report that there are two. Now, put one behind your back. Ask again. The person in front of you only sees one, but actually knows that there are still two (or course). But what should they say—one or two? At that point, they might ask for clarity. *"Is the question how many do you have, or how many are seen?"* They won't be able to answer clearly without that information. So you might say that this situation exemplifies a simple rule of 4D: There's a consistency in reality that supersedes what is perceived.

In an older consciousness, all we could tell you was that you had divinity standing next to you called guides, and that your perception told you there were two or three (for example). In this old energy of linearity, that's all we could convey. It was overly simplistic, but it was the way of things before the completion of the grid shift. When we told you that there were two or three, or even none (in the case of a temporary condition during an energy shift), we were giving you the best description we could of what your own perceptions would verify. In fact, you were feeling the energy of the "guide soup," something that's always there, but that changes as you do.

We can tell you now that guides are an infinite number. We can also tell you that they are as much a part of you as your hand is, and also as much as your Higher-Self is. They are *always* there.

Some of you have asked, *"Okay, but even if they can't be counted, who are they?"* This is the most difficult question of all, since the very concept is not an Earthly one, and goes far beyond what you wish to consider or hear.

In a past example, we told you that you can't number a soup as it sits in front of you. You cannot ask, *"How many soups are in my spoon?"* The real identity of your soup is the flavor instead of a numerical identification. So, the guides are that way. They're an infinite number of changeable energies that appear to clump in a grouplike fashion, and are part of you forever. They're felt, not numbered. They're energy, not entities.

The actual guides are just like you... they exist on both sides of the veil. You're a group, and so are they. They're part of your spiritual makeup, but their energy can change daily, if that's how often you change your vibration. Think of them as a helper energy group that is as much *you* as your Higher-Self is you. The real *you* is angelic. It's interdimensional and infinite. It's a piece of God.

When you come to Earth, only a part of who you actually are comes into 4D. The rest exists in an interdimensional state, and part of that energy is what you've called the "guides and the Higher-Self." Therefore, the answer of *"who are they"* must be *family*. This also must mean that the God part of you is far larger than you think.

Begin to understand that the duality works overtime to keep you isolated so that you can make independent choices and not be biased by the group that you belong to. This is all part of the test of Earth, and the grand plan of being a Human Being.

Perhaps you might now be ready to understand that being "part of God" means that you're actually immense in your energy potential... just like the master said. The truth is that all those you loved and lost in your lifetime are part of this guide-set, as well as those in what you would call "past lives." The truth is that you're also part of others, and will be this way even after you leave the earth-plane. This is more complex than can be explained, but filled with awe and wonderful potentials. It's all there for your enablement, and not as a hindrance of any kind. It's there to complement your vibration, to help others and the planet, and to amp-up when you need it the most. So the answer to the question about whether there are guides or not goes back to clarifying the question: *"Do you mean the reality, or what is perceived?"*

This energy that you call guides is being redefined as you move into ascension status. The new energy of the earth is beginning to turn on the light and expose what they really are—a piece of God—a piece of you.

If you're still confused, it's time to relax and know that you're never alone. Sometimes it's okay to just know how things are without having to understand all the mechanics of them. Does it bother you to step on the accelerator in your vehicle and not know the inner workings of the automatic transmission that's allowing for the transfer of engine power to the wheels? The answer is obvious. Just drive the car... you have places to go!

The next time you see 11:11 on the clock, just say *"Thank you."* All is well, as that interdimensional guide part of you taps you on the shoulder to remind you of their presence and their love.

The Human is encouraged to stop numbering and naming everything. For that practice will keep you forever in 4D.

Meditation

"Dear Kryon, there have been some that say that all meditation is over. We have to throw it away. In fact, they say that we're

not supposed to meditate anymore. Who's right and who's wrong? Did it change or did it not? Is it old or is it new?"

Again, we'll turn to the interdimensional truth. There's nothing like it when you sit in ceremony and speak to Spirit! God loves it when you dedicate time to just sit in the presence of family. Can this be any clearer? Do it!

But there's so much more! There's a new invitation to communicate interdimensionally. Spirit will never tell you to stop meditating. But we've invited you to change the modality from where you meditate once in a while or once a day, to that where you have a 100-percent connection!

Think of it this way: In an old energy, meditation was tuning in to a radio station. In the new energy, that station got stronger and increased its frequency. Now, with the same radio, the old station seems to be gone! Did it really stop broadcasting? No! Instead, it became more powerful, with a new identity that's beyond the senses of the old receiver. It invites you to turn the dial and find the new frequency. When you do, you'll reach up and take the hand of Spirit and never let go.

It's not once in a while anymore. It's all the time. And that, dear Human Being, is one of the keys to ascension. If you're going to move into what we've called ascension (which we will speak of in a moment), you're going to have to have a constant connection to Spirit.

So, like the guides, we're telling you that if you define meditation as it was a decade ago, then you would have to say it's old. If you define it within the scope of the new energy and the changes that have occurred, then it's new. But communication with God is what it is, and that will never go away. In fact, it just got much stronger.

Intent

The power of intent is the divine catalyst for co-creation. It drives humanity forward, as it's the power behind Earth's response to the consciousness of humanity.

Although the power of intent has changed, and there are new ways to modify it into a more powerful tool, it has always been the driver of your reality. It was Human intent that caused the new energy of Earth. It was Human intent that voided out the Armageddon. It's Human intent that's creating the conditions on the planet right now that will lead to the potential of The New Jerusalem.

Dear one, if you find any human or entity who tells you that intent is old and not needed anymore, you should examine that message carefully. That's far from the truth. Some will tell you that intent has graduated into something else. Yes, it has... more powerful intent!

Under the category of old and new, intent is very, very old... and profoundly needed in the new energy. From the beginning, it's been seen as the one thing that could be measured within humanity to make history itself change. It's the divine tool of creation, placing the ultimate power within the purview of humanity to rewrite history, and therefore change the vibration of planet Earth. We've taught for 12 years that the power of intent has always been one of the keys to personal co-creation. Pure intent is seen in the Human Being as divine energy. It's awesome. In the energy spectrum, it's gold—and precious. Intent is everything! This teaching hasn't changed in all our messages to you, and will not in the future.

In a new-energy Earth, with new magnetic and crystalline alignments, the power of intent is being reshaped completely. It's becoming a grander and greater tool. What's your intent for your biology? How often do you talk to your cells? How often do you tell them what the boss (you) wants them to do? What if you were to tell them to revert to a pristine condition similar to when you were ten years old? You may laugh at that until you start doing it. Start talking to your cellular structure; start talking to your blood groups; start realizing that the cells are listening to intent of your own mind, and then take your blood tests regularly to verify what you're doing. Create your own 4D proof about intent in this new energy.

When you start chasing away the imbalances within, and the diseases begin to retreat, you'll remember where you heard this. Intent has to do with tuning in to that new station. The nine items in this message are all related. They're in a circle of nine. Within the question of the old versus the new, which it is? Sometimes it's both!

Blessed is the Human Being who practices pure intent in all aspects of his life. For this is the one who will climb the stairs of ascension. This is the one who will see the face of God, and it will turn out to be his own! This is the one who will reach up and take the hand of the guide groups that are around them and will never let go. Intent is the energy of the New Age. Not all that is old is to be cast away. Sometimes the oldest is the newest. Such is the way of the now.

Ascension

There's more being given this year about ascension than at any time. In these last two months, we've given you two parts of information and training that we won't review here. But we must revisit the definition. *Ascension* is defined in the new energy as stepping into the next life without death—taking control of your biology, of your chronological age, of all the potentials you came in with, rewriting your contract, vibrating higher and living a longer life. Some of you will even change your names, and some will actually become different people.

Way beyond the concept of a walk-in, ascension status includes many things. But let me just give you the summary of it: It represents a divine energy represented by the Human who takes the hand of Spirit and never lets go. It's the energy of the masters who walked the earth, the ones who told you that you could be just like them.

"Peter, you can walk on the water, you know? Do it!" Did you hear that? Do you remember reading that? [Chapter Two] It's about enabling a Human Being to go beyond physics. Go read it again, for Peter did it, and he did it without help, until he doubted the reality of it.

The energy beginning to close in on some of you is literally a return to the earth of a collective master energy. It's part of the energy that's shifting within the guides, meditation and intent. It's part of what you're feeling, which is energy shifting, and it's part of what some of you are actually feeling as "anxiety." We told you of this potential all those years ago. Remember, there's no predestination. There's only predisposition, an energy that says that you have a direction, but one that can be changed at any time.

So the energy of the ascension status is indeed a very new concept for humanity. Before, this exact energy would vaporize Humans. Now it enhances them. That's a result of the grid shift, and of the crystalline rewrite. It's an awesome new tool in the divine tool group that you're being given in response to what you've created.

*****

The energy in this room is ripe for change. We've only spent a few hours together, yet there are those who will walk from here differently from how they came in. They'll go from here with a full understanding that there's an energy with them that wasn't with them when they arrived. Those entities and helpers who came three days ago, came with the intent to leave with you if you allowed for it. There will be some who will recognize them and say, *"Yes, this is what I always wanted. I want to leave with more than I came."*

It's nothing that God is going to do for you, you know? It's an allowance... attributes given with your permission. It's you with you. It is the recognition of the divine energy inside you saying, *"Indeed, I deserve this. It's why I came to the planet, and now I remember."* And so it is about remembering, is it not? Collectively, why not remember this, Human Being: You are a piece of God, divine in every way, enabled in every way. It's time to move forward. It's time for solutions. Patience is the key. Intent is the catalyst, and even when you're finished reading this channelling, the energy of what you have remembered is with you.

That is our promise... that you're never alone. Some of you will establish tendrils, connections with us, where everything is connected to everything. And you'll begin to understand The Lattice, the physics of it, the divinity of it, the beauty of it. That's why we're here. That's why we speak to you as we do. Let it be known this day that we came to see you... and in the process, we weren't disappointed.

And so it is.

In the face of war, in the face of anxiety, in the face of all the things that are your reality at the moment, there's a peaceful, sacred spot that you can be in—where you see the appropriateness, where you hold the light, where you send the light where it's needed most—to Africa, to the Oval Office, to Afghanistan, to Palestine, and to Israel. Send light, one family member to another. Don't send politics, and don't send your own ideas. Send light. Light will make a clearer path for those who make free choice decisions in partial darkness.

Does it make a difference? It already has, dear ones. It already has.

Live Channelling

"The Mount Shasta Experience"

Channelled in Mt. Shasta, California
June 2003

Chapter Eight

The Mt. Shasta Experience
Mt. Shasta, California - June, 2003
Chapter Eight

Greetings, dear ones, I am Kryon of Magnetic Service. The energy is strong here. We picked a time and place that had even higher energy than my partner expected, so I'm asking him to center [speaking of Lee]. There is much today that will require that he go slowly. There will be concepts presented that he's never seen before, names he's never heard. The following is the kind of information that can only be delivered in a place like this—a place with Lemurian energy.

We will speak of these things more as we go, but for this moment, we wish to tell you that the entourage that arrived three days ago is active among you. There will be those who would ask, *"Can such a thing be? How could we know that any of the esoteric subjects discussed this night are real or true—where is the proof?"* We're going to tell you this: This entire evening's message will probably be the most esoteric ever given by my partner. If it's proof you're looking for, you may have to wait years, or you could follow your intuition and believe it tonight. You could also call upon those who stand next to you to help you with your own discernment [speaking of those unseen].

Tonight is very different for my partner. He has done this for years and years, yet this one is different. It's a throwback, is it not, my partner, to some of the days when you were filled with anxiety before the event? For you did not know what was happening next? Such is the way of the love of God. Such is the way of "the now."

We are here, you know? So many of you feel us here. This group of beings that comes before you has only one purpose—to support humanity. We often tell you that you're not alone, and we tell you about the gifts of divinity that are yours. Yet so many of you say, *"Who, me? I'm so ordinary."* The duality hides it all. It hides it all! There won't be a day in your life that you will have proof of your sacredness. There won't be a day in your life that you will look in the mirror and say, *"Oh, yes, I see that divine face."* There will always be the duality at work—pieces and parts of you, pulling and pushing—always wondering if such a thing could be.

Even the most enlightened of you, the ones who vibrate at the highest level, will have your moments. *"Dear Spirit, you said I'd never be alone, yet today I feel alone!"* We've heard you in your darkest moments—in your sorrow, and the lightest moments in your joy. We've been with you to celebrate when you danced in the light and cried in the dark. It is one of the reasons why, as long as we are here channelling through my partner, that the theme will be this: that *you are dearly loved*—loved beyond all Human measure that you can imagine, dear family. There is so much hiding in your grandness.

The theme of the Kryon has been, and always will be, this: that you have changed the reality of your planet. In the process, you have enabled a situation... one that was waiting for you. We told you this: that at the end of the magnetic grid shift, the work of Kryon would really begin. All our work in the last 12 years about being the *magnetic master* had to do with the *changing* of the grid, but now it's not about the changing of the grid. Instead, it's about what happens next after the grid has settled. And it's time to review that.

If we're going to give you good communication about what is taking place, we must take it in careful steps, especially the message this evening. So here's the first step. We told you about the magnetic grid and the crystalline grid—two grids of the planet next to one another, in line with each other. We also told you of the third grid, which is Human Consciousness. That grid is one that will move with the Crystalline.

When you gave permission to change the reality of the planet, one grid had to move first, and the second and third are moving now. Twelve years ago, we told you that now would be the completion of the magnetic grid of the planet, and it is. We gave you the dates and the energies around the shift, and they proved out. Even your geologists see it, and the navigation instruments of your planet responded to it.

Then we began to tell you that there would those who would give you far more information about the next shift, that of the Crystalline Grid. And they are doing so. We told you that you are in a new dispensation, the "dispensation of responsibility," and it has the energy of number *eight*. Eight is an interdimensional number that suits the interdimensionality of the energy that you are moving into. [It reads the same upside down, and on its side it represents infinity.] One of the biggest subjects that we have ever had in all of the channellings has been the interdimensionality of Human DNA. Over and over, we have channelled what this means. We're going to do it again.

The Crystalline Grid is being shifted. Perhaps you would ask, *"What does that really mean? What is the major shift?"* It is a shift in information and Earth energy. Think of things that are crystalline, such as the crystals you love. They hold energy, don't they? More than that, they may hold information. And what would be the largest piece of information that the Crystalline Grid would hold for planet Earth? It is the records of *you* and your ꞁ mirrors what you've done. Within the Crystalline Grid, you might say is the history of this planet and all of Human records of the past. The Crystalline Grid also contains the records of who you are, who you have been, and what you're doing right now. It's the past catalyst to the future, for it does not recognize time. It records energy, which then manifests into the "now." Immense in its storage ability, in interdimensional ways it continues to create and enhance the reality of humanity.

The magnetics changed first [the magnetic grid of the planet]. They are the catalyst for DNA activation that will be starting with the completion of the stages of the Crystalline. One shapes the other, and the biggest thing that's going to take place within the Crystalline Grid is the *rewriting of the past*. Yes, even the physicists were right! They are questioning the meaning of time and asking the question, *"Does it even exist?!"* You're dealing with interdimensionality, and therefore you must suspend your belief in the linearity of time itself. This will help you understand how such a thing could be... rewriting the past of the planet in order to change the "now."

It's something we told you is needed and necessary. It indeed has the potentials to create something that we have called The New Jerusalem. Although this portion of this message is a quick review, it's a necessary one for those of you who are not familiar with it. And now you know that something is afoot. The energies are starting to move, and we even told you about this year (2003) being the "year of change." In all appropriateness, the things that you're seeing on your planet are unfolding even faster than we thought they would. It's no accident that finds you sitting in a Lemurian energy at this moment, listening to the message [to those in Shasta who are hearing the channelling]. We will tell you what the connection is in a moment.

That is the review of what has taken place in the last 13 years. The magnetics of the planet have moved. They've postured themselves in a way that has actually lifted the veil slightly, and under that veil has poured energy to the planet... a new energy that will continue to unfold for another 12 years. It's an energy of a type that some of you never expected. I'm going to discuss that.

Some of you say "new" energy, but the word is used so often in your language and culture that it may not even be meaningful to you. What does "new" mean? The last channelling we gave you, one that will be published, was one that gave you the information of "what is new and what is not." We ask you now to look at that, for it will tie in to what we tell you today. God is slow, and the wisdom of revelation is slow. Good things are given in this way, and you know this. The ancients knew it, too, and the wisest societies on Earth still honor the process of things that take time. So the "new" energy on the planet actually means one that is different from the energy of the past millennia... one that will be "new" for this entire dispensation. It's also one of the most profound changes and shifts of all Human history, and it will take time.

Honoring Those Who Are Part of Mt. Shasta

It's time to speak of this area [Mt. Shasta]. There's no better time to speak of an area than when you're sitting in it, and it has much to do with the planet as a whole. It has a great deal to do with those listening and reading, also. Let's start with those who live here. I'd like to greet and celebrate the Guardians. This is a name we're giving to those who have vibrated higher almost all of their lives. They were born with the Lemurian energy, they could hardly wait to get here [Shasta], this is where they were drawn, and this is where they stayed.

They literally nursed the information of the mountain, the Guardians did. You might say they were the forerunners of the Lightworkers. But oh, they're more than that. They anchored and held the energy and kept it fresh around this mountain. It's fresh to this day! First-timers to the area: Are you aware of the kind of energy you walk within? Those of you who have trekked up the mountain know that it speaks to you. Did that surprise you? There's much going on here, and we're going to even rename the process.

The Guardians—who are they? They're the Human Beings who've lived in this mountain area for years and years and years. They've watched the comings and the goings—they've watched all of the energy around the mountain—they've seen the truth and they've seen the non-truth. They've seen the frivolity come and go, and they've remained anchored, keeping the mountain precious... holding it for what it's going to do.

The Guardians. These are the ones to whom we say, "Well done!" These are the ones to whom we would like to say, "And if you wish to leave now, you may. Permission is granted, and you may pass the torch." In fact, some of you are tired, are you not? You think we don't know this? Now that the grid has settled and we move into the crystalline energy, the interdimensional active parts and pieces begin to move. It's a different energy. You Guardians are finished. You did it... held the energy to the manifestation of what it was designed for, and you've done a fine job.

Why move? Because you're about to see a shift in this Mt. Shasta area. There will be great comings and goings even within the next three years. Those who have lived here for a very long time, for whatever reason, may choose to leave. I'll tell you something: There are Guardians here who would never come to a meeting like this! They don't think they're spiritual, but even *they* are holding and anchoring. Much of it is intuitive... they're drawn to the area lifetime after lifetime and are keeping watch over it. Even those who don't hear this message will feel it in their bodies, a surging intuitive feeling that their job is done. Although it's a precious place to be, some of the Guardians will leave anyway, not even knowing why.

We celebrate the Guardians, and we tell you that these Humans do not reflect old energy workers. They are the forerunners of you, Lightworkers! If you call yourselves Lightworker, then you are the ones who will take the mantle of the Guardians. An influx of energy and humanity is about to happen here. Guardian, as the energy begins to be realized and the reality of what is taking place begins to manifest, you'll no longer be able to keep Mt. Shasta a secret. Don't be alarmed, however. Yes, there will be growth. Perhaps there will even be commercialism. The mountain remains the mountain, regardless of what you do. It cannot be spoiled, for the Guardians have done their job. So we celebrate the Guardians, and some of you are here. Don't be surprised if you're pulled back to this spot for an annual trek of your own choosing, coming back to visit the family that resides in the mountain. There's a great shift occurring here. When you return, remember: Climb the mountain before you decide what has changed and what has not!

Realignment and Shift of Mt. Shasta's Energy

Many of you have always known about the energy of this place. But did you ever know of the timetable? What about the prophecy of the mountain? There's a shift taking place that even the most esoteric of you are not totally expecting.

Let me ask you this: If you think about those on the other side of the veil, you'll know intuitively that there's no gender there as there is on Earth. Angels may appear to be male and female, but they're neither. We've told you repeatedly that Kryon and all of the family around you are genderless. Gender labels and names in spiritual matters are something given to you for energy identification. When you speak of spiritual gender, you're speaking of attributes around energy. It gives you something to relate to... this thing is masculine, or something else is feminine. It becomes a communication identification tool, and not a biological designation.

Get ready for something you didn't expect: That system is over. There's no longer any reason to give elementary information in parables to those who are enlightened in this new energy. So we tell you this: Something is going on in the mountain. Mark my words right now so you can refer to it later. In the not-too-distant future, the ones who identified the male and the female portions of that mountain behind us [Shasta] will have to reevaluate it. The energy around it is melding. It's melding. Some of you have been aware of this for a while.

There will come a time when you can no longer say that this particular portion "is masculine" or that this particular portion "is feminine." Although those are the energies that have always been part of the mountain, the mountain itself is melding those energies. It's changing. It's changing because it's time to change.

Oh, there's more. We're going to give you a new word. Some have asked the Guardians: *"Is this Shasta mountain a vortex or a portal?"* Some of you locals have thrown up your hands trying to explain this. It has the attributes of both, does it not? How do you explain it, then?

There are other places and parts of this planet that have featured strong male and female energies as well. But with the magnetic grid shift, some of these attributes have "moved away" or melded. Let me give you an example. The area you call Sedona has changed greatly in the last 12 years... so much so that you will no longer feel what you felt the last time you visited there. Those of you who visit repeatedly know of this. That's what the grid shift did to this profoundly energetic area. It did the same with the area in Machu Picchu that many visit regularly. Things are beginning to change even within some of the most well-known energetic areas on Earth.

Well, let me tell you what it did regarding the mountain behind us. It activated it. It has been waiting all of this time for the shift of the magnetics of the planet. Is it a vortex or a portal? Neither. It is instead something new: It's a *vortal*. A genderless vortal. And to some, especially those who call themselves Guardians, they're not going to like it. After all, it's the mountain they grew up with, and it's changing. Guardian, there is no judgment for leaving this place, only celebration. If you're one of those who's disturbed by the energy shift and the population increase, there's absolutely no judgment around your decision to leave. You've done your job, steward.

For those who don't believe this melding process, I ask you: Why would you be shocked at this when the energies of the planet are shifting so greatly? Where does it say that the polarities always have to be the same geologically forever? With a huge shift in magnetics, wouldn't you expect the polarities of masculine and feminine to adjust? Where does it say that things only work one way and stay that way?

Some say that the earth is moving into the fifth dimension. We told you before that we don't like to number dimensions, for they're not like peas on a table that are things to be numbered. However, since you're in 4D now, it's the next logical number for you to refer to dimensionally. For now, and for clarity, we'll also call it the fifth dimension... that dimensionality that you're moving into that represents a big shift in reality.

The prophecy regarding this mountain has spoken about those within the mountain who are fifth-dimensional. What's going on? What's happening to the land? This prophecy is beautiful. It's esoteric. To some, however, it's eye-rolling. Could there be proof? Some prophecies would indicate that there's an interdimensional city in the mountain, one inhabited by fifth-dimensional beings with Lemurian energy, they say.

God bless the Guardians who brought you that information, for they were right on the mark. We'd prefer not to call it a city. That makes you compare it to what you're used to. We'd like to call it a "gathering." It's a constantly shifting and changing interdimensional gathering of beings of the fifth dimension. (Again, the five is for you.) There's more prophecy, too. The most unbelievable and eye-rolling portion to some is this: There will come a day (they say) when the mountain will disgorge those who have been in there for eons! There will come a time (they say) when these fifth-dimensional beings will walk the streets of Mt. Shasta! That's what they've said.

Well, perhaps you can celebrate this truth with me in an esoteric way, for it's beginning to happen. As you sit here, the city within stirs. Don't be frightened. It's a celebration of you. Let me give you some things to think about: For years, we've told you about a time when your DNA could be activated in an interdimensional way. Some have said that it would be activated into the fifth dimension. Again, that term stems from the idea that you're moving out of 4 (your reality) into the next one (which, to you, is 5). That has been the information. So, what do you think this activation includes? We're going to give you just one attribute of "activating DNA."

What if today's scientists are right, and you actually have interdimensional matter within your body [a teaching from the seminar of the day]? What if the things that you cannot see, but which are there, might include beings (angels, to some) who have stood by to come forward when it was proper and the energy was right? They come to literally be part of the Lemurian family and to be part of the very DNA that you carry with you. Think about it for a moment. Do any of you feel incomplete? Are you waiting for something or someone to join you? And what is all of this Lemurian talk about?

I'll give you some answers, but before I begin, remember this: You've given permission for this. No matter what I say or do, there are some (who see conspiracy and drama as their way of life), who will say that this is a takeover. "See," they will say, *"Kryon has tricked us to allow the Lemurians to take us over!"* Let's get this out in the open where you can look at it so it's not a *secret.* Use your intuition, common sense, and free choice. When God fills you with love, is it a takeover? No, it isn't. It's a transformation.

The Lemurian Connection

There is a core of humanity that has always been here... that's never left. Lifetime after lifetime after lifetime, it has in-carnated into expressions of humanity that emanated from the continents and many societies you called Lemuria. It was one of the greatest civilizations on the planet. Although it was small compared to today's standards, it was enlightened, almost to the end. It had great leaders and scientists, almost to the end. The first group of you who emerged could be found in the Indus Valley in yet another great civilization—almost all composed of Lemurians. However, it was not in your best interest to "clump" into another advanced society, so you were scattered yet again, this time all over Earth.

The core of the group that sits in front of me tonight, and many who are reading this, are a part of this original family. These are the ones to awaken first on planet Earth—the few of you who carry the stamp of the Lemurian and Indus culture. It surges within your DNA, Lightworker. Are not aware of this?

Some of you have memories that you cannot explain of your time there. It is the core group that is interested in these things—the one with the Lemurian DNA that awakens first. Like some kind of broadcast receiver, the DNA in most of you is being activated at a level that tickles your free will, and is asking you to take a look at everything, because something is different. Feel anything lately? Are you the same as you always were, or is something stirring? Do you feel that time is speeding up, perhaps? Seeing 11:11 on the clocks?

I'll tell you what's going on: For many of you, there is the awareness that you're now ready for those of the *fifth dimension* to join you. What am I saying? There's a great deal at work on this planet that you've called *fifth-dimensional energy*, including entities all over this planet who are waiting to enhance you, to join you in a way you cannot even fathom, in an interdimensional way. Don't make this sound like an invasion! It's an invitation through free choice, to accept the angels who are standing by to become "part of you." It also includes the energies of all the masters who have walked on this planet. Many of them even told you of their return, and that they would "fill you" with their presence.

Many of you wondered if the ascended masters would return and walk the streets of this planet. Well, Human Being, when you leave this place, or the place where you're reading and you walk outside, that's what's happening! That's the reality. Are they walking the streets? You answer that. Are you walking the streets? It's about you, and it always has been about you. Many of you are beginning to understand our channellings over the years. You're now becoming aware that the ascension of this planet, and the return of the masters, is beginning to happen within you! Go back and revisit *The Journey Home* parable. It's about a Human who became divine, simply though pure intent and a transformation of being through knowledge. It's about ascension!

Many spiritual Humans wish to sit back and have the earth and God "do something" for them. They wish to watch it, feeling that they're only Human, after all. Not this time. Those days are gone. You want to watch the handiwork of God? You're going to have to look *inside, where God lives*. That's where it's going to be—all of it. And so we tell you this: All that is here in Mt. Shasta—all the prophecies about the beings waiting for a certain kind of time and energy on the planet—is being realized. The entities in the mountain are lining up to be part of you. Pieces and parts of them will become pieces and parts of you. Family will join family.

How can we explain this to you? Will *you* change? Yes, it's called ascension! How did you think that was going to be accomplished? It's accomplished with profound help and beautiful love. It's all part of an energy on this planet that we told you about. Do you know what happens to a core group that goes through that? They change the very dirt of the earth, and the reality of the planet. The consciousness of the children are all part of it, and they're changing too. It's all part of this decade, one of the most profound in Human history, where you'll decide what *peace on Earth* really means. That's what's happening here.

DNA: The Beginning of an Elaborate Explanation

We cannot stop the conversation now without discussing DNA. Let me tell you about it. You've named it for your 4D visibility and chemistry: deoxyribonucleic acid—DNA. That's what you see. It's what is in your reality of perception. It's 4D, and a description of your Human genome. To most of the earth, that's the extent of it. We've spoken of it time and time again. When we say DNA, we don't mean the layer of chemistry that you can see. We mean *all* the layers. Here is the basic information. We've given some of it to you before, but we'll enhance it now. And we'll do something else, too. It's time to meet someone.

DNA is 12 layers deep. Each layer has two attributes—the one you can see in four dimensions (the double helix) we will call the *bottom layer*. Although bottom and top don't mean much in an interdimensional aspect, that's just for you. It's to give you an idea of where it belongs. It's on the bottom. The two attributes of it we will say are the sides of the ladder, connected with a chemistry that you're well aware of that bridges both of the attributes and creates the bonds. On top of this layer, there are 11 more. Therefore, there are 12 layers total, with 24 attributes. Each layer, even the interdimensional ones, have two sides. They're balanced very much like the one you can see. We told you that there would come a time when we'd discuss the other layers. And we will. Complex, it is.

In order to do this properly, we'd like you to meet somebody. It's a surprise. Get this right, my partner, this is critical [Kryon talking to Lee]. We wish to celebrate Yaw-ee today. Yaw-ee is here [speaking of someone in the crowd]. Yaw-ee is a Lemurian name composed of nine glyphs. The Lemurian writing, much like Sumerian, which became part of the Asian culture and the Indus culture, was glyph writing. That is to say, the letters themselves had meaning. They were concepts and not just sounds. Nine of them composed the name of Yaw-ee. Yaw-ee was known to all of you as one of the greatest architects of Lemuria who ever lived. Beyond that, Yaw-ee had a gift. You see, Yaw-ee built the

Temples of Rejuvenation that were present on the mountaintops. Yaw-ee knew all about DNA. He was given visions—visions he's still being given today. I would like to introduce him to you, for he's here in your group today. A surprise, even to Yaw-ee!

You know him as Dr. Todd Ovokaitys. Doctor, are you here?

[Pause]

Speak out if you are.

"I'm here." (A surprised Dr. Ovokaitys answers from the audience.)

And so we will address you as Yaw-ee. We bring you into this because we want to review your vision, and we want to tell you about your future. It's no accident that you find yourself on the planet in this place at this time. For an awakening is beginning. You can only go so far with what you've known. We wish to take you back to the vision that you had in this lifetime that set you on the course that you're currently on, a profound vision it was. Do you remember it?

"Yes."

Yaw-ee, do you remember the door we took you through?

"I do."

There, you were shown living DNA in the inner workings of a Human Being, which was alive and functioning. There, you were shown the magnetic resonances and more that are part of a ladder in four dimensions. Did you ever wonder, Doctor, why we took you into a room to show you something that's not in a room?

"Yes!"

And now we'll tell you: It's a metaphor. I'm going to give you information that even you, Doctor, will not understand yet. The shape of all DNA together, all the interdimensional DNA when placed together with interdimensional eyes, as a complete and total shape, is in the form of a six-sided cube. It fits within the Merkabah, a very designed place where a cube should be. And that's why you were given the metaphor of the room. That's why there was a door to take you into a place with six sides, all equal in dimension. Now I'll ask you some more questions. Were you aware of the twists?

"Yes."

Did you count them?

"No."

Let me tell those listening and reading about Yaw-ee. He was known as the *Twist Master!* There's a secret here, Doctor. It's given publicly because you have the answer. I will tell you something about this. Many have asked, *"What causes the twists within the twists in 4D DNA?"* Some say that it's obviously the chemistry that pushes and pulls on it in certain ways to torque it in certain ways. I will give you the answer to what causes the twists, and then I'm going to tell you about the *Twist Master.*

There are four elements, all of which are interdimensional, which twist DNA. DNA's relational twisting is from the interdimensional pull upon it. *Time, gravity, magnetics,* and one other, which you've called The Cosmic Lattice. But we will call it *Ascended Master Energy.* It's the divine energy of the cosmos. It's the pieces and parts of what you've called *Human consciousness.* It's an energy that you're starting to discover.

All four of these energies are present in other dimensional DNA layers, and they push and pull upon the dimension you can see, and they twist the ladder and provide the twists within the twists. It's time to count the twists, Doctor, and it's time to also see which direction they twist, although that is well known. For we have information: When you start looking at the twisting, you're going to see some correlations... some things you didn't expect. Count the twists in the Indigos, too. Here are things that no one suspected. How different are the Indigos, really? Are there basic core biological differences? Yes.

Yaw-ee, you will have two more visions within your lifetime, if you wish it. They will occur to you as you move from place to place, for you have taken a high vibration where these things can now be "seen" in ways that no longer require ceremony. Two more are granted to you.

Yaw-ee, welcome back to Lemuria! There were songs about you. It seems that you applied your own science to your own body and lived a very, very long time. Even before the scientists of your time believed you, you were applying it and you outlived them all. If the culture was still there, there would be books about Yaw-ee, one of the greatest scientists that ever walked the planet. And that's the truth, Doctor. It is one of the reasons I asked my partner to speak to you often and channel to you in private. It's also one of the reasons why you have other visions about a past life that you've never told anyone about.

More about DNA

Let us finally (for today) speak of a layer of DNA that's next to the bottom—an interdimensional layer that all of you are feeling. It's difficult to explain this, but this particular layer that has a specific name and a color (neither of which we're going to give you yet), floats in and out of four dimensions. Yes, it's interdimensional, but it has attributes that interface with your 4D DNA. You might describe this piece as *intuition*... a layer unto itself that is also the one responsible for fear, joy, and for love... and the responses those emotions carry to the bottom layer. Why do you cry when you're fearful and when you're joyful and when you're in love? Isn't that odd? There is a similarity, is there not, to your reaction to all three? This layer is responsible for it. It is interdimensional, and it touches the four-dimensional layer that you can see called the Human genome. It's the layer we described in the ascension channellings, which must be rewritten with ascension status. It's one of the layers that those in the mountain are interested in. It's the layer of your future and your past. It's the layer that is ready to be rewritten, and even redesigned and reactivated.

It's the reason that some of you are feeling an interdimensional DNA aspect in your 4D layer. One of the biggest things that you're feeling is this: Dear Human Being, you are without a future! You were born into an energy where you knew you had a future. Just ask the prophets. Well, it didn't happen, did it? So where are you headed now? Your future is being written right now by *you*. The prophecies about the future are being written by *you*. And this is most uncomfortable for many of you. After all, only the masters can write a future for Earth. Is this becoming a familiar theme?

For some, you have depended on an emotional status that has a future that was prophesied, and that belongs to you... good or bad. To be on Earth without a known or prophesied future is to be a ship without a rudder! It's why some of you wake up at three in the morning and want to know what's wrong. *"What's different?"* you might ask. Pieces and part of that DNA are being stripped away and reactivated because you asked for it. Had any interesting dreams lately? What's going on? Oh, celebrate the miracle! A time that some thought would never come is before you. It's a time when the land celebrates you. For eons there have been fifth-dimensional beings who did nothing but wait for you, and now they want to join with you to create an Earth for the potential you were born for... designed for, and yes, that even your DNA knows about. Now that's profound.

All of the layers of DNA, interdimensional and not, are labeled for you. They're the names of God. Eventually, we'll give them to you. I've asked my partner to seek help from others so that the names will be familiar to him when they're channelled. But you're not ready for that yet. This layer is the closest one to the ones that you would *feel,* as opposed to the ones that are etheric. The next channelling we will give will expose the third one, and the last one in the first grouping.

There are layers that are active, and there are ones that are waiting to be active. There are layers that are informational only and set a stage. There are also ones that are only "stored potential," like batteries waiting to be used. There are even ones that communicate. Part of your divinity is wrapped up in what you call the DNA. And that's the truth.

What is the overview of this as we close? What a puzzle that is coming together! Here you sit this day with the architect that some of you sang songs about, yet you don't remember it. Such is the duality that hides things, family. You are Lemurian, every one. You are core group, every one. You're the ones who have changed this planet. The duality is strong, and many of you reading and listening still don't believe it. That's called free choice. But I know your names! Blessed is the duality that lays upon you, for it keeps the play fair. You're going to have to decide if it's real. When you're most alone and when that time is upon you where you ask about the others, we ask you to stretch out your hand in an exercise we've told you before and let us touch you. Feel the tingling, feel the massaging and the love. *"Are you there?"* you might ask. "Oh, yes, we are, dear Human Being. Yes, we are! We're always there."

We support the love of God. That is the essence of those who wait to become your partners. As you walk from this place, many of you will embody and manifest that. That's why you came. Some of you will do it and some of you will not. It's about the journey, not about judgment of what you do while you're here. That's why we love you the way we do. There has never been a time on the planet where so few will do so much for so many. And I'm looking at them.

So why are *you* here? What's bothering *you?* Will you have abundance to sustain you? Yes. We've defined *abundance* before. It's when you get fed every day. Abundance is the love of God in your hearts. Can you walk through life healthy? Yes. It's called the love of God in your DNA. When you realize who you are and why you came, everything starts to change. The invitation for ascension? Yes. We've even defined it.

The first ones to take that graduate step of ascension will be Lemurians. You have survived eons, lifetime after lifetime. You were monks, nuns, and shamans—killed, burned at the stake—just so you could keep it fresh. And here you are. It's your time.

Make it count! Reader, listener, you will leave here different from how you came. Within the spectrum of free choice, each of you, to whatever degree you wish to accept it, will walk from this place different from how you came. You can't help it. You're Lemurian.

And so it is.

You're in a different reality—one that has no prophecy around it, and one that's absolutely new. There's not one entity on the other side of the veil who knows what you're going to do tomorrow or what's going to happen to this planet. Instead, it's held in your hands. The days of turning to ancient prophecy for your guidance is over.

Live Channelling

"Self-Worth"
Kryon Annual Healing Conference

Channelled in Del Mar, California
August 2003

Chapter Nine

Self-Worth
Del Mar, California - August, 2003
Kryon Annual Healing Conference
Chapter Nine

This channelling was given at the end of a very special and unique healing meeting where **Peggy Phoenix Dubro** *of the EMF Balancing Technique° and* **Dr. Eric Pearl** *of The Reconnection° presented together in a full day of lectures and questions.*

Greetings, dear ones, I am Kryon of Magnetic Service. This very day you've heard of the prophecies of healing, and the beginning of the discoveries on this planet of your real power. So what exactly do you think your role is? What do you think about those entities who are in this room with you now... the ones who are interdimensional, whom you cannot see? They have been here all day, you know. And what do you think our role is here? Many of us arrived three days ago because we expected you, dear Human Being, to be here. What do you think the role is that we play?

I will give you the answer: We weep in joy! That's our role. For we're beginning to see a balance on the planet start to move from where it's been for eons, to something that only the new-energy readers are seeing, and we're going to speak about that. It's a new paradigm where humanity begins to be empowered more to the degree that matches why they came. In other words, many of you are actually beginning to feel the planet's energy start to match yours instead of fight it... something you had only hoped for since you were born.

Many have already taken the *Mantle of Spirit*. We speak now of the teachers who have presented this day [Dr. Eric Pearl and

Peggy Phoenix Dubro]. Both of them are in love with Spirit! Both of them are so focused on what we've given them that they spend little time doing anything else but teaching. The Mantle of God is upon them, and they see humanity differently than you do. They see those who can be enriched and enabled. They don't look at you in judgment, and they don't look at each other in judgment. For they understand the integrity and the intent of the heart. And so it is that there has been no accident that on this day, these two profound healers were brought together in the same room with Yaw-ee, the Twist Master [Dr. Todd Ovokaitys]. [See the Mt. Shasta channelling for more information about what this means.]

More on DNA

So we'll talk about DNA yet again. In order to do this properly, we must speak about a piece and a part of it that is not difficult to understand. It's "in your face." We'll do more plain talk, more teaching of the core information that you're ready to hear.

Within the last few transmissions, we've given you the names of two of the three layers of DNA that you've been working with and studying. None of you are being given any information past layer three at the moment. Ask either of the healers who presented their divine information today, *"How many layers are there?"* Their answer? *"Twelve."* Indeed! We've given you this identical information. We've also taught you how these layers are organized. We told you that they're not strands, but rather, are layers. We've told you that in all 12 there's only one that's in your dimensionality, but we didn't name it yet.

Lately, we told you about the second layer, which carries much of the emotion. [This was a channelling not in this book, called "Activating the Third Layer of DNA," given in Philadelphia.

It's on the Kryon Website - *www.kryon.com*] Interdimensional, it is, but you understand it because this is often where you feel. Sometimes it's the feeling of anger or worry, and sometimes it's the feeling of love. Sometimes it's the experience of the love of God. It's the emotion layer. We asked you to think to yourself, does emotion affect chemistry? The answer is an obvious yes. Worry, love, anger, and drama will all drastically affect your biology. So layer two is a key layer for balance. We told you its name was **Torah E'ser Sphirot**. Its meaning is "Divine Blueprint," or "The Blueprint of Law."

We told you about the third layer and gave it a name, also. It was called **Netzach Merkava Eliyahu**, which means "ascension and activation." We told you it was the "ascension layer," and that it greatly modified the other adjacent two... almost as a catalyst does in chemistry. Then we gave you stories that were very hard for you to understand. We told you about the wisdom of the master, and we invited you to understand it.

But we never labeled and named layer number one, even though we've talked about number one more than any of them. Number one is the human genome, the biochemical layer that is within your dimensional perception. I will now give you its name.

You might ask, *"Kryon, why didn't you give us the name of layer number one sooner? You gave us the names of two and three, but not the most common one? Why now?"* And the reason is that we wanted to give it to you in the presence of the healers whom you honored today, and who know all about it. They know how it's affected by the energies of the Universe. They know about the divinity in the Human body and what happens when you claim that sacred energy. Their entire purpose is to try and teach it while showing that it's common and available, so it's not frightening or scary. They're trying to show you how each of you can practice it within your own divine power.

The name of the first layer of DNA is **Keter Etz Chayim**. It means "the tree of life." All of these names are given in the core spiritual language of the earth. Each name is meant to be heard as a spoken phrase, strung together for the full meaning in Hebrew.

More about Layer Two

Today we wish to speak more about layer two. Hiding in layer two is a duality attribute that you deal with every day. If we could rewind this day of teaching and listen to the questions that have been asked of the healers on this very stage, they would often be about the hows and the whys and the doubts of life. Some have said, *"I feel this way, I feel that way, why can't I do this, and why can't I do that?"*

If you could again listen to the healers as they told you about their lives, you would even hear expressions of their own doubt. They asked themselves, *"Am I doing it right? Am I doing it wrong? What should I do next?"* They expressed a situation when they didn't always know what to do. So in retrospect, you might ask yourself, *"Why does such a condition exist? Why is there so much doubt and difficulty, even with divine direction?"* With this question we open a subject that we've never identified before in this kind of detail. It's for the Lemurians in the room, which accounts for almost everyone here [speaking of the attendees of the healing meeting].

Human Being, examine your heart. Talk to your cellular structure and ask it: *"How many times have I been here?"* The answer may surprise you, for most of you have been here long before the experts in Human history perceived the possibility of your existence. There are pieces and parts of the layers of your DNA that you haven't discovered yet, which know all about every single past expression [past life] that arrives on Earth with you. It's part of your biology, and it's part of the chemistry that's interdimensional. It encompasses all the names you've had and all the lives you've lived. So we have a room filled with old souls, and you know it! We have young people here who know it. We have seniors here who know it. For a moment right now, you're all one age, and that age is forever in both directions [past and future]. That's what an interdimensional being has in common with another interdimensional being.

You pretend not to know each other here in this room. When you stand up in a few minutes and leave this place, you'll still pretend not to know each other. The truth, however, is that here are moms and dads and cousins and grandmothers. Don't look at the gender, don't look at the race, and don't look at the nationality. Instead, look at the wings. We have seen you before. You've seen each other before. So the invitation is given right now to feel this, and the teaching begins in these moments.

Self-Worth—Core of the Duality

We're going to talk about self-worth today, and it's about time. We've told you over and over that the duality of humanity features a balance of energy. We're going to get into a subject that's difficult to describe because we only have several English words that will work. We talk about the balance of "dark and light," yet we don't mean what you think. Some have called it a balance of energy. Some have even called it old and new. But none of those labels are correct. Instead, we see it as an energy quotient, a seesaw of added and subtracted attributes created in much the same way as a puzzle... a puzzle that creates a struggle of one kind of energy with another.

For eons, this particular self-worth balance in the Human Being has been biased toward the *dark side*. In review, I'm going to make a statement, and I hope that you fully grasp and understand it.

DARK: There's nothing on this planet more evil or more dark than what is possible to conjure up in the Human mind. There's no evil that stands by itself on the planet. All evil is contained in the consciousness of humanity. There's no dark entity or group of entities that stands around waiting for you to slip and fall so they can take you away or capture your soul. Such stories are fear based and do not reflect the magnificence, power, or responsibility of the true Human situation.

But there is darkness, isn't there? It's created with free choice by those Humans who choose to take their consciousness to a darker or denser side. So, dear Human Being, the darkest place on the planet is therefore what Humans have created by choice.

Remember this: You are creators of energy. Humans have the power to create darkness just as they create light. There's no judgment about this from anything around you, so the very elements of the planet will actually respond to this kind of energy and create the kind of dark magic that so many Humans are afraid of, and what many feel comes from some kind of dark place, or storehouse of evil. It doesn't. It comes from Humans.

Also remember what we've been telling you for years: Dark and light are not equal energies. If you have a dark place and light comes in, darkness does not creep away into another dark place. Instead, it's transformed! Of the two, light is the only one that has an active component and a physical presence. You cannot "beam darkness" into a light place! It can only be the other way around. This is because they aren't equal. One is the absence of the other.

LIGHT: The most divine place on Earth, where there is the most light on this planet, exists in the Human mind within Human energy. It's within the angelic part of humanity that wishes to show itself, enable itself, and claim its divinity. There's no group of bright, white angels who are standing by to take your hand and whip you into heaven should you choose to go. No. Instead, they're standing by in full regalia, willing to celebrate and love and press upon you with their energies to let you know they're there. The planet of free choice is like that. It's the Human who's enabled, and it's the Human who will make the difference in the history of the planet. It's the Human who has the responsibility for dark and light, not an outside force that's vying for your soul. But you've always known that, haven't you?

But with all this, isn't it odd that you arrive on the planet with your self-worth attribute like a flag at half-mast? It isn't balanced, is it? Why? Because your self-worth is tempered by the quotient of the energy of the planet. It's a measurement of what you've developed through the actions of humanity—what you've done and what you're doing. Therefore, personal self-worth reflects a planetary energy balance.

The New Self-Worth Balance

Did you ever ask yourself what happened on Earth that would have voided your Armageddon? Did you notice that despite all the prophets' predictions, the Armageddon didn't happen? This prediction of Kryon, given many years ago on a hill right in back of you, is now your reality. [The Kryon work started not far from where this channelling is being given.] In those days, I came through my partner and said, "You've changed tracks or reality, and changed the essence of Human consciousness. There will be no Armageddon."

(Many religious leaders will tell you to ignore this message of Kryon, that Kryon is a false prophet, even though the events on Earth unfold as we told you they might many years ago. They will tell you that the Armageddon is still going to happen—and soon! Our answer is this: We don't ask you to do anything but look around and judge for yourself. Why do they postpone their own prophecy? Use your own discernment, and meditate for answers that are correct. You can "wait them out" if you wish, riding the fence just in case they're right. If you do, however, you'll have to make this decision again and again as they try to explain why an old Earth paradigm of their doctrine didn't take place. Meanwhile, you will have lost years of action, a wasted potential of using your own divine power to help create peace on Earth.)

We told you of the enablement of humanity, and we gave you information regarding a 10 to 12-year window of time where the magnetics of your planet would change... and they did. We told you that the weather would begin to change... and it did. Four years ago we said that there would come a day when the greatest religious leaders of your planet could no longer say one thing yet do another [speaking of the current challenge of priests molesting children]. Now, all of this is your reality. Have you noticed? Are you beginning to "connect the dots" for yourself?

The Armageddon that didn't happen sits within an earth you are no longer on! Now, here you are, dear ones, in a new energy. Yet there is still the issue of self-worth. It's not automatic, you see? Your personal self-worth represents an energy at your birth, not a changed Earth. A new self-worth doesn't automatically take place just because of your new path.

Why Is Life So Difficult?

Don't you find it interesting that most of the religions on your planet see you as being born dirty? It's an odd posturing, is it not, for a creature of divine creation? Does it even sound reasonable that you would be born into a spiritual system where you didn't have a chance when you arrived because of something that happened eons before you got here? Does this really sound like being "made in the image of God"?

Is it not so that there are nonspiritual industries all over the earth—large ones—spending great resources trying to help Humans out of the hole of self-doubt? You call it a self-help industry. Why would this exist at all if you had come into this planet equipped with good, balanced self-worth? The reason? The self-worth that you possess was given to you appropriate to the energy of the balance of light and dark on the planet when you were born.

Now that the energy of the planet is vibrating faster, this planetary dark-light balance has changed. Let me give you information that's going to make sense: There's a newly created energy on the planet, one that you began in 1987 and that you'll finish in 2012. This is the 25-year energy window that you're working within. You were born in older energy. That's why your self-worth attribute is at half-mast. But for the Humans who are born right now, it isn't that way at all. Who am I talking about? The new children! We've called them Indigos. Some have called them Crystals. Some have called them Children of the New Earth, Children of the New Millennium, the New Kids—call them what you wish.

Everyone's noticing, aren't they? The children are different! They arrive enabled in the self-worth department. Their flag of self-worth flies high and proud. What happens when you take a child with high, balanced self-worth and put them with adults who came in with theirs at half-staff? The children seem a bit headstrong, perhaps? Maybe it's because they know who they are! Has a child ever looked at you curiously and you could see in their eyes that they're asking, *"Why are you that way?"* [Laughter] It's one consciousness looking at another! It's an enabled consciousness that comes in balanced, looking at one that came in in an old energy of uncertainty and doubt. They are your kids at the moment, which makes it worse. These children don't mean to be difficult! But to you, who have never had the attributes of balanced self-worth, they often seem overbearing.

The Truth

Do you wish to know the truth about the balance between the duality—you and the spiritual you? Go back and read the parable we gave you called *The Journey Home* [Kryon Book Five]. In the parable, there's a man called Michael Thomas. Michael stands for the archangel Michael; and Thomas, for the Doubting Thomas. When Michael stood in that last house [in the book] and saw the last angel coming down the stairs, the angel was so grand that Michael Thomas could hardly breathe! All through the parable, the angels he had formerly met said, *"Wait until you meet the last angel. It's going to be the best one. Wait—just wait."* And when he did meet this angel, who revealed himself slowly, it was the most divine one of all in his journey. Gold was the angel's color. When the angel came down the golden steps and his face was revealed, it was the face of Michael Thomas. Michael saw himself as the face of God, and he was astounded.

You see, dear Human, that's the truth, yet you arrive without the ability of seeing it. Born dirty? Oh no! Born hobbled, maybe, only in your awareness of who you are, but not dirty. Instead, you are born divine, but with a puzzle before you to discover it, including navigating the traps of believing those who wish to tear your divinity down to nothing.

Creating Balanced Self-Worth

How would you like to take that imbalance and correct it? How about taking that imbalance and making it equal? It's possible, and the invitation is extended for you to begin, and there are seven attributes that can help you with this. Some of them are easy, some of them are hard, some of them are simple in their explanation, and some of them are not. Some of them are going to sound overly simplistic. *"Well, I knew that,"* you might say. So I will say back to you, "Then why aren't you doing it?"

Here are seven attributes that we guarantee, if you practice them all regularly, will begin to increase your angelic awareness and provide self-worth balance.

1. Get Creative

The first is this: Do something creative! You may say, *"I have nothing whatsoever that is creative."* Yes, you do. All of you do. How many of you have tried channelling? And you might say, *"Well, now, I don't think I want to do that."* Why don't you try it when you're alone? Why don't you try it on paper? Why don't you see what your cells and your Higher-Self want to say to you once you let it flow out? You might be shocked and surprised. You don't have to show what you do to anyone, ever.

Doing creative things takes that God-part of you and spills it in to the duality part of you, and it's interesting to watch the light develop. Do something creative. Perhaps you don't consider yourself a singer, so instead, write a tune. Let someone else sing it. Perhaps you're not a painter? Paint anyway. Let the child out to paint pictures that you painted when you were a child. Do something creative. That's number one. It sounds overly simplistic, doesn't it? You watch how these things will meld one into another, when number one becomes number seven. The circle of attributes that I'm giving you now will be far more profound than they sound now. Creativity accomplishes something for you that almost nothing else can. It knocks at the door of the God-self, and begins to exercise the parts of you that need to be awakened.

2. Help Others

Number two: Help others. This one sounds simple until I elaborate on it. So I'll just get right to it: We challenge you to volunteer in a place where people are dying. Go find the darkest place in the hospital you can find, Lightworker. Go find the place where the children are dying, and plant yourself there. Find those dying with the cancers and viruses, and put yourself there. Read to them, hold their hands, and tell them stories. Volunteer. You have time for the children... and you know it. Have you ever thought of this?

"Kryon, you've just given us a horrible thing to try to accomplish. We cannot. I could never go there," you might say. *"I would sob at the door and be no good to anyone."* Dear one, this is a common misconception... that humanitarians could not help because they're so sensitive. So I'm going to give you a postulate and then ask you to go prove it for yourself: When you stand at the door of that place where those children are dying, and you open that door, your light spills into that area and their love spills onto you. You will feel uplifted and blessed. You may sit and hold the hand of a child when he dies, and you may weep for his life, but you'll feel enhanced and uplifted because the divine in you touches the divine in him. There's nothing like it, Human Being... nothing like it. You become part of a divine process! Can you celebrate being there and helping?

If you wish to touch the family, that's where you do it. Go volunteer where the seniors are, where they're close to passing. Read them stories. Ask about their lives. Celebrate their youth, and be there when they pass over. Your divinity will celebrate their divinity, and the two of you will be enhanced.

Helping those in passing, no matter what their age, creates and stimulates a part of you that will surprise you. You will ask to do it again and again, understanding that what you're doing is truly sacred work.

Dear Human Being, those are only two of the points, and already you're going to start feeling different. *"Maybe I am someone!"* you might say. *"Perhaps there really is something to this."* The dark parts of you will begin to diminish as they see the light begin to develop in areas that were dim before. That's number two. Go help someone.

3. Exercise and Meditate

This is the most difficult one, and the one you're not going to like. Exercise! In your culture you're no longer chasing animals for food! [Laughter] You need to balance this lack of activity with exercise. Biologically, when you exercise there is chemical balance that is shifted and changed. In addition, you take in much needed additional oxygen, a necessary fuel for the body for a Human Being trying to enhance new parts of their thinking. Oxygenation has been overlooked in the past. This is very needed!

Let me give you another secret: Go exercise, then follow it up with meditation. Watch what happens. An oxygenated brain creates a new palette for the artist of meditation. That's the order of things. Get it right: Exercise, then meditate. Don't cheat. Some of you will say, *"Let me see, that's meditate and meditate, right?"* [Laughter] That's number three, as important as any.

4. Personal Verbal Affirmations

Number four may be difficult to explain to you, and it's oversimplified. Watch what you say! The words out of your mouth are constructs of energy that are divine. They go into the air and they're fulfilled, as best can be, by those energies in your body, and those around you (who you cannot see) try their best to fulfill what you wish to co-create. Perhaps in a negative situation you might say, *"Oh, great! I knew that would happen."* Your cellular structure says, "Did you hear the boss? She liked it!" The entities around you hear it, too. "Did you hear the boss? She thinks it's great. Let's do it again!" Did you ever think of that? The cells hear it, and they'll do their best to make sure it happens again!

Watch what you say. Instead of negative posturing, give yourself affirmations. Blessed is the Human Being who understands the power of Human speech. Who are you? Say your name out loud. *"I am [your name goes here]."* And put the emphasis on "am" and watch what happens. Let me tell you what that phrase means. If your name is Paul and you say *"I am Paul,"* the first two words are the statement of who you are. *"I AM."* Paul is then the added identifier of what you're called. It's two statements in three words.

You manifest the energy that you place into the air through speech. The very elements "hear it" at a universal level. You're so used to making a great noise only when things are challenging. Try to balance that! It's time to speak your joy!

5. Challenge Your Darkest Part

This sounds like a frightening thing, but it isn't. Listen: Challenge the dark side of you to a fight! Throw the gauntlet out. Tell it where you're going to meet and at what time, then wait for it. Dare this part to meet you head-on. Do you have parts of yourself that you don't like? Of course you do, since you're in duality. I just gave you that information. Do you have dark parts that you'd like to scrub clean or perhaps put away or defeat? Well, then, challenge that darkest part of you to a fight. Set an appointment. Do you really want to be brave? Then challenge it to a fight in the dark, on its own turf! [Gasp].

And the reason we tell you this is because these dark and horrible parts are not going to show up! They're afraid of the light part of you, and especially the parts that are becoming stronger. You will have won this fight just standing there in the dark and daring them to show up. Soon, there you will be, in the dark, singing! Unafraid, and laughing at this whole situation. If you remember nothing else today, it's that this energy that you think is so ferocious is actually afraid of divine intent! The intent to balance will defeat this dark part every time. Empower yourself, and the dark parts of you begin to abandon ship. They don't dare show up, and they won't.

6. Claim the Angel Inside

After you realize that the dark part of you is a coward, it's time to claim the angel that's always been there. This is about understanding who you really are. Although you may never be able to see this angelic part of you, it's the true self, and it's ready to be claimed. Again, use your power of speech if you want to enhance this process. Hold a ceremony if it helps you make this process real for yourself.

Do you understand how the above attributes are fitting together? Here you are being creative, helping other Human Beings, exercising, watching what you say, realizing that the dark side has no power over you, starting to feel your own life potential, and now it's time to call your angel out of hiding (hiding only because you buried it)!

Reader, listener, you think that this is just "channel talk," don't you? You just wait. How would you like the drama in your life to go away? How would you like to be able to face any situation and know that you are absolutely 100 percent safe in your truth? Nobody can mold you in any direction, or in any way, when your angel is in charge. When the angel has come out, the third layer of DNA begins to be activated. We talked about that last time. Self-worth is no longer an issue. You know who you are. It's empowering to know of your divinity. It creates a situation in your life that's joyful.

7. Melding

The last one, number seven, is about melding polarity. Right now on this planet, one of the things that's going on with the earth, with the rocks, with the ground, with the portals, is a blending action that you can share in. There's beginning to be a meld of masculine and feminine. Those attributes of your gender that you've taken for granted—one gender is this way, one gender is that way—they'll never get together in thought—is beginning to change. Each of you is here in one gender, so we ask you to begin to accept the attributes of the other. You just thought I asked you to look at another person, didn't you? No. I want you to see the attributes of the other gender in YOU.

You exist with the ability to meld a healthy balance of both genders within yourself to allow you to understand and therefore co-exist with the other gender on the planet. It makes you a far better Human Being to have a balanced mind of both polarities, even though you're the obvious biological gender of only one of them.

Let me tell you what this balance does. It brings humanity closer together! It's called consciousness melding, and it's the start of another Human consciousness change on the planet.

We spoke about portals and vortices becoming vortals. We talked about the yin and the yang [opposites] coming together and creating something you haven't seen before... a new kind of Human balance. You may not fully understand what we're telling you at this moment, but we're telling you something that some of you are beginning to feel—women becoming stronger—men becoming more sensitive—together, looking at each other differently and sharing the planet far better for it. Stop seeing each other as opposites or as adversaries, but rather as a spiritual family. Stop seeing the other gender within you as a weakness! Begin to understand how each of you needs the consciousness of the other. The result? The balanced Human Being is now able to see an overview of balance because she sees with different eyes... ones that are walking in the other's shoes, and ones that have awesome self-worth! We wouldn't tell you these things unless they were so.

So it is we have reached the end of this teaching. Some of you came today saying, *"If I can sit in this energy long enough, perhaps I'll leave differently; maybe I'll even have a healing. Perhaps I'll learn something and get rid of this or that. I'm tired carrying it around."* Indeed, this power is in your grasp right now. Reader, listener, if you want to interview any of the healers who spoke this day, they'll tell you that it's in your grasp right now. Perhaps it's a healing of attitude, or of anger, or of worry. This shift is yours for the taking. There's no greater time than this for you to reach out and grab this self-worth, and the healings that come with it.

And so we have come again to this place after all these years, to celebrate the seeds and the core of the work. In 1989 we worked here to bless and help my partner begin the work of Kryon. We never returned until now. Now, in 2003, we have Lemurians awakening on a changed Earth that you've created (if you noticed). Much of what we taught could happen, did. Much that we taught about that might be accomplished, has been. Note that we didn't create anything. You did. We just watch and help in your grand plan.

Blessed is the Human Being who sees the planet's glass half full, and who understands that the changes on the planet are needed and necessary. Blessed is the Human who also understands that in order to create a new temple, the old one must be removed, and its foundation scrubbed clean. The new temple is called *The New Jerusalem*, a metaphor that means "peace on Earth." And just like those who wondered in 1989 if the things we told them would ever happen, so it is that you might look around in 2003 and wonder about what we say now. Could it be that things are not what they seem? Could it be that historians will speak about these revolutionary times before the great awakening, the shift of humanity... as the beginning of a time that created a more peaceful Earth?

Only the Lemurians will be able to tell you the answer to that.

And so it is.

Please see Appendix A on page 383 for a discussion of the Hebrew DNA names, included in this chapter.

Blessed is the Human Being who practices pure intent in all aspects of his life. For this is the one who will climb the stairs of ascension. This is the one who will see the face of God, and it will turn out to be his own! This is the one who will reach up and take the hand of the guide groups that are around them and will never let go. Intent is the energy of the New Age. Not all that is old is to be cast away. Sometimes the oldest is the newest. Such is the way of the now.

Kryon

Live Channelling

"Frustrations Part I"
(Plus the Harmonic Concordance)

Channelled in Toronto, Ontario, Canada
September 2003

Chapter Ten

Frustrations Part I
(Plus the Harmonic Concordance)
Del Mar, California - September, 2003
Chapter Ten

Greetings, dear ones, I am Kryon of Magnetic Service. There's a sweet energy here, do you feel it? It's a sweet place where Lemurians gather together. The scope of who you are and what is happening on this planet is far beyond your comprehension. But right now there's a sweet energy here. The entourage that came in this morning is now being given permission to move between you—to touch you, if you choose; to sit next to you, if you choose. As the energy is developed, we give permission for some to see the colors both on the stage and in the group. That's what happens when angels come together. It's a cosmic joke, you know, that you would sit in front of me and I would speak to you as I am. It's a duality that totally and completely hides what's really going on.

When angels speak to angels, there is not one that is above the other. We all speak together. Dear Human Being, I know your other name. I've said this since the beginning. There's a name you cannot pronounce—a name we sing in light—and that's you. Far beyond the strife and the frustrations of Earth, the *real you* exists. You exist in this temporary form, performing a test for the Universe, one that you agreed to perform.

You're eternal, you know? Your life on Earth is very temporary. It's a series of temporary events, much like you would think of as a number of bus rides. You're always in transit, never home, but always going somewhere purposeful while you're on the planet; it's profound.

I want to remind you of something you need to hear, and I've said it before: Every single one of you was born into this planet when the prophecy and the energy was gearing for its end! You were to grow up and then experience the horror, the doom, and the death. Every single one of you arrived on purpose, by choice, in that energy. Do you remember? Now remember, you had to give permission to come, and we've told you that you metaphorically stood in line to be here! So you might say to yourself: *"It would seem like a pretty bad decision. I could hardly wait to get here to do what? To perish in the Armageddon?"* No. Lemurians knew better. One of the postulates that's literally a test of the earth is this: When enough Human Beings decide to change the energy of the planet, it changes. You set in motion the tests and the changes. You set in motion the times where humanity was questioned [the convergences]. You were the ones who set the time lines. In those planning sessions that none of you can remember, you're now fulfilling what you set out to do.

What happens to an earth when angels arrive but their sacredness is hidden? What happens when the playing field is evened up and there's no God-bias? What energy will be developed? Which way will it go—to the dark—to the light? Will the "angels disguised as Humans" see their sacredness? Will they understand the *prints* within their DNA [the hidden math]? Will anybody bother to try to unscramble the mysteries that are there? Will they do the numbers that tell the stories? Will they see the codes? Will they understand that within the DNA there really are messages that are sacred? If they do, will it make a difference?

Well, here you sit, Lemurians. Welcome to a new planet—one that didn't move through the predictions at all. You made the difference. For when you came into this planet, you knew you could change it. Regardless of the prophecies, you came in willing, arriving at an auspicious time when the earth was preparing itself for the end. It was something that you had helped set up, by the way, but you came in to change it, if it was appropriate.

Part of the change of the planet began in 1987, and you called that energy the Harmonic Convergence. In those moments, to us, there was an actual poll of the Higher-Selves of every Human on the planet. Perhaps you didn't remember that? You wouldn't, for it wasn't in your reality. At that time, the Higher-Self of every Human Being was asked the question: "Are you ready to make the changes of the energy that you've set up?" This was the first time it was ever asked in the history of humanity. The answer was yes. The result is what you've seen in these past years.

The Harmonic Concordance*

Kryon arrived within Lee Carroll in 1989 (two years after the Harmonic Convergence—also called the 11:11), but this energy wasn't a stranger to my partner at all, for he helped set the grids, just like some of you Lemurians. In 1989, many of you began to *feel* the differences. You began to feel the enlightenment taking place. If you take a look at the calendar and how this occurred, you'll see striking coordination with many who were being "awakened" at that time. Many found their way and their path in those early years after the 11:11. The reason we bring this up is because many of you aren't aware of what will happen on November 8 and 9 of 2003. There is something similar, something just as profound, and something that spiritual historians will speak about in the future.

---

*Also see page 288 for Kryon's remark after the Harmonic Concordance was complete.

November 8 and 9 will be the Harmonic Concordance. This Harmonic Concordance is the next step after the Harmonic Convergence. There will be another poll, and I'll tell you what that question will be: *"Do you give permission to have your DNA changed? Do you give permission, humanity, with free choice, to have the tools available for its spiritual alteration?"* We already know the potential answer, since it's written in the now. If we had a reading of the energy of that question at this moment, it would be yes. It's going to be yes. But we go through the protocol of asking, since it suits the linear process of your time line, and it's a ceremony of great importance.

There has been a change within the magnetics of the planet since 1989. This now-completed change is cooperating and synchronizing with the new authoring of the crystalline grid. This combination is an allowance for the DNA layer called *Layer Three* to be activated. It's an allowance, not a mandatory shift, and you won't feel anything immediately. A door opens, and enablement begins. It also begins a cooperation with the earth that is new. It begins a meld of masculine and feminine energies of the rocks themselves! It also releases processes that have been part of ancient Lemurian prophecy for a very long time.

"Kryon, how does this fit in with free choice? What if there are Humans who don't want this?" You have to understand the dynamics here. At a spiritual "knowing" level, what you call humanity has indeed given permission for this new energy. But it's presented as a tool. Think of this metaphor: You are a carpenter. You go to sleep one night and wake up to find that your old tools are still there, but next to them is a case that says, "There are new power tools in this case." There you stand with the decision to open the new case with free choice, or not. Do you understand that the new tools don't change anything as they just sit there on the floor? Some won't want the new tools.

Some won't believe that they're real, and some will actually fear them. It's Human nature that some will go on a quest to find out who put them there before they'll open the box, and others will wish to have a book written on the best way to open the box. Still others will simply open the box, since it was obviously a grand gift with their name on it, and "see" the splendor of the potentials of the new tools. Then they'll learn to use them and build new and wonderful things. This is free choice of the individual Human, but with a scenario that was allowed and enabled by the whole.

When enough of you open this metaphoric box, something amazing happens. It's something that some of you won't understand, and something that we've only spoken of one other time. For those of you who have understood that the changes in the crystalline grid of the planet is the rewrite of the memory of the planet, this will begin to make sense. Remember that all crystal structures, both physical and interdimensional, contain memory.

More on the Cave of Creation

Very early on in our work we spoke to you about the Cave of Creation. It's a real place that will never be found on this planet. It's in your reality, in 4D. It has to be. It marries the spiritual to the physical, and the interdimensional to the dimensional. It's a place where there are crystalline structures within a memory vault called the Akashic Record. It's where your essence comes and goes from when you arrive to when you pass over, and what happened while you were here. It's the first place you go, coming and going. You pick up the essence of the memory and take it to the other side of the veil.

When you choose to come back [and Lemurians almost always do], the first thing you do is reactivate that record, placing that crystal, metaphorically, in the cave again. This custom crystal unit of your record tells you (1) that you're on Earth, (2) that Earth knows you, (3) what you've chosen for yourself this time as your starting energy [potential contract], (4) what happened before this time [past-life solutions], and (5) what the potentials are if you choose to change your starting energy. All this information is also in your DNA! The crystal in the cave is a passive record that coordinates with the living one (you). But *both* will change together as you change the living one.

Did you ever wonder why there's a cave at all? Couldn't these things be done on the other side of the veil? The answer is no. Consider this: You're a part of the dirt of the earth. The planet knows of your existence, and the first thing it does, like a mother in the womb, is to accept the essence of a Human Being. It might say: "How wonderful! You're back, and we accept you. Now return to the surface and let the action begin."

With the Harmonic Concordance, which is a quantum event, (interdimensional) comes permission to rewrite the Akashic Record. That's part and parcel of what all this new energy is about. For with the rewrite of the Crystalline Grid, the crystalline portions on the Akashic Record will also be rewritten, and so will the crystalline sheath of your DNA (which we've spoken of before). Some of you are going to feel it. Within that rewrite is also a change of vows. These are the Human spoken vows [which carry spiritual energy] that were taken in past expressions [lives] that are now surfacing in the "now" time, and which are becoming hang-ups in your 4D linear existence.

Some of you have asked how it is that you might change these vows if the past and the present are melding. You've asked, *"If we're coming together and the past is so profound, even within my present, how can I rewrite these vows? What can I do? What should I say, and to whom?"* Like so many other things we've spoken of, the answer is far easier than you might think. You need to be alone. Then with pure intent, come before the family [Spirit] and state your case. Whatever you say is then the beginning of the rewrite, since the energies of Earth respond to Human free will. Speak it out loud so your cells can hear it, too, in the air. State that you drop the old vows and then give a new one... perhaps one where you'll now take the vow of master-hood? Perhaps you'll pledge yourself to the benefit of all humanity? In the process, you'll need peace in your life, without drama. You will need sustenance [abundance], and loving relationships with those around you. This drops the vows of poverty and celibacy, and all the other old-energy thinking regarding what Humans originally thought God wanted from them. Do you know what God really wants from you? Partnership, family awareness, and love.

A vow of master-hood gives permission for the energies to change within you, for the tool box to be opened, and for Human Beings who have always thought themselves ordinary to begin to activate the *ascension layer* of their DNA. The door to a peaceful planet begins to open, and only a few will walk through at first, then more and more, should they choose to see. It's free choice. It's often slow, and it's frustrating. But it starts one Human at a time.

Changing Old Concepts

We'd like to give you some news today about master-hood. In the process, it may help to explain more about some misconceptions of old Earth-based spiritual concepts, and also explain some frustrations. Before we begin, we'd like to give you some postulates. [From Lee: The definition of *postulate* from the energy of Kryon is this: "A spiritual rule of absolute truth."] Here are some postulates. You should hear these clearly, Lemurian:

1. The Human Being, who vibrates at a high rate and has pure intent, is not destined to be in suffering on this planet. That is not a plan of God. You're not in a suffering mode in order to achieve great things on this earth. Hardly. Gone is the old concept of suffering somehow creating solution.

2. Human Beings who vibrate high, calling themselves Lightworkers, are not those who are going to be in constant pain. Pain is not part of an ongoing spiritual scenario, dear Human Being, no matter what you've been told.

3. The Human Being who vibrates high and calls himself a Lightworker is the Human Being who will not be in fear and sadness. He will instead stand in the light of wisdom.

Perhaps you feel that you have to have pain or must suffer to become sacred or help the planet. That simply isn't the way of it. Don't confuse this information with what we've told you about those who have elected to sacrifice an expression [die in this lifetime] for the enablement of others. That scenario is different. We're speaking now about those who believe that they must remain in suffering and pain while remaining on Earth, and that it's just part of their "life lesson." The irony here is that the Human's real life lesson is really "how to *get out* of pain and suffering"!

The whole idea of "suffering for God" is of Human origin. You'll never find that in any real channelling from Spirit from the other side of the veil. Instead, it's just the opposite! Humans have created this, even placed it within some holy scriptures, in order to produce control over other Humans. It never was a spiritual message of truth.

Dear Human Being, you're an angel of the family, and you're my friend. I know you, and you've been here forever [Kryon's way of saying that you had no beginning]. Can you imagine this bond of angel-to-angel? Can you begin to conceive how much love and planning have gone into your being here? When you're on the surface of this planet in duality, walking in biology, you don't see things in angelic terms. For us, to think that some of you feel you must suffer and be sad in order to be spiritual breaks our hearts! Maybe it's time you reexamined this entire suffering scenario. Oh, you may have challenges. Indeed. These challenges may be what you think your contract is all about (we'll speak of contracts in a moment). But being on the planet in duality doesn't mean you have to endure sadness. Joy is the invitation. The real challenge is this: Can you be joyful in whatever the challenge is you're in? If you can, it's one of the chief catalysts of the solution of the actual challenge. That's the way the new energy works.

Contracts

I want to talk about *contracts*... an overused word in spirituality. There are Lightworkers who walk around saying, *"It is my contract to have these challenges in my life."* And they say, *"It is what I chose a long time ago."* No, it isn't! I'll tell you the way it works, and you should hear this clearly: Is there such a thing as a contract? Yes. However, it's not a predestined thing that you would come here with a lifelong contract of unhappiness, or some kind of sacred agreement that you would find, discover, fulfill, adhere to, and play out all of your life. We know this may be confusing for some of you who truly believe you're here to suffer and somehow help Earth, but again, does it make sense that a loving family would send you here to be unhappy?

Listen: This is different from having a lifelong disease, or a disability. Indeed, you may have chosen these things to set an energy around you, but it doesn't mean you then have to accompany it with misery and unhappiness. The invitation for joy and peace belongs to all of you, no matter what is happening with your physical circumstances. In some cases, the invitation is to discover how to heal physically, and in some cases it's to discover how to heal emotionally. Many times it's to heal spiritually, bringing about a complete change in your attitude and your life. But the invitation is to change it! Each one of you is unique.

Instead of predestination, contracts are a predisposal [predisposition]. They're only a starting place of energy. They're an opportunity for you to fit into a set of circumstances, predisposed to be there, and then using free choice to decide to stay there or not.

I hope you understand what I'm saying. All of you Lemurians have free choice about what you wish to do. You may say that there's a contract for this and for that, but the reality is that you're constantly rewriting them. Every time you shift vibration, passions change. *"What does that do to contracts?"* you might ask. They change!

Some of you have been part of a very long, educational Earth-based process that eventually has brought you an academic degree. This often puts you in a place where you exercise what your passions are, and that becomes your life. Some of you will call yourselves doctor or healer. Some of you are esoteric healers, and some of you are 4D healers [certified by the system], and that is your passion. Suddenly, the earth shifts and you shift! You discover new energies as the "light is turned on" in your life. Oddly, sometimes the result is that all that you've gone through and everything you've done looks meaningless! You receive a new facilitation, a new passion, a new contract. Think of that. This has happened over and over to many Lightworkers, and it has brought them joy and not frustration! Why? There's nothing like being in your sweet spot.

Others around you may shake their heads and say that you're "wishy-washy." They say you can't decide who you are, or what you want to do. Instead, perhaps they're the ones who are stuck, anchored in an old linear reality that says that a Human is only supposed to do one thing. Think about it. Who's flying here? Perhaps the "wishy-washy" Human is the one with the wings, flitting about in the joy of co-creation. The others are stuck in the mud, which they call "normal."

Co-creation

Let me give you another concept that's often misunderstood. When you co-create something, have you ever wondered about those around you? You can't co-create in a vacuum, you know. How many of you have ever gone to a sports event to watch one team play... alone [without the other team showing up]? The game wouldn't be very exciting if only one team showed up to play and win! There really couldn't be a game at all.

So you should understand that everyone around you is affected by what you do. Have you ever wondered about that? Your co-creation is always a part of another person's reality, and perhaps their own co-creation. It's a huge puzzle, isn't it? It's a puzzle that's filled with complexities that are being worked on 100 percent of the time by the pieces and the parts of you that aren't on the earth. That, by the way, is part of your frustration. You'd like to see a different kind of timing, wouldn't you? We have channelled about this complexity before, but there's frustration around the process of co-creation.

If indeed you're moving into master-hood, how are you going to cast off some of these fears, worries, and frustrations? This subject is so large that it will take still another message [another channelling] to complete. But for now, I'll give you some of the questions we get: These are from Lightworkers on their knees, ready to move forward. Many are saying, *"Dear God, how can I get rid of the fear in my life? I'm always afraid to co-create or move forward spiritually. I always seem to be in fear that if I change, I'll lose something I really love."* Not all Lightworkers ask this, but many do.

It wasn't long ago that we gave you a full channelling on seven steps to gain self-worth. [the last chapter] It's unusual that we'd refer to another channelling, but if you will find that message, it will help. For the fear goes away when self-worth is achieved. Most of you were born in a situation where you didn't have much self-worth. When you were born, you weren't given much of the energy of true self-worth, so many in your generation represented right here [and reading this], come in with low self-esteem. When you start to build self-worth and redeem your magnificence, the fears go away. Do you understand that there's a giant darkroom, metaphorically, with all of your fears in it? When you go in that room and begin to enumerate them, it's scary. That room represents the energy of Earth when you were born.

Now, however, a light has been turned on, representing the new energy you've created for the planet. The room is still there, but when the light was turned on, it illuminated everything in it. Behold! What was hiding were the solutions for every single fear in the room! These were hidden completely by the darkness of the old energy. So in the same room with your fears are the solutions. Does that surprise you? It's the balance we promised you. You created the fear, so why not the solutions? It's just that the fears are felt more strongly when there's darkness. You know that from your childhood, don't you?

Some of you won't want to visit that metaphoric room, but we encourage you to anyway. Within the channelling message on self-worth, we asked you this: "What is your largest fear? Why don't you ask it to meet you in the backyard for a fight? Face off with it, and you'll find that it won't even show up! It's a fake, a fallacy, yet so real to you." Start working on your self-worth, and the fear will dissipate and disappear. There will come a time, dear Human Being, when everyone who has ever asked that question will wonder why they didn't discover the joy sooner.

Do not fear the love of God! Within this message, Spirit and family are here to visit you, to hug you and hold you, to move between the chairs in this room, and the place where you're reading. We know why you're here. We know why the reader's eyes are on this page. We know what you've been through. Oh, it's a good time to start something new. It's a wonderful time to be healed. Can you feel the sweetness here?

Abundance Frustration

Many Lightworkers are still saying, *"Dear God, when are we going to get our abundance? I know it's out there."* Do you think we haven't heard you? Dear Human Being, I'd like to redefine *abundance*, yet again. This area is frustrating to you because you think of it as something you wish to store up. Abundance is *sustenance*, like it was for the Israelites who walked in the desert. Do you recall the story? Every day they were fed by Spirit. Generations went by, and they were fed, every day for years and years. They got used to it, you know? Can you imagine the scenario... 20, 30, 40 years of being fed every day by God? Can you imagine how large the storehouse was to do that?

Now, let me ask you: What do you think their reaction was to this consistency? I'll tell you: Every day they wrung their hands and said, *"Will it happen again tomorrow? We're afraid. What if it doesn't?"* That's Human nature! And here you are, asking the same thing.

Look at what has happened in your past. Look at the way things were moved around for you. Abundance is sustenance. Every day is your first and also your last. Will it sustain you? Is there food and shelter? Is there love? *This is abundance.* It's not what you call a storehouse, and yet it is. What if I told you that your storehouse was absolutely 100 percent real? It's just that you only get to peek at it and use it one day at a time. You don't ask God for your abundance; instead, you *create* it. You create it daily by what you do, and with the voiding of fear through the realization of self-worth. Then, when you start to balance the energy around you, which we've called The Cosmic Lattice, abundance and sustenance take care of themselves. Maybe you didn't know that [see Kryon's channelling about *Singing in the Choir*, presented in Chapter Four in this book].

Your Path

Here's another frustration. Lightworkers often say, *"Dear Spirit, when am I going to find this path that I've been shown I'm supposed to be on? I'm tired of waiting for it. I get glimpses of it, but it never manifests itself."* Well, perhaps it's time for some plain talk. You wouldn't be in this room, listening to the voice of this angel who loves you so dearly [Kryon] if you weren't walking a portion of it right now! Did you think of that?

You might say, *"Well, maybe you don't understand, Kryon. I have a job I don't like. I don't have much money in the bank, and I'm standing around waiting for something good to happen. You're telling me that this is it?"* No. I'm telling you that there's more here than meets your understanding about "path." Why are you really on Earth? Didn't you come to do some work?

Are you walking in a dark place? Is there strife where you are? We'll say this again: How many lighthouses have you seen on calm, serene bays lately? None, you say? Why is that? Is it perhaps because they're needed specifically in places that are challenging for others to navigate? Yes.

Maybe you're the only one at work with a *light!* We've said this so many times before. The frustration in your path is due to a misunderstanding. Maybe it's time you found joy *where you work*. If you could find joy where you are, self-worth begins to develop, and fear goes away. Abundance starts to come in, and co-creation begins to work. It's about the *attitude* of the path that you're *in*, not the one you wish you were in.

It's your last day, your first day, your only day—what are you going to do with it? Make each day count. You've heard this before, yet these are the spiritual truths that often sound trite, don't they? And that's because they're real!

When you create peace with what you have, then you begin to manifest motion and change in your life. You're not stuck in the bad job. Instead, you're simply "working it" for a while to enhance the lives of others around you, and the energy of the job itself. Be aware that sometimes the "bad job" becomes a miracle! What if the energy dramatically changed around your work situation? Would you still want out? What if your peace and satisfaction with something formerly intolerable gets the attention of someone who needs to engage a peaceful person in a better surrounding [a new job for you]? Do you understand how, when you change energy, it actually brings about co-creation of something else? Things aren't always as they seem, and sometimes you create the perception of what's bad or good by your fears or attitudes within your own reality. Again, everything that's before you has been sanctioned by you and created by you. It often lies there begging you to work with it. Energy is like clay. It can be formed into a beautiful statue or just lie there on the floor. In both cases, the clay is still the clay.

Joy

"Dear Spirit, when am I going to find joy? I'm a sad person. I want joy. I deserve to have joy. I'm trying so hard!"

Let me tell you about the chicken. A very concerned chicken sat on her egg and worried. *"When is this thing going to hatch?"* Other chickens around her hatched their eggs, and beautiful little chicks came out. But not this chicken. She was sooo concerned! *"When is my chick going to hatch?"* She agonized. *"I'm sitting... sitting... sitting"* She never took a break from sitting. She sat and worried, sat and worried. Finally, after a very long time, the mother chicken had to take a break from sitting. *"I have to take a break!"* she cried. *"This is far harder than I thought."*

She got off the egg momentarily, and immediately the egg burst open! A half-grown, very hungry small chicken popped out, looked the mother chicken in the eye, and said, *"What's wrong with you? I couldn't get out!"*

Dear Human Being, stop trying so hard! Let the love of God into your life! You don't have to create this yourself, or know the integral inner workings of the joy process to experience it! You don't have to analyze it or launch an investigation about what it might entail, or intellectualize what it might mean. You don't have to wonder if you deserve it, or ponder the ramifications of what might happen if you receive it! Do you get the picture?

Also, you seem to have multiple reasons why you're unhappy, and we get to hear them enumerated constantly! *"Because of this, and because of that...*" Would you stop and let the love of God into your life? That's where the joy is. It's behind a door you're holding closed! Perhaps it's the "fear of being happy"? No. It's the lack of self-worth, a lack of the realization of your own splendor as an angel in the universe. Blessed is the Human Being who lets the joy of God in their life, because this breaks down the door of duality and lets in the truth. The Human Being who doesn't have joy is the one who's holding it back. Again, you create your own reality. That's the truth.

Peace on Earth

Let me tell you about one of the most profound frustrations of master-hood. The Lightworker often says, *"Dear God, when are we going to have peace on Earth?"* I love to talk about this, because that's why most of you are here.

Dear Human Being, this is one of the biggest frustrations of all, since it's your passion, and you can't seem to see any progress. You're here to facilitate peace on Earth. In order to do that, you're invited to change yourselves to clear the fear and to make your self-worth higher than it was when you were born. You can experience satisfaction with your sustenance every single day, and have an understanding that the Universe will cooperate with you as you create and manifest for yourself. As you walk an uncertain path, still you find joy and take care of yourself. This creates an increased spiritual vibration. Yet... where are the results of all this?

When enough of you claim your master-hood, dear Human Being, you're going to change the very essence of Human nature. You already have! The children of the new Earth [Indigo] represent a new Human consciousness. This is a consciousness that would never have happened on the planet without the returning Lemurians... you!

Blessed are these children, for they will be known as the peacemakers—the spatial thinkers—the "Teslas" of sociological change on Earth. They will find solutions where there seemingly are none. They will become very different Human Beings who think differently. You watch. The situation on your planet is critical, and you're frustrated by the lack of progress. What is the hold-up? You're waiting for these new children to grow up and become your leaders! You're the ones who brought them into the earth, and you're the ones who changed the earth's vibration so they could be what they are.

Blessed is the Lemurian, the old soul who keeps coming back and keeps coming back. We do not see the time line as you do. We see your lives, your futures, all in one energy. That is why we smile when you ask, *"Is peace on Earth possible?"* It's not only possible, it's probable... even in your lifetime, perhaps. Oh, there will always be dissension. Free will is like that. But true peace on Earth is when the hatred is no longer there as you see it today, and where the large issues have been settled and there's a consensus of humanity that to exist is to have peace. Believe me when I tell you that there may even come a day when a peaceful existence and the health of populations may even be considered a virtue of humanity.

Things may seem to get worse before they get better, for that is the "scraping of the foundation" as you rebuild the structure of your civilization. It's not a pleasant experience to have some of these ugly and very old energies brought into focus, is it? Yet that's one of the attributes of turning on the light in a place that has harbored so much ugliness in the darkness. Blessed is the Human Being who looks upon these things and understands the entire scope of what's taking place, yet still has joy. Blessed are the Human Beings who still have the wisdom and the knowing that they were *built for peace on Earth*, despite all that's taking place around them.

It seems like an interesting challenge of dichotomous energies doesn't it... that the more people there are on the earth, the more likely humanity is to settle the peace and health issues? The genesis solutions are closer than you think.

So why don't you go from this place changed? How about turning frustrations into solutions? Why don't you leave this place healed? Why don't you get up from your chair, put down this book, and take a moment to claim your magnificence? Isn't it time?

There will come a day when I look at you and you look at me, but the *bodies* won't be the same as they are now. Instead, you'll have the ones that are really yours. That is when we really celebrate. Are there parties on the other side of the veil? Yes. Grand ones. I wouldn't tell you these things if they weren't true.

And so dear ones, it's time to depart... and again, we don't want to go. You think this was for you, don't you? You've come to a meeting, or you've read a book. So you think it was all something for you? What about those who have held your hand during this time? Do you think they're anxious to back out of the room, or to leave your energy? We've said it so many times. Doesn't it give you pause to wonder who came to see whom? Did you ever think of that? Could it be that angels stand on the other side of the veil and they crave the ability to touch their family? And the answer is yes. These are the times when we can touch you, so we're having a hard time leaving.

And so it is that we remove ourselves from this place and move back to the other side of the veil. But not all of us. Some of you on this day have accepted energies that will go out *married* to *you* for the rest of your life. These are energies of master-hood and love, wisdom and understanding. These seemingly Human attributes are yet another piece of the puzzle that will change the dirt of the earth, in a remarkable time that humanity has never seen before.

And so that crack in the veil opens and we retreat [pause]... and it's difficult. For we want to stay and touch you more. But we honor the protocol of the time that you've set. Reader and listener, let the love of Spirit lie over this place as long as you choose to be in it. Let some of it go home with you, or marry to you as you raise from the chair. May it be remanifested every time that you call upon our name... that of family or what you call God, of which you are a part.

And so it is.

Dear Human Being, this family of whom you are a part loves you so deeply! We give information that will enhance you, and promote you to graduate status. We give you information that you need to hear and which puts you in a place where you'll be able to enhance it yourself, validate it yourself, and continue the learning yourself. And that is enablement! It doesn't subject you to sets of rules that would enslave you, put you in boxes, or ask you not to look around. It's just the opposite. It's about release, and it honors both the emotional body and the intellect. It honors spiritual logic and intelligence.

Kryon

Live Channelling

"The Interdimensional Universe"

Channelled in East Rutherford, New Jersey
November 2003

Chapter Eleven

The Interdimensional Universe
East Rutherford, New Jersey
November, 2003
Chapter Eleven

Greetings, dear ones, I am Kryon of Magnetic Service. God is not linear and neither are you. When you're not here [on Earth], you participate in an interdimensional life-force called God. We've given you this information for years, yet it has never been so important as it is now.

The energy of Kryon has been here all day long [speaking of the all-day seminar]. It's part of the entourage that came here three days before you did. Spirit is also like that, you know? The potential of your visit was known. It was not known as a pre-destined thing, but as a potential where you gave permission for today as part of your free choice... just like the reader right now has free choice to read or not to read.

As I mentioned earlier this morning, you were greeted and celebrated when you arrived. Those of you who came later were greeted and celebrated when you arrived, too. Some of you felt it profoundly, and some of you did not. Perhaps readers know right now about the changes going on around them? This is the basis of free choice. How much you wish to participate in an event that features your own divinity is up to you.

Many of you know others who "would make wonderful Lightworkers." You wish they would read this book or that book, yet all of their lives they just "hang on the periphery" of spirituality and never wish to open that spiritual locker, so to speak, and put on the Lightworker suit. They are "hanging back," yet there's an appropriateness in these things. There's respect and ceremony and free will involved. We've also told you that there's no judgment of family in these things. There's also no rule that says you have to make them open that locker. This is their choice this time around. Some of them are very spiritual, too! It's part of your frustration, isn't it... that you see the giant in the small body and wish they could see what you do?

Each of you is here doing the work, and walking through Human life is not an easy task. If you've chosen to open that spiritual locker and be a "light house," you find yourself meta-phorically shining a light on the rocks—helping others to find their way around the challenges, wishing they had the same light you had. The more your light shines, the more you have compassion for those around you.

All of this is to say that all of you are "known by God—fully and completely." You're part of the whole. "Known by God" ac-tually means "known by *you*." If there was no you, there would be no *God*. You're not just known; you *ARE*. The phrase "I am that I am" seems to be circular in logic. It is an interdimensional phrase that claims your own divinity. It's one that's difficult to explain in any language on the planet, for it's given in a reality that you don't study or live in. Humans will always perceptu-ally separate themselves from God, for this is part of the duality. The joke here is that this would be like Humans deciding that their own thoughts belong to someone else, since they can't "see" them.

Let me tell you more about *you*. You're here at a special time on this planet. This last weekend ushered in an energy that many of you knew was coming [the Harmonic Concordance]. In addition, accompanying the energy of not only the alignment of the Star of David but the eclipse was something that some of you noticed. The sun is in an 11-year radiance cycle, and you have amazing energy being delivered to the planet's magnetics by the solar flares. Now, there would be those who would say, *"What a coincidence that this is taking place at the same time a spiritual alignment on the planet is also taking place."* Naturally, there is be no "proof" that the two are aligned. However, let me give you something to think about. These convergences are like bookends: the *Harmonic Convergence* (the 11:11 which we have told you so much about) and the *Harmonic Concordance* (which you just went through) are indeed like balanced bookends. Both of these events asked questions of humanity, both were windows of opportunity, and both delivered to the earth necessary energies.

Now, I challenge you to go back, scientist, and tell me when the last time was that there were solar flares that approximated the intensity that you experienced this last week or two. When was it? You'll find that it was in 1987! Oh, what a coincidence! [Kryon humor] And there you are with the bookends. This is not simply a spiritual event. This current delivery of balance to the planet is what some of you actually came here for! It's the beginning of what you've worked for. It involves the heavens, the solar system, the alignments, and the energies of all of them combined.

Let me tell you that all over the Universe they know about this. Family in different places, whom I cannot describe to you, know about this. All divinity watches this planet of free choice. And you? Well, here you sit thinking that you're the ordinary Human. Yet again I tell you this. Ordinary or not, these are not ordinary times. Old souls are being awakened, and hidden consciousnesses are coming out of the actual planet to facilitate what's coming.

Human Being, some of you waited on the other side of the veil. You wouldn't come in until you could be this age right now. Did you hear me? "This age right now." Some of you have said, *"Well now, I'm older than I should be in order to generate the energies I need to participate fully in these things that Kryon is speaking of."* Oh, really? So why don't you stop aging? This is beginning to be well within the purview of your ability, Human Being, to slow down that biological process.

Aging is only an *agreement* with the cells. That's all it is! It isn't even fully biological. It's part of the DNA that has an *agreement* with your divinity that states: "Here is the potential of how long you'll last." That's very changeable, you know? At the same time you drop those old vows, why don't you also tell your body to readjust the clock. You think we're kidding? Wait until science catches up with this knowledge! Then perhaps these words won't sound so odd. Will you remember where you heard them first? At a future time, we'll discuss *The Agreement.*

Let the energies of the healings that you've come for, descend upon this group. Let there be healings in abundance, relationships, cellular communication, and personal growth. How long does it take to heal a body that's been injured? Perhaps it's time to throw away the old experiential concepts. Why don't you cut that time in half? You know who I'm talking to, reader. Why don't you prove it to yourself that you can talk to your own cells, to promote healing long before it was scheduled within an old paradigm. All of this is possible.

Let me tell you something interesting, Human Being: You're about ready to broach interdimensionality in many, many ways. What this last weekend was about [the Harmonic Concordance] wasn't just energy delivered to the planet. It was also about a slight *lifting of the veil.* It was about *allowance of things unseen.* Let me tell you that we're going to take a trip. We're about to become scientific, kind of.

Step with me into the middle of your atomic structure. Pretend for a moment that you're the size of a proton. It's very, very small, you know. There you are, in the glory of atomic structure. Now, you might say, *"Well, I think I can pretend what that's like. If I'm the size of a proton, I'm going to see those electrons just zipping around. There's probably going to be light, and it's going to be like fireworks, and there's going to be a wonderful show."* Think again. It's dark. Real dark. If you [as in Human size] really represent the size of a proton in the middle, those electrons are a mile away! Did you know that? You're going to have to hike to find them! That's the average scale of atomic structure. There's a lot of very empty space in each atom's makeup.

Most scientists are still puzzled about this. Why would the basic building blocks of your reality feature a structure where the objects involved are in a proportion that are an alarming distance apart? Perhaps you weren't aware of this fact. If you were the size of a proton in a helium atom, you would walk and walk and walk with your little proton legs before you would ever see anything that even resembled the electron haze around atomic structure (still pretending, please). And the entire walk would be in the dark! Then you might say to yourself, *"Well, this isn't what I expected. It's actually kind of boring."*

Indeed! In past scientific channellings, we've indicated to you that the micro and the macro have many things in common within their physics. Even within your biology there's an order that follows the larger Universe. Let me tell you what's in that space that is invisible between the protons at the center of the atom and the electron haze, which, proportionately, is very far away. It's packed with information! It's packed with physics. There's matter there that you cannot see; some of it we will even call "spiritual matter." Your interdimensional awareness is yet to manifest itself. You still look at everything in a linear fashion within your four-dimensional reality. So when you take a look at the mathematics at the center of the atom, you only see what four dimensions will tell you is there. You will not see what is *really* there.

The difference between your old energy reality and now is this: Pretend you're still a proton, taking that long journey to find your tiny friends, the fast-moving electrons, who you know are circling. In an old-Earth energy, you will "see" nothing until you finally reach the outside circle where they're whizzing around. Now, however, within a new energy, and a slightly lifting veil, you're actually beginning to "see" something in this vast void in your journey from the middle of the atom to its outside circumference: You're beginning to "see" other dimensions! They show themselves at first as "shadows" that vibrate. Now, reader and listener, this is a fantasy voyage, correct? Yes. However, I just gave science a hint about what interdimensionality may look like as your science begins to broach the visualization of it as well.

Dear Human Being, there are very real pieces and parts of this "interdimensional sight" happening right now in this very group. Some of you are becoming interdimensional! Oh, not fully, but you're broaching the issue of the "unseen." One of the most fun questions we ask about humanity is what will happen when some of these things start to occur where you see the shadows of something that you never saw before, within places that you've been looking for years. Out of the *corner of your eye*, motion may occur that in the past would have frightened you, but which is now appropriate. We've told you for more than ten years that you're "not alone." Oh, that sounds wonderful, doesn't it? Perhaps to some it's scary? When you start seeing what's really there, what will your reaction be? Fright or celebration? We're not talking about ghosts here; we're talking about the love of God [Spirit]. We're talking about you with family and interdimensional things that are going to be able to be seen—some clearly, some not. You just wait. And it isn't just for Lightworkers. Some will see this in laboratories, and some will see attributes of it all by themselves.

Does it make sense to you that when the earth reached a point of high vibration where it earned this kind of delivery system [the Harmonic Concordance], it would only be for a few? No. It's for all of those who wish to examine it. It's humanity-wide, this new energy of Earth.

There's more. I just took you on a trip to the center of a simple atom and told you that there's far more there for you to see than how it appears in 4D. Let me give you a prediction: Scientists will begin to understand this on a grander scale as they continue to look at the Universe. There's something missing within the energy measurement of "everything that should be there" for the motion and scope to exist as you see it. So what's missing? Why can't you see it? Already scientists are postulating the possibility of *dark matter*. This would be matter you can't see, but which must exist to enable the energy equation to be balanced. No one has said anything about interdimensionality yet, but they will. They have to, for the elegance of the math eventually will show them very clearly that perhaps what's going on in the Universe is interdimensional in its scope. What's missing in their energy computations is very real interdimensional matter.

Who said that the cosmic lattice was linear? Who said that the energy that you can't see follows the same paradigm as what you can see? Oh, before this channel is over, I'm going to give you some puzzles. So here's another prediction: Science will begin to look for missing dimensions to explain missing energy! And it's about time. And that's the way of it. So it's time to reveal the shape of the Universe, and the push/pull action within dimensional shifts that cause your Universe to do what it does, and show you what it does. Many of the things that you continually observe are hints of it, but they're misinterpreted.

In four dimensions, your physics makes a lot of sense. When you step out of 4D and become interdimensional, however, all those logical rules of physics change. We even told you the last time we were here that when you get small enough, the laws of basic physics changes, too. It also changes when you get very large. It also changes with time frames. Stay with me here, for this will be simplified in a moment

Before we get into the puzzle of the actual shape of the Universe, I have another prediction. In order to give it, however, I have to lay the groundwork. Let me engage in some plain talk here. I'll give you one of the postulates of your modern scientific thinking: The speed of light is absolute, and everything, speed-wise, is measured against it, since it's the fastest thing you can see or measure. It has become a yardstick of astronomy and a standard. The idea of "time" being variable (and it is) is also dependent upon how fast you travel. All of this has become your reality using that magic number, the speed of light. Watch for this; it's going to happen. There's going to come a time when there's an acknowledgment that the speed of light is variable! The reality is that it is indeed different all over the Universe depending on the dimensionality attributes of where it's being measured. There are many speeds of light, and it depends upon where you're standing and what you're looking at.

Now, this statement is at considerable odds with almost everything that you've learned, and with almost everything that has been postulated about the way things work. So the idea won't come easy, or fast. But it has to come. It also messes up the distance measurements in astronomy, but it's about time. Look for it—it's just around the corner. Some will start to issue the proclamations that the speed of light must be variable for things to be the new way you're seeing them. As the eyes of your astronomers get better (meaning the equipment), so it will be that you will have to change the reasons behind what you're seeing. Look for postulates of multidimensional areas in space, and also postulates of light changing its speed from place to place, depending upon the formula around localized reality, especially the time frame. By the way, this will also begin to explain why there was no "big bang," but instead, a "big revelation." Again, I ask you this: When unseen things become seen, does that mean that they didn't exist before you saw them? Think about it.

Your science gave you the postulate that when you travel almost at the speed of light, your time changes. So work that backwards: What happens to the speed of light when you change your time instead? It works both ways, and magnetics and gravity play the role of changing time.

All of this "new sight" and understanding is actually tied in to what happened at the 11:11 (1987). At that time, you gave permission to change your time frame, if you've noticed. All of these years later, we can say to you that your train of reality has sped up. We told you in 1989 that the magnetic grid of the earth would change, and it did. We told you in 1989 that the future, the potential of the earth, would feature massive weather changes. Have you seen any? The vibration of the planet is vastly different from how it was in 1987, isn't it? And what about your senses? Is there anybody here, perhaps those who are reading this as well, who would admit: *"Yes, I've felt the speed-up of time in the last two or three year"*?

The Human Being has felt it, the earth is physically showing it, and here you are in a time frame that's different from the one you were raised in. You're not aware that the speed of light changed for you, are you? It did. That's what happens with a higher-vibrating planet (and everything around it). The potential of science is to begin a new understanding of relativity... one that reaches far beyond anything that has ever been postulated before. However, if everything is relative to everything else, then where's the constant? There has to be one for the wise scientist to breathe easy and know that chaos is not the way of such a grand plan. There is a constant, and it's called the "love of God."

The Shape of the Universe

We'd like to explain the shape of the Universe to you. This becomes difficult, and again we'll say this: In scientific discussions of this nature, I can't give you interdimensional information within a single-digit reality. There's no way I can present to you the way it is without giving you oversimplified metaphors and analogies. Some of you will understand this despite the fact that you're functioning within a single-digit dimension with a metaphor that's only *true* to a certain extent. There have been those who would say, *"Kryon, what is the shape of the Universe?"* The shape of the Universe, in your dimension, looks like a toroid. Now, for those of you who do not know what a toroid is, it's a shape that looks like a tire or a doughnut. Within any 4D toroidal shape, there are mathematical relationships that are unique. These relationships have to do with efficiency and distance, and you're also going to find them (the relationships and toroidal shapes) within your DNA. This is only to say that the macro is similar to the micro within nature, as you observe it. This is no accident. We invite you to study why this might be.

So I've just given you the shape of the Universe, but it hasn't helped you one bit. Even so, now I'm going to complicate it. The Universe as you know it is pasted upon the inside and the outside of this toroidal tube. You look out and see the Universe as a shape that suits your expected reality. You don't see the curves, since light is supposed to travel in a straight line. It doesn't... it never has. In an interdimensional paradigm, you could be looking at something where the light from an object comes to you through a convoluted, twisting path, but within your 4D reality, you would swear that it was a "straight shot" to the object, since this is what you expect to see. The truth lies within a scope of reality outside what you expect or have experienced, so it's tough to describe it to you.

Now, in a closed, contained 4D shape like a toroid, there's no path from the inside to the outside. (Think of it as a closed pipe in a circle, with the ends connected together.) Yet, I've just told you that your Universe exists on both the inside and outside surfaces at once. So you might go to a model of a toroid and examine it to see how this might work... to have something on the surface of the inside and the outside at the same time. However, there's nothing you can do in 4D to create that path, even if you snip the toroid, straighten it out, and experiment with reconnecting the ends in clever ways. But no matter what you do, the inside surface always ends up connecting to itself, and the outside attributes are the same... no matter how many times you might twist and turn the ends and reconnect them. And here's where it gets very strange and interdimensional. We'll describe how it works, but you won't understand it.

Some of you understand the attributes of a Mobius strip. We've discussed this before. A Mobius strip is a ribbon, except that it's been snipped with a half-twist and re-pasted together. This creates an interesting situation. If you consider the ribbon as a road, you can travel this ribbon and walk and walk, eventually walking on what used to be both the inside and outside surfaces of that ribbon. It's a very efficient shape. This Mobius strip is a well-known phenomenon in mathematics and physics.

Now, what I'm going to tell you makes no sense at all. Nothing will make sense from here on in 4D. You've never heard of a Mobius toroid, have you? Well, that's exactly the attribute of the interdimensional toroid that is your Universe. Multidimensional physics is different from your 4D physics. It allows for paths and portals outside of your linear thinking, and it seems to allow for objects (and light) to be in two places at the same time. They're not, but when you take away linear time, it looks that way to you.

Let me give you an example. You're used to linearity and to the elements around you behaving in a certain way every day. When you sat on the chair tonight [speaking of the seminar in a hotel], you knew its shape. You knew that it would support you. You knew how to pick it up and put it in a stack, if need be, for storage. These are the kinds of things you're used to. But what if I told you that there's a situation where you could place the chair on the top of a chair-stack, and it would become the bottom chair! That doesn't make sense, does it? You can't have matter going through matter. You can't have things connected to other things that "go through themselves." Not in 4D, anyway. Let me tell you why the chair really stays on the top in your reality. It's because you placed it there last. It has less to do with the fact that it's solid, as the linearity of the time frame it's part of. In interdimensional things, their "place" in the Universe is often driven by the time frame. Objects in the "now" always think they're together, even if you think they're galaxies apart!

Your reality contains two attributes that are strongly interdimensional. Both violate the rules of 4D physics, only because you don't know what the actual *rules* are yet. The two things are *gravity* and *magnetism*. Isn't it true that gravity *goes through* everything? It doesn't seem to matter what you have, or what element you present, gravity always wins [affects the object], if you've noticed. Gravity is an interdimensional force that's related to time and the shape of the Universe itself. It's actually very related to the toroid. It goes *through* everything, almost as though your dimension was invisible to it.

Magnetism, to some degree, does the same thing. In your reality, magnetism is the basis for all of your broadcasting. You broadcast a modulated magnetic frequency, and it goes through buildings, through walls, and most objects, and it comes right into your home. If you have a receiver, you can manifest what it contains in your reality. It's an interdimensional thing, this magnetics... just like gravity.

Your science still doesn't understand either one, so apply these principles to what I'm about to show you, metaphorically. The shape of the Universe is upon the inside and the outside of a toroid, yet they're connected in a way you cannot visualize in your four-dimensional mind. Think of your Universe as having the same attributes of gravity and magnetism, which seem to be able to permeate almost everything. With that in mind, the pieces and parts might be like the chair that somehow goes to the bottom of the stack, even when placed on the stack last. It goes through the others because there are rules of interdimensional physics that demand that it find its true *universal location* based on things other than what you think they should in 4D linearity.

Universal Distances

Here's something you can visualize that may help you understand what I'll call the *deception of one dimension looking at another*. I'm going to show you how the Universe isn't really that big.

Take this toroid we've created in our metaphor, and visualize it. Now, change the metal-pipe scenario to one of soft cloth.

The toroid is now flexible. Take scissors and cut it anywhere you want. Straighten it out so it's a tube, like a tube sock. Make it big enough so that you could put your hand inside.

Reach in through the tube, and grab the other end and pull it through. Visualize doing this many times from each side until, instead of a pipe that used to be a tube sock, you now have collapsed it until it's a fraction of its original size and shape through pulling the ends through the sock many times. When you're finished with that, cleverly connect the ends again. You can do it. It's not that hard. You can wrap one end over and connect it to the one inside. Question: Is it still a toroid? The answer: Yes. The shape is the shape, and it has only been modified in three dimensions. Also, it still contains the mathematical "magic" of the toroid, only it's now collapsed.

Now, let me take you to the middle of this collapsed toroid for a moment. You're the size of a molecule, inside the sock. Metaphorically, there you are in a special Universe, vast beyond belief, yet layered and collapsed. If you begin to "walk" the surface of the toroid (inside or outside), you'll still have to walk and walk and walk to make one full round-trip journey, even though the sock is collapsed. Why do that when the adjacent layer is only a fraction of an inch away? The answer? You can't get through the layers. You can't even *see* through the layers to know where you are. So you're stuck with walking and walking and walking to get anywhere at all.

What we're telling you is this. Your science and logical observation tells you that you're literally hundreds of millions of light years away from objects. But what if this is an illusion, and a multidimensional Universe has attributes of the model tube sock? Could it be that what appears to be a linear 100-million light-year trip might be next door? The answer is a positive and strong "yes." Although difficult to conceive of, yes, the vastness is real, just like the perception of the molecule that believes it has to walk the entire interior of the sock to get where it wants to go. The universal shape is also curved in such a way that there's a predictable and mathematical way of broaching the "wall" (just like gravity does), that allows you to jump to other parts of the socks inner and outer surfaces.

That is the shape of the Universe. Now, however, let me give you some more information about "broaching the wall" between the layers of the collapsed toroid (are you still with me?). The Universe is a push/pull arrangement of energy. It's constantly creating itself. It's never destroying itself, but rather simply moving between dimensions in an arrangement where time and magnetism and gravity demand that it rebalance itself. There are facilities within the Universe to take away and replenish matter. Entire galaxies may seem to disappear and come back (as viewed from one dimensional paradigm). Dimensional shift is therefore the engine of your Universe, and all that you currently see in 4D. It's responsible for what you feel is the beginning of your Universe, although it doesn't have anything to do with a "bang," What you call "black holes," which are present at the center of every galaxy, are part of the engine of dimensional shift. They are the portals that broach the walls of the tube sock. We've also told you that in each galaxy center, there are at least two black holes. They always come in pairs, and one pushes and one pulls. Only one, however, is obvious to you. The other one belongs to the other side of the wall and hides. However, you'll see it soon.

Dimensional shift is also the engine of The Cosmic Lattice. You're becoming interdimensional, Human Being, because you've shifted your reality on your own planet. You are the only creatures in the Universe who are in duality, but also able to change your planet's dimension! Many can change it with machinery and for travel, but only *you* can change your entire reality scenario.

Let me give you another hint about the mechanics of your Universe. We've talked about gamma-ray activity for almost a decade. We told you to "look for intense gamma-ray activity." We told you that when you see it, you'll know that there's *creation* going on—something special happening. Now we identify this as dimensional shift. It's always accompanied by powerful gamma rays, specifically of extreme high intensity. This is an attribute of dimensional shift, and also tells you that something is happening. You see this at the edge of your galaxy, and you know that something is changing there. It's a "mini-big bang," if you want to use your own terms. It's part of a constantly changing Universe, one that's moving in a push/pull fashion.

Although it may seem to be billions of light years away, it isn't. It's really in your backyard, but you're never in danger, dear Human Being, of having a collapse of time around you, or a new Universe showing up in your solar system. The physics of it keeps it separate and in its own time frame. This also means that the "center" of the Universe is everywhere.

However, there's a special, sacred place in your Universe, and it seems to be in a very ordinary place. It's a place called Earth that exists with angels upon it disguised as Human Beings. They're there working a puzzle for Universes yet to make a shift. They're called "the only planet of free choice"... the only one that can change its own reality. It's the only planet where the inhabitants can take control and change the time frame of their reality and actually create dimensional shift. And this fact, dear Human Being, is the difference between yesterday and today.

This last weekend [the Harmonic Concordance] was significant, just like the Harmonic Convergence was significant.

Human Beings decided to change the way they've been. Even at the cellular level, this will be felt. DNA's "permission" structure will actually change because of what you've done. How can I tell you this? How can I show this to you? You're going to have the beginning of interdimensional sight, which is going to aid with your co-creation. Each of you has the ability to co-create a reality for yourselves that will match the energy of the planet, and those around you. Perhaps this reality means bringing peace in your own life while you work on the puzzles that have given you the most challenges?

What if you had interdimensional sight—the kind that could reveal the things that are hiding, but which are literally the sustenance of what you need? What if I told you that the secret of co-creation is subtraction? *"Kryon,"* you might say, *"you're talking nonsense again."*

Wo and the Block of Granite

We're going to give you still another parable of Wo. We haven't given a parable of Wo for a long time, and so with this we close. Wo is a Human who is genderless. He/she is a Wo-man, but we will call Wo a "he" for the purposes of this story.

Wo was disappointed with his life. Oh, he was working hard and was also a Lightworker, but he was depressed. He said, *"I want something precious in my life. I want something meaningful and beautiful in my life."* Wo knew that he could manifest. He was just a little unsure of what he would manifest if he tried. He also didn't really know what to ask for within his manifestation. He was cautioned never to ask Spirit for anything specific, but instead to say, *"Let me manifest only what I need, which is appropriate for my own divine plan."* Wo had the wisdom of a Lightworker, so he prayed, *"Dear Spirit, I want to manifest something large in my life. It's time. You choose what it's going to be, God, Higher-*

Self. You have the wisdom... choose what it's going to be. I need to manifest something large so I can get on in life."

And he did! One day Wo came out of his house to find a large cement block in front of his door! It was 30 feet by 30 feet. He was mortified! *"Is this what I really needed, Spirit? What is this?"* And Wo's Higher-Self said, *"We're not done yet, Wo. Just wait."* Wo waited, but the block just stayed there. He became impatient, as always, and thought that perhaps he had misunderstood the messages. Then his neighbors started complaining about the block. Wo was certain that a mistake had been made. Really! Spirit shouldn't deliver a block of cement! It's not really very Godlike. So he brought in a large mechanical crane and tried to move the block. It wouldn't move. He then brought in all manner of granite-block-moving-experts.

"Can we please move this block?" Wo requested.

"No, we cannot," they said. It's just too big.

Then it happened. Wo heard a knock on his door, and he opened it. There stood a small man with a chisel.

"Who are you?" Wo asked.

"I'm sorry I'm late," the small man replied. *"I'm the sculptor."*

"I didn't order a sculptor," said Wo. *"We've been trying to move this block and get it out of here. Can you perhaps break it up?"* The little man was horrified!

"Please, please, that's a beautiful work of art—you can't destroy that! Isn't that what you asked for? Isn't that what you wanted? You're about to have something valuable and precious and wonderful and forever in your front yard. It will be in a place that you'd like, and all will admire it and come from distances to see it." The little man was panting and out of breath. Wo just

looked at him and paused.

"It's a block of cement," Wo replied slowly. *"Why would anyone admire such a thing?"*

"No, it isn't. Can't you see it?"

"I see a large, irritating, and unmovable block of cement," said Wo. *"It's killing my lawn."*

Although Wo didn't understand, he tolerated the little man in his font yard for the next month or so, and slowly began to understand. The sculptor didn't see a block of cement at all. He saw art! He proceeded to remove all of the cement that didn't belong around the art sculpture the artist "saw" inside the cement. Carefully, he chiseled away what wasn't precious until finally an object of art appeared to take shape, which was much, much smaller than the block had been. Oh, it was beautiful!

Wo was so happy! *"I have something precious in my life that I never knew existed in that ugly block! I can't believe I tried to take the block away. How silly!"* Wo's neighbors noticed immediately, and came to "ooh" and "aah." Wo was very proud.

When the sculptor was finished, he came to the door.

"Well, now it's time," said the man.

"Time for what? Do you have to go?" asked Wo.

"Oh, no. It doesn't work that way, Wo."

"You mean I'm going to have to live with you being in my front yard?"

"Oh, it's even better than that," replied the man with a smile.

With a flash of light, the sculptor transformed. He became part of Wo, taking his place within the angelic attributes that

Wo perceived as *guides*. He became a soul mate, a spiritual twin-flame, and an advisor. His disguise came away, and his divinity shown brightly.

It's funny, you know. Wo never asked the sculptor's name. Now he realized that the sculptor's name was *Wo!* Not only did Wo receive the manifestation he wanted, but he also got an active wisdom partner to work with at the same time! Wo had just been given a new perception: Perhaps what is *unseen* is of the most import, and it's what gets subtracted from reality that allows for miracles.

The Zero

There will come a day when your science will honor the zero within your coming interdimensional math. Right now, you see the zero as nothing. Some have said, *"Well, we know that zero doesn't really mean nothing. We think that an interdimensional zero will be infinity. That's what a zero is."* No, it isn't.

We've told you about 12-based math for over a decade. The elegance of it will astonish you, especially its computational simplicity. It's the only math that "shakes hands" with nature. You cannot consider 12-based math without making the zero an integer of special value. It cannot be a placeholder; it cannot be "nothing," and it doesn't represent infinity. Again we'll tell you this: The zero is the magic of interdimensional math. It's the magic of base-12.

The zero is the *potential of all that ever was, is, or can be.* It's the "now" of universal math. It represents potential, or an energy of possibility. Therefore, the zero is variable depending upon the equation. You're not used to this. You're used to mathematical equations being empirical, and you wish that to remain. But it can't be that way when you begin to compute outside of linearity. Within that scheme is revealed the elegance of the math. The zero removes what is not needed, and reveals the solution. It becomes the facilitator of the reality of the puzzle itself, and is often the core number. We don't expect you to fully understand this. In fact, we don't expect any understanding at all. Not yet.

The Harmonic Concordance

Finally, I'll tell you what really happened last week. There's a place on this planet called the Cave of Creation, which we spoke about the last time we were with you. That was our name for it early on. But you have called it the Akashic Record. It's a precious place, where the lineage of *you* is stored. I wish to take you there for a moment. The walls glow. The crystalline is everywhere. It's cool, even though geologically it shouldn't be. There's a crystal for every man, woman, and child on the planet. Many of the crystals are very old, but they don't look that way. When you come and go, your many expressions (lives) simply update the crystals. You might say that there's a system there that even goes beyond what we've talked about.

Some of you have indicated that you feel that this is your last lifetime. For most, it isn't. What you don't know is that for most of you, "this is what you do" in the Universe. You might say you're universal professional Human! Why? Because you're in love with the earth! You're in love with the family! When this play is over and your "life" ends, you just change energies. Part of you becomes another Humans' guide; part of you goes on the other side of the veil, comes back, and reincarnates. The group that is you is always working. You'll do it again and again, and it's because you refuse to miss the ending! You worked too long, Lemurian, to miss this. You've been part of this for a very, very long time, and you've seen and shared the love of God. You've seen it work. You volunteered for the hard things, and here you are yet again in one of the last waves that no one ever, ever thought would take place.

In that Cave of Creation, over the weekend, crystalline energies that are the very life-force of who you are were changed. Only two or three times in the spiritual history of Earth has the Cave of Creation and the Akashic Record been altered. This was one. The crystalline grid of the earth is starting to be rewritten and realigned. So, therefore, will be the crystals that have your life-force and your lineage and your records of the soul on this planet. They changed, too. It has to be this way. There comes a time when the esoteric is also the physics. It's a system that has to be updated, for you see, the Humans are getting a lot closer to being angels. It was the same with the 11:11. Did you realize that? That's why we wash your feet.

Today we've given you interdimensional information about science. You might say, *"Well, that's not my subject, Kryon. I would rather have pure spiritual information."* You'd better get used to this, for this scientific information would never, ever have been given to an earth in a lower vibration. There's a reason why this is given in a spiritual venue. You're about to broach many changes, including a grander explanation of the Universe. This is so you may eventually go places you never thought you could go. A grander explanation of your reality is needed so you might do things with your biology that you never thought you could do.

The earth is in the process of being repaired—counterintuitive, perhaps, to what you see on your news, but there is great hope for peace on this great planet. There is hope for the end of hatred as you've seen it in these past years, and for an understanding and wisdom that has not been here before. There are those who sit here who give energy and light for the earth, and we wash your feet for this.

And so it that the entourage has removed itself... all in appropriateness.

And so it is that this message is complete.

Live Channelling

"Frustrations Part II"

Channelled in Newport Beach, California
December 2003

Chapter Twelve

Frustrations Part II
Newport Beach, California - December, 2003
Chapter Twelve

Greetings, dear ones, I am Kryon of Magnetic Service. *"Oh, how could it be,"* you might say, *"... that Spirit could speak through a Human Being?"* Let me tell you: It is the way of it. All the sacred scriptures of Earth occurred this way, did you think of that? You're seeing it now in a form that's personal. Did you know that one this very night you can go home and sit in front of Spirit and quietly, within the process of meditation, call upon the same energies that are here? This is the miracle of your divinity. The entourage again takes its seat beside you.

There is a sweetness here, which is the love of *God*. Whatever that word means to you—*Spirit, family*—that's what we wish to speak about tonight, among other things. There is one here who's saying at this moment, *"This cannot be so. I don't want to believe it."* Dear one, so you really want to be an island, cut off from all of the wonder and the love that is your family? Is this really what you choose? Through your intellectual judgment, do you wish to isolate yourself from healing, from peace, and from joy? If so, we bless you! For there is no judgment of free choice, dear one.

But at the very least, we ask you to stay with us. Perhaps during these few moments you might feel the touch of the hand that is not the one next to you. Maybe there will be *an invasion of the heart* when you finally realize that who's speaking to you now is your spiritual family. It's the core of all existence. What you call *God* is here! What you call God sits in the seats in this room!

The duality presented for the Human Being—part of the challenge—working the energy of Earth—to many, seems like a fruitless thing. Some say, *"We come and we go, and we come and we go. What's the purpose?"* Let me tell you: You're sitting in the middle of the purpose! Dear Human Being, there have been no prophecies about this day. What can you say about sitting right now in an energy on the planet that had no prophecy? What does it mean to you? It ought to tell you a lot. If there was no prophecy about what's taking place here, could it be that something changed? Could it be that the prophecy is now being written on a clean slate by the ones who sit in the chairs in front of me, as well as the humanity that's also outside this room? Is it possible that what we've said is indeed so—that humanity has changed the very reality of Earth?

There would be those who would say, *"Well, Kryon, that's not what we're seeing around us. It's chaos out there, and it's not positive."* Perhaps things are not as they seem. We'll talk about that in just a moment. But now, let's take a moment to posture the energy in this place, for we're almost set for the information to begin.

Who is it who comes here [speaking of the meeting taking place]? You might ask yourself, *"Who is it who sits in the chair I'm sitting in?"* [speaking now also of the readership] You might ask yourself, *"Who am I?"* You might ask yourself, *"Who am I to think that I can change things?"* We say that you are the angel who has come to Earth, fully willing to walk through the Armageddon! Impossible? Did you ever think of that? When you were born, that was the prophecy. Yet here you are! Why would a sacred creature who "knew" the potentials of a horrific future actually choose to come to Earth when you did?

The reason we continue to speak of this, as we have for the past months, is to trigger your "spiritual logic." Asking yourself "Who am I" is for this very reason. Perhaps it will occur to you that you're here on purpose. All that's here before you is on purpose. You arrived with a plan, and came with free choice—with predispositions that you have indeed walked through. Now you're starting to understand what *free choice* really means. Could it be that you can change your own cellular structure with your intent? Could it be that you can talk to your cells? Could it be that you also might create peace on Earth? Let's talk more.

More on DNA

In this last month of your calendar [the meeting was in December] it's a time of resolutions—a time where you'll promise yourself that you'll do things so that next year you can promise yourself again! [Laughter] It's Human nature, is it not? We told you sometime ago that there would come a moment when we'd reveal the names of the layers of DNA, and we've begun to do so. In review, we've also told you interdimensionally what some of the DNA "looks" like. As we told you about the twisting, we also gave some of the names that have now been published and some of the identities and purposes behind the layers. Did any of you see the reality that all of the layers are in a circle? They are. And you might say, *"How are they arranged one with another?"* Our answer is yes. [Laughter] How can we show you interdimensional things when your thought processes are limited to a single-digit dimension? As much as we've tried to give you examples, they just don't make sense. We even pointed to your artist *Escher* to give you an idea of what it must seem like to you... reality beyond your perception. Escher's perspectives don't make any sense within your reality, and neither does the your 4D physics around DNA. But we continue the best we can with our metaphors and the names.

We gave you the name of the second layer. *[Torah E'ser Sphirot]*. The name of the third layer was also given *[Netzach Merkava Eliyahu]*. The name of the first layer, we gave you later *[Keter Etz Chayim]*. If you noticed, they were all names of God. If you go back and study the published information, we were very careful to give certain information in those places where we know the information will be transcribed and published. What follows has been given at least twice before in unpublished venues, but it's time for the information to be written. We did that so that my partner [Lee] could get used to seeing and saying the words. It's too important to be left up to the moment. This is the way of it. With this new information, even my partner needs to practice the channeling!

So what we give you now is further information of the 12 layers of DNA. In review, they exist interdimensionally in four groups of three. Three elements or layers are in each one of four distinctive groups. Each group has a different purpose or energy. The first group we told you about involved layer one, which was the only 4D layer. It's the one and only one that you can see under a microscope. We also told you that there would come a day, when interdimensional exposition is at hand, when the *shadows* can be seen of the interdimensional layers. Look for this. It's a certainty. For as you begin to look into the interdimensional, some things will start to show themselves, even upon the double helix. Look there, because, dear ones, all of the layers are together in a circle, interdimensionally. Therefore, they all can be *seen* on the one that's in 4D. Their shape together will not make any sense to you... much like the Escher painting. The grouping of fours and threes will also make no sense.

They're shaped in a circle that fits in a box, and the box is the one in the middle of the Merkabah. This won't make sense until you observe the geometry of the Merkabah in 4D and find the box in the middle. Then perhaps it will begin, even in 4D, to be more meaningful than these words are.

Layers Four and Five of DNA

It's time to reveal layers four and five. Their names will always be in Hebrew, and this fact will eventually give you some hints about their purpose, but let's do a review of the first three.

The first DNA group of three work together and are about a *grounded* DNA. This group contains layer one, the Human genome, which you can see and which is the biological blueprint of the Human Being. It exposes all the chemistry involved in your life-force. Within this first layer, we told you to look for the "fours, threes and sixes." We told you that they all relate to a base-12 attribute of all life. And they're there for you to see, even in 4D. They'll even show in a greater way as you understand more of the chemistry involved in the twists. They'll *shout* about *12*, hopefully giving you even more evidence that what we've been telling you for over a decade about base-12 being the math of the Universe is indeed so.

That first group of three included an interdimensional third layer *[Netzach Merkava Eliyahu]* that we've called "The Ascension Layer." From this, you can see that even spirituality is included in the grounding layers. We told you in past channellings that the attribute of fear was also involved. We also told you what to do about self-worth, and how important it was to the entirety of your growth. All of these things were involved in the first three layers of DNA.

As we gradually expose all 12 layers, don't be surprised if we get to the ones that will be the imprints of your past life experiences. Even your karmic attributes are there, and all of them are *changeable!* The most confusing part of all of this for you will be something that we haven't discussed yet: As you change one of the layers in any way on any plateau, all of the others "know" it! Like complex chemistry, you cannot change one thing without the reactions of the others also changing something. In this chemistry metaphor, DNA is the same. If you activate the third layer, all 12 know it.

Within the scope of what has formerly been given, we now reveal the names of DNA layers four and five. Within this knowledge, we'll again say that these layers can't be isolated within your study. You can't study number four alone, or number five. You only can study four and five together, for they're a pair. They can never be separated, for it's an interdimensional certainty. It's the way they work with the other layers, and that's the best we can do to explain their process and how they relate to the rest of the 12.

Some might say, *"Well, Kryon, why are they two layers if they act as one?"* I'll answer you with this question: Why is the double helix, layer number one in 4D, made of two distinct sides of a ladder, when they can only work together? You can't study them alone with any success. The sides of the ladder are "married to what's in the middle." Again, it's difficult to describe what interdimensional properties are. So let's just say that they comprise the structure for what's in the middle, which isn't a layer at all. They support an energy of divine law.

Layer four is called ***Urim Ve Tumim***. It describes great power and great light. It's a name of God, and it's never to be taken alone without the fifth layer. The fifth layer is ***Aleph Etz Adonai***. It describes God! It describes a tree of life. Together, these two strands are part of *the divinity group*. Group one (the first three layers) was *the grounding group*. It included the Human genome (layer one). Group two is the divine group, and is layers 4, 5, and 6. Now you've already *stacked them up*, haven't you, within your mind? Well, try not to do that. They're not stacked at all. They're intertwined among themselves.

Layers four and five together are the essence of your expression (this specific life on Earth), and your divinity on the planet. They represent the "name" on the crystal on the Akashic Record. Let me tell you in one sentence what layers four and five mean: *The primary and most important spiritual attribute of all is the tree of life, which is family.* It's a divine grouping, one that *talks to angels.* Layers four and five together are in a divine grouping of three, but the last layer in this group, layer six, won't be presented tonight. But some of you already know that it's still another name of God, and a phrase that you've heard over and over, which modifies four and five. We now talk esoterically. We don't expect you to understand, so if you're going to take from this place one message about what has been presented tonight about DNA, know this: There's a portion of your DNA that's as divine as God itself. Call it the *Angelic Grouping,* if you wish.

Why would such a thing be? you might ask. Can you even for a moment consider that part of your biology is divine? Well, you'd better get used to it. How else do you think co-creation takes place? How else do you think you can manifest and change matter? [As the science section of the seminar clearly showed] How do you suppose those things get accomplished, Human Being? Moreover, have you put it together yet that even without intent, your consciousness and the field around it changes energy around you! When you sit next to somebody in a theater [or even right now], you have a field that speaks interdimensionally to their field. The same is true when you pass someone in the grocery store. Did you know that as your own energy fields passes within another, and both *touch* one another, there's an *intelligence* of one that interacts with the other? It's subtle, but it is so! Think about that the next time you walk among others. You think this is ridiculous? Just wait for science to validate the "picture" of your interdimensional life field. They will.

What kind of energy transference is there from Human to Human when you get close enough to interact in this way? Let me tell you: This is not an invasive transference. This divine grouping portion of your DNA is the one that shouts divinity wherever you walk. It's the ones that tells those around you that you're vibrating higher—that you're starting to awaken. It's not invasive, but informative. How many of you have had situations where you'll meet people for the first time and they'll be back on your doorstep over and over, until finally you'll say, *"What is it that you want?"* And they say, *"I just want to stand next to you. I don't know what you've got, but I like it, friend, and I want more of this."* They may not even be able to describe it, but they like what you have! Perhaps you don't even want them around, but they're there anyway.

Some of you attract and attract. Rather than invasive, this energy is often just the other way around. This energy of balance and wisdom in the *bubble* that walks with you is so attractive that other humans know it and feel it—even the ones who would never come to a meeting like this, will wish to be with you. Someday we'll cover some of the basics of this.

So that's as far as we'll go today regarding the DNA. One of the upcoming meetings we have will feature the name of layer six. For some, it won't be a surprise, because it represents the name of divinity at its highest. Understand, dear Human Beings, that the information about DNA is highly esoteric. What are you going to do with it? So when you have all 12 Hebrew names—and you can't pronounce them any better than my partner [laughter]—what are you going to do with this knowledge? These names don't stand alone. There are also *pictures* and *colors*. Perhaps there will come a time when all of this will come together and it will be more meaningful to you, even though it's interdimensional. Perhaps you'll start seeing the divinity within, and understand where the miracles actually come from. Perhaps you might even find out how to pronounce the ancient words, and feel the energy they contain when spoken.

Frustrations Part II

We'd like to speak to you about six more frustrations of Lightworkers. Naturally, we're not going to discuss all the rest of them tonight, are we? [Laughter] Only six more. [See Kryon's channelling—*Frustrations Part I*—Chapter Ten]

Number one: *"Dear Kryon, I'm very distraught about what I'm seeing on the news. It doesn't fill my soul. It makes me worried. I try to hold a positive attitude. I look at peace on Earth, but everywhere I look where they're broadcasting the news, it seems like everything is flying apart. You know, it's getting worse, Kryon! Just at a time when you said the energy was being delivered to the earth, where we would see improvements, where someday we could have the real solutions, instead it seems we get horror! How do we justify these two things? It's frustrating. Not only that, even if I could justify it, how do I talk to my friends about it when they come over and they cry for those who are lost, when they see hatred and war; when they see it getting worse instead of better? What do I do, pat them on the head and tell them the energy is changing? No. I want real answers."*

First, dear one, get a grip on your divinity! Understand what's taking place so that you can emanate peace. Do this so no matter what's on the news when your friends come to see you, you'll still have the peace of God in your life. You are an *ambassador for the divine.* Intuitively activate the layers of DNA that will give you peace and divinity in the face of uncertainty and frustration. This is first. YOU are first, even before the explanation you seek. Learn to accept that even when it seems like everything around you reeks with challenge, there's a quiet spot called YOU where friends can sit and find solace in your energy. This is what a lighthouse does when the storm hits... it leads others to the safe harbors.

Let me tell you what's going on, and I'll use a metaphor. What if there was the most corrupt nation on Earth? All of it was corrupt. You don't, but pretend with me. Pretend there wasn't a piece or a part that wasn't corrupt, and it's been corrupt for a hundred years. Plain talk: Everybody was *on the take*. The common person didn't have a chance to get anywhere unless he or she joined the corruption process. It was a way of life.

Now, into this make-believe scenario steps a new leader, who has integrity. Remember, this is a metaphor. Now pretend for a moment that *you* were that leader and you began to try your best to do what was correct and wise for all. Let me ask you this: Do you think you'd have any trouble? Some challenges, perhaps? [Laughter] Absolutely you would! What to do? The answer is that you could never do it alone. You'd have to start with those around you, and you'd have to show them your light. You'd have to show them the difference by living it. Once they felt safe with you, they might see something within you they wanted... integrity. Pretty soon that might rub off and you'd have a Cabinet that had integrity. Then maybe they'd spread it to their Congresses until you had more and more who came on board who saw the wisdom of it all. As you raised the "integrity" bar and they saw the treasure that had been hiding, they'd get excited. Fifteen years ago, this was brought to you in different words within "The Parable of the Tar Pit." That's what this is all about.

Now stop the story for a moment. Let me tell you what the metaphor means so far. Who is this new metaphoric leader? The leader is *Human consciousness*. It has shifted quickly. It has changed, and it's an energy of its own that literally lies like a cocoon around all of you, begging to be discovered. When the earth changes energy, it doesn't force choice upon you. That's a staple of your Human free choice. It doesn't convince. It doesn't prod you. It lies there, should you wish to look upon it. That's an honoring, is it not, of the process of duality? This new leader called enhanced Human consciousness is here, and it's saying: *"I have for you, peace on Earth. I have for you, health for the countries who need health. I have for you, concepts no one has ever thought of to provide compromise and solution for the unsolvable. I have for you, the end of ancient hatred. I'm here to feed you, should you be hungry for the truth."*

In a room like this, full of Lightworkers who are responding to this consciousness, it should be obvious to many of you that things are shifting... a great deal! Why is the news so bad? Here's the next part of the story: Within this metaphor, once you, as the leader, get a few others to help you with this integrity quest, you turn on a bright light (after all, you're a Lightworker, right?). Suddenly in this bright light, all the ones who felt that darkness was their friend are caught where everyone can see them! What would happen in a perpetual dark place if you turned on an incredibly bright light? I'll tell you. Dark energy would scamper, trying to find hiding places! You would expose the worst of the worst. There would be outcries, change, and suddenly the dark things that had always been there would suddenly be looking at you! Some might attack you. But there would be no place to hide. Slowly they would have to shift, too... to accept the new light, or to go find another dark place.

For reasons that have already been discussed, Human nature likes drama. You'll notice that there is no *good-news channel*. Wouldn't that be something? A place where you could tune in and hear the good things of the day, and where you could hear stories of how people helped people? Imagine a broadcast where you could hear about victory, joy, and common positive experience! Wouldn't that be something? And you might say, *"Well, who would tune in to such a thing?"* And the answer is, not enough at the moment. We know that. But when this occurs, and it will someday, you'll understand that a part of Human consciousness has indeed changed.

So the answer to the question about being frustrated with the media is this: Understand what this shift is creating. In your "fair and balanced" news, you're receiving "fair and balanced BAD news." You're only getting one part of it, since this is Human nature. It's covering the "scampering," and the increase in negativity is due to the increase in light! Intuitively understand that the other part is there, but just not seen. In your own consciousness, understand the joy that's also there, in order to balance it out within your own logic. Understand the impossible task of the metaphoric leader, stirring up all the old energy, with the dust of darkness suddenly choking everyone.

Number Two: *"Kryon, I'm tired of people and am frustrated with them. What's going on in the last year or so that would create a situation where people would change so radically? I don't understand it! Many I've been with seem to have polarized themselves one way or the other, and they're changing."*

Well, Lighthouse [pause]...

Let me ask you some questions about that. Are you sure they're changing, or are you? What if it were a situation where you have asked for enlightenment and you've received it... in a very soft or precious way. What if you become wiser and you look upon your friends and your family, not in judgment, but in wisdom, and you perceive a separation? What if it was you who changed and not them? So again, we call upon this tolerance and patience as you move... but they remain as before. So there will be a chasm that opens since you're moving and they're not. The chasm can be bridged with what we have called, metaphorically, *The Bridge of Swords.*

Now, this is old information, but suddenly it's on your doorstep. Now it's your reality, whereas some years ago, when it was given in the Kryon teachings, it was *just in a book.* There's never been a time in your life where you've seen the polarization of humanity like this. Had any personal betrayals lately? What does that mean to you? No more fence sitting! It's starting to show, is it not? What is really felt and thought by others is starting to show. So you're now seeing Human Beings start to move apart and isolate themselves into what they really believe, whereas it wasn't so obvious before.

Now it's your turn, as that part of the leader of Human consciousness, to show your love, compassion, and tolerance of these who would pull away from you... even the ones who would betray you. Can you do that? Let me tell you what happens, dear Human Being, when you take and look in the eye of the one who's betrayed you, and you love them anyway. When you do this, a specific energy is created as a third energy between the two of you. This energy is divine, and it goes right into the earth—right into the crystalline! Memory is stored of what you did, and the wisdom it took, and it changes the planet. That's how it works.

Start looking at people differently. Look upon them *through the eyes of ascension.* See them as *family.* Within normal society, no matter what they've done to you, understand that they're part of the whole. If it's their choice to move away from you, so be it. But understand that they're loved as much as you are. Can you do that? It's one of the hardest things we've ever asked of any Human Being. Look at the betrayer and love them as you love yourself.

Number Three: *"Kryon, I'm tired—really tired. I don't seem to have the energy I used to have. You know, Kryon, you're teaching about the energy being delivered to Earth, finally unifying with Lemurian energy—Lightworker energy! I should be feeling stronger, not weaker! Why am I always so worn out? Am I doing something wrong?"*

Not all of you ask this question, but enough to warrant this discussion. How do I tell you this, dear one? The next time you feel exhausted, the next time you feel as if you just have to sit down and perhaps lament the fact that it wasn't always this way, I want you to know something: There's an entourage around you celebrating your life, watching you put down the weights that you've agreed to carry! Don't you understand that as the energy begins to draw near to what you waited for, you go to work?

You've come here to do some of the heaviest spiritual lifting of any Human Beings in the history of this planet. Lemurians, are you listening? As this new energy comes into the planet that is commensurate with your energy, you're lifting it right into the planet's reality by the bootstraps. It's part of your day-to-day walking around! Some of you are saying, *"Well, Kryon, all I did today was fill up the car and do errands! Big spiritual endeavor, huh? Well, I'm tired!"*

Listen, in the process of your day-to-day existence as a Lightworker on this planet, there are multi layered parts of you that are carrying energy for the Earth. The very fact that you're here in an enlightened state creates energy! It doesn't matter what you're doing. In a dark room, lights that walk around pretending not to be lights still illuminate the room!

Perhaps you might awaken in the morning and you're really tired, so you decide to take the day off and it makes you more tired! Sound familiar? Ah, you're doing the heavy lifting! What an honor for us to sit with Lightworkers like this! You actually came in with a willingness and a plan to do this, remember? The next time you feel tired, why don't you greet us and say *thank you* for this tiredness. You might take a moment and say, *"I understand now that I'm somehow doing planetary work, and I'm happy and joyful to be part of the family of God. I recognize Urim Ve Tumim. I recognize **Aleph Etz Adonai**."* When you do this, the spiritual DNA grouping gets activated, and you start to understand what spiritual *heavy lifting* is all about.

Tired? Yes. It isn't going to be this way forever. These are the times that we spoke of. They're not in the future anymore. They're here. So do the heavy lifting, and understand that this is why you're here. This is also why we love you the way we do. Then later... take another day off!

Number Four: *"Kryon, I'm concerned about what I'm seeing in the elements of the planet. There's global warming. The glaciers are melting. We're hearing stories about weather changes. I'm afraid... or at least concerned."*

Dear one, what did you expect? When the bell rang and the fight began, did you come out of your corner expecting nothing? When the earth vibrates faster and your time frame changes, geological changes also take place. Go back and read the original transcriptions. [referring to past Kryon books] We told you that there might come a time soon in your lifetime when on parts of the planet, nothing would grow in fertile areas, and where former deserts would bloom. We told you of a geological increase in time and activity. We told you of the quickening magnetic grid movement, then we told you to also watch for severe weather changes.

So now that these things have now occurred, what does this add up to in your mind? Let me tell you, if you haven't figured it out already, that you've changed your time frame! You're seeing geology increase. The time frame has increased so that you're seeing things in your lifetime that you wouldn't have seen otherwise. That's what an *enhanced earth* does. The actual **earth** is changing. It isn't some esoteric change that only a few "enlightened ones" can see! It's real! We told you this. We also told you that the earth responds to Human consciousness, and now you get to see it. And now you're telling me that when you finally see it, you're worried? Bless you... the duality really works!

Again, I'll give you this information. Global warming is a product of the oceans of the planet and not the atmosphere. We look forward to scientists finding this out. When they do, we ask you to remember where you heard it first. Maybe it will bring credibility to this event for those of you wondering if this channelling is real? We also tell you that this warming would have occurred anyway, even without the fossil-fuel problem that you have. Then in the next breath I'll say to all who hear and read, please continue to clean up the fossil-fuel problem anyway! But it isn't what's causing the global warming.

All of this will settle since the earth is dynamic. Listen: There's no divine plan afoot to take the earth and make it uninhabitable! Would that seem right to you, that the earth would not support what you're doing? No. The earth is a partner in all this. It's the same as when you see the news. It's frustrating, and it doesn't make sense. It's time to turn the worries into celebration and joy. There's irony here. The very things you're concerned about have happened because of what you've done to change the consciousness of the planet!

Number five: *"Well, Kryon, a moment ago you said with the changing of the earth, and with the light turning on, that there'd be a lot of those who scamper seemingly from under the rocks. In other words, we're going to see a lot of evil in the earth. We're seeing it now. Is this the reason we're seeing a lot more hatred and evil than we ever saw before?"*

Yes. When the light is turned on, and what was always there is revealed, it's hard to sit on the fence, isn't it? That's exactly what you're seeing. Two years ago we sat in this spot and told you of this very potential, and now you're experiencing it.

"So you might say we're going to need a lot of help because of this. What can we do to protect ourselves from all this evil that seems to be crawling from under the rocks and coming forward? How are we going to protect ourselves?"

I will say it very firmly for publication one more time: Dear Human Being, protection—spiritual energetic protection—is a relic of the old energy. It's based in covert fear, and whereas there was a time when you might have wished to shield yourself from the energy of others, that's no longer needed. Again, we use the metaphor of the room that's dark: When someone comes into the room emanating light, the dark goes away. It does stay! It doesn't try to attack back. Instead, it's transmuted. Dark becomes light, and *you* are the Lighthouse who creates this. So again, dark energy isn't an active energy. It completely depends on an empty place to exist... and that empty place is where fear is found.

You're the one who carries that light! It's automatically generated when you begin to vibrate higher and develop your divinity. Wherever you walk, your light will transmute any dark energy in your path. There's no need for protection. Use the light that you have to completely saturate anything that's inappropriate that you come into contact with. This is a reality and a promise. This is something we have told you many times before. Please understand that your light is not an invasive force but a neutralizing force. Again, the dark room is illuminated, and in the process there is sight. This is only invasive to the dark!

Don't be frustrated and fearful about those around you who you believe are carrying darker energies. In this new energy, even the darkest Human Being whom you can imagine in your presence won't have a chance to pierce the light you carry. They can't *shoot a dark gun* at you! Those who try to project darkness need an empty space with no light for their darkness to exist. That, by the way, is why there's so much frustration within so many of them. Those who carry dark energy around with them by choice simply won't get anywhere when they try to do what they've always done... influence everything around them and create fear. When they can't seem to affect you, they get very angry. Did you notice? They get angry because you don't react to their darkness, Lighthouse. We'll talk about that more at another time.

It's very interesting how humans work with humans, especially when one of them is a Lighthouse. Some get very angry in your presence. You might do nothing at all, and even say nothing at all. But by simply carrying your light from place to place, you often create their frustration. This is all part of the interaction of your personal interdimensional fields that we have spoken of earlier in this teaching. Perhaps this of all things this evening would be one of the exposures of what is going on in your life with those who betray you and turn their back on you, Lighthouse. They carry an energy that's not commensurate with yours. You frustrate them, did you know that? An irony is that this is listed as one of the frustrations of a Lightworker when you frustrate them.

Number six: *"Kryon, I'm frustrated by having to learn the same lessons over and over. Won't I ever get it right? Why do I have to keep doing this?"* Let me ask you a question. Before some of you came here today, you ate a grand meal. It sustained your body, and here you are in the seats. After this event is over, you'll probably leave this room and do it again! What's wrong with you? The first one wasn't good enough? [Laughter] Didn't it sustain you? It did. Wasn't it good? It was. Understand?

Dear one, you're in a growth mode. When you repeat lessons, you're not actually repeating them. Instead, you're sustaining your life on the planet. Don't look at it as a repeat. You don't look at your meals that way, do you? Do you sit down with your food and go, *"Oh no, not again"?* Don't you look forward to the sustenance and joy of sitting with family? If you started looking at your challenges in the same way, dear Human Being, this world would heal itself a lot faster.

Look at what seems to be repeated learning as a confirmation of learning. Understand that you're not in an endless spiritual cycle any more than your body is in an endless biological cycle. It's life-sustaining to eat, and it's life-sustaining to have spiritual knowledge created from circumstances in your lives that need to be solved. It's part of life.

That's our message. So let's take this sweet energy as we close, and turn it into something else. There are those of you who came here this night for a healing. Maybe it was for emotional healing, perhaps physical or situational healing.

"Dear Kryon, I've got an impossible situation. There is just no solution." Oh yes there is! You're not giving credibility to Spirit for knowing about these things! How do you know that what you're asking for isn't in the process of being created by somebody else who's manifesting synchronicity that will solve their problem, and in the process, yours too? That the way it works. Did you think of that? Dear ones, you continue to isolate yourselves and think you're alone. Somehow you feel you have to solve everything alone! That's the duality at work. You're not alone, and your challenges aren't particular to you alone.

The truth? That group of DNA we spoke of, is the spiritual group, literally hooking up every single Human Being interdimensionally to every other Human Being on the planet! It's not just DNA that can't be seen in your reality... it's a force that's divine! It's a web of complexity we haven't even begun to describe to you, which is even beyond the information of The Cosmic Lattice. You're connected to every other Human in existence. That creates a web of *co-creative purpose and synchronicity.* That's how it all works. As you might imagine, it's incredibly complex, with the Higher-Selves of humanity doing things that you can't imagine... all joined together while you sit there feeling that you're all alone!

Tonight, let's turn this sweet energy into manifestation. What is your challenge? How about manifesting energy that's appropriate for your life... right now? When we talk about co-creation, we're talking about solutions to life's problems. We're not talking about manifesting material things for your pleasure. No. You live in a culture where many material things are necessary and needed. We understand that. But what is before each Human who sits here reading and listening is unique. It's more about balance than anything else. So let's turn this sweet energy into a healing for you tonight. It's been done before, many times, with groups who sit in front of Kryon, just like you.

[Pause]

You have free choice, dear Human Being, and among all the freedoms you have is the freedom to embrace the love of God in your life and to walk out of here differently than you came in. And that is the truth.

And so it is.

Kryon

Please see Appendix A on page 383 for a discussion of the Hebrew DNA names, included in this chapter.

"Questions & Answers"

From the Kryon Website
2003 & 2004

Chapter Thirteen

Questions and Answers
From the Kryon Website
Chapter Thirteen

Here are questions and answers selected from the hundreds on the Kryon Website. If you like what you see here, there are many more, updated each quarter. Please see the Kryon Website address: [*www.kryon.com/questions*].

Question: *Dearest Kryon, on October 28, 2003, there was a huge coronal mass ejection from the sun pointed straight to the earth, as well as a smaller one on Thursday, October 30. I also understand that there were several significant flares before then. When I originally heard this, I immediately felt that something important was happening and that a tremendous gift was being given to all of us on Earth. Such joy, happiness, and gratitude went through me. Can you please tell us more about this phenomenon and its effects on both the earth and us, spiritually and physically?*

Answer: Dear one, congratulations. You have immediately summed up the situation. There are many who would generate fear over something so profound and spectacular from your own sun. Instead, you correctly assumed that there was actually more happening. Let me give you a hint about what's taking place. According to your own scientists, the last time you had solar activity like this was in your year 1987. Do you remember what took place then? It was the Harmonic Convergence, or what you now call the 11:11. Your current situation has you experiencing the alignment of what is now called the Harmonic Concordance. The sun's activity is once again at a peak (an 11-year radiance cycle), and is delivering energy to you. This is not a coincidence, and it's not an accident that it again coordinates with a strong spiritual event.

We've spoken before about the magnetics of your solar system. Your sun is the center, and it radiates information to the planets. In your case, this directly affects your magnetic grid, and your grid is what saturates your existence, including the instruction sets to your DNA. This is how the planet's energy is postured and changed, as Human consciousness on the planet steers it.

If things stay the same in the scenario you've set up, expect something else of this nature in 2008.

Question: *Dear Kryon, in your books and Q&As, I have not yet come across information about ancient Egypt or the pyramids. There have been some recent claims that the famed Hall of Records has been found beneath the Sphinx. Is there anything appropriate you can tell us at this time about ancient Egypt, the pyramids, or the Hall of Records?*

Answer: Don't confuse the Hall of Records with the Cave of Creation, where the Akashic Records are kept. Although physical, it will never be found, and it's nowhere near Egypt.

The Sphinx is not anything more than what it seems. What is *under* it may be discovered, but it will only be important to Egyptologists. What is *in* it, is actually more profound.

The pyramids may also interest you, especially the relationships of mathematics and solar alignment, but most of this is a result of superstition, cultural religions of the time, and the preoccupation with worship of the solar system. Add to that something that's very mystical and some important missing pieces of your history, and this puzzle begs to be discovered. However, there are very competent Humans who are in the process of revealing some of this. Our teachings, instead, focus on a very different kind of Human on the planet at this time... you. That is why our information spends very little time in your ancient past.

Some of the things we've told you regarding your history have even brought about divisions within your own belief system! Some have even discredited Kryon, weighing what they were told about the past with what I have revealed. My information wasn't the same; therefore, the old information "won." That's how "hooked" many of you are with respect to what you think happened. You "hang your spiritual hats" on what some have told you happened, taking you out of the paradigm of the "now," and also keeping you from experiencing new information about what might have really been. This propensity on the part of many of you to anchor yourself to something you felt happened is why we don't often give you information about what really took place. Instead, we wish you to look around you now, and experience what is happening today. We encourage you to drop the old fears.

Let the proof of what we're telling you now anchor your belief. See if what we've said in the past ten years makes sense to the Earth energy of the last ten years. Use intellect, logic, and intuition together to make this decision, not what someone told you in a past discussion. You're in a totally new paradigm of existence. None of your prophets told you anything about what's happening now, did you notice? Therefore, isn't it possible that even your spiritual reality changed? Are some of you so stuck with an old reality that any other information must be a "trick"? Think about it. Some of you would be shocked to know what your history really is. When you eventually find out, what will you do—deny all evidence as it churns up out of the earth?

What happened in your ancient past is no longer the issue. We'll leave that for others. The only thing that is important at the moment is the work you have as a Lightworker now.

Question: *Dear Kryon, my two sisters and I are triplets. We've been told that we are one soul in three bodies. I was under the belief that each body houses a separate soul. I think my ego is upset that I'm not an "individual," if this is true. Can you enlighten me on this?*

Answer: The most difficult thing to explain to a Human is the concept of how something singular in appearance can be many things in reality. You appear to be one soul because you have one body. When angels are drawn in your books and paintings, even though they are multidimensional beings, you give them skin and wings and call them one name!

So you continue to believe in "one body, one soul." The reality is that every Human alive is multidimensional and is in many places at one time. Even as you sit there reading this, parts and pieces of you are in other places doing other things. Is that, then, one soul in many places, or many souls? The answer is both. Your single-digit dimensionality limits your concept of how this is, since everything before your reality is singular.

So the very premise of your question can't be answered, since nobody on the face of the earth has one soul. A better question would be, "Do your sisters share a singular purpose with you?" The answer, as your intuition told you, is no. They may have the same astrological aspects, but each Human is a separate piece of God, multidimensional and therefore not singular. Each is a different piece of God, on Earth in lesson to be independent.

The confusing part in all of this is what you *do* share with your sisters. You all share a common thread of divinity that might actually look like "one soul" to a reader (in 4D). This thread is your karmic bond, and why you all came in together the way you did. This has to do with potentials, past energies, and your current expression of lesson. But it's not the "same soul."

Again, we liken this to a bowl of soup. It is singular in appearance, yet fluid inside. You can't ask how many soups there are in the bowl. It's different for all, but each bowl is singular. The soup is the divinity. Don't ever let the container fool you. It may be the same size and color, but the soup in each is diverse and tastes different. It's composed of many parts that make up what it is. It might be nourishing or poisonous. Only the soup can decide what vibration it will be.

Celebrate this with me! Isn't it a wonderful situation that you have? The connection to your sisters is unique to humanity. Only twins and other multiple-birth Humans have it. This is why you will always be "connected" as long as you live. When one of you leaves, finally, watch what happens: You will still be connected! Multidimensional things are like that.

Question: *Dear Kryon, I have a question regarding the EMF Balancing Technique™ and The Reconnection® energy. Are they the same thing?*

Answer: No. They are two profoundly different approaches to the discussion and development of procedures around one thing... the power of the Human Being.

Both disciplines are new to the planet (in the last ten years). Both are discussions that actually start out by asking you to "feel" the energy within you. Both are divinely inspired, and both are stewarded each by one Human Being who was born to do just that. And... both facilitations can work together if you wish them to.

Humans are diverse. Your brains are designed to be different from one another. One's approach to excitement in life is often the other's boredom! You know this, for you see it every day. This is why there are many religions on the planet. Did you ever think about that? If God is God, and you are actually pieces of God, then why are there so many different ideas of what to do about it all?

Therefore, you'll continue to see many roads to the realization of the same thing. Some will travel one, some will travel the other. Some will even wish to travel them all! So weigh which process is meaningful to you and study it. Then when you're finished, see if you wish to study the other as well. They do not conflict with respect to what they teach... that the Human Being is capable of divine power within, and can create in ways that an old energy thought was impossible. The basic premise of both is that you're a master on the planet.

Question: *Dear Kryon, in your channeling in Redding, California, you told us that holding pills in one's hand can be an effective way to "heal." Question: Will that eliminate harmful side effects? Is it safe to hold Prozac? Can I hold a painkiller without negative after-effects?*

Answer: We've been speaking about this for years. The Human Being has the ability to link to "cellular intelligence" in order to hold medications and benefit from the results. This is perhaps one of the strangest of all the Kryon teachings. However, it also forms the foundation for kinesiology, and in some ways, even homeopathy. In both those cases, cellular intelligence, beyond your own understanding, is activated to bring about changes in your chemistry or give you answers or messages that only it has.

We've told you that you might experiment with this by holding in your hand the medication you've been using. Just as in kinesiology, the body "knows" what you're holding. Call this strange if you wish, but even your own science is beginning to validate the process of meditating to change body chemistry. This gives validity to consciousness over matter, or in the case of what your science has seen, "the ability to significantly alter your own cellular structure through consciousness alone."*

Your body knows what your intent is, and also what substance you're holding. It is therefore possible to imbue the properties of the intent of using the substance into your cells. You're not actually using the substance, so there are no side effects of a drug, for instance. The body is reading what you wish the drug to do, and it is "seeing" the properties of the drug.

Be wise here. This is out of the experience of your normal reality, isn't it? Then if you wish to try this, go very slowly if the substance is important to your health. This will work on a case-by-case basis within the consciousness of each Human and the

*Editor's note: If you wish to try this, do it slowly and with ceremony. If you find that it's not working, then stop. Don't do it "cold turkey." Use common sense here, and experiment. But be aware that many have found it to work. Just think... a bottle of aspirin or antacids will last for years!

path they're on. But it will work with aspirin or insulin—substances with two very different purposes.

There have been those who have heard these words and have reduced their insulin levels substantially over time. They still need to actually inject some of it still, but only a fraction of what it used to be. This is the same principle as homeopathy, where one part in a million of a "cure" can be "seen" by the body. What the body is doing is reacting to your intent, the substance, and the consciousness around it.

Question: *Dear Kryon, I have a new grandson. He's going for his first vaccination in the next few weeks. If we're beginning to transmute toxins with reconnections to our endocrine system through our DNA, then what happens to our babies, who by law have to be vaccinated? What are your thoughts on this subject?*

Answer: First, know that vaccinations are a God-given science that humanity earned. They're a tried and proven homeopathic method that have been with you for years. You were probably vaccinated yourself, and it worked.

We have three answers:

(1) God is not in a vacuum. Even the vaccinated Human Being who's older can modify and rework their DNA. So there's no time limit, and there are no rules that say, "Once vaccinated, you're ruined."

(2) The Human who is of the age of awareness can say, even as they are vaccinated, "Let nothing inappropriate enter my chemistry." This is a conscious instruction given to your "intelligent cellular structure" (the same one responsible for kinesiology and homeopathic results). This will result in your cells only using what they need and casting away everything else.

(3) Finally, about babies: There has been a push by your science lately to vaccinate against many things at the same time. You'd be advised to seek out a doctor who will only vaccinate your child for the basic diseases that have been known in the last 40 years. Eliminate the vaccinations for the new ones. This leaves you with approximately seven or eight—the very ones that have been used for years. What your science is not appreciating yet is the results of combining all the vaccination substances together. There's a problem that will show itself in time. Stick with the basic ones.

Question: *Dear Kryon, it seems to me that from time immemorial, the soil in Jerusalem has been covered with the blood of the thousands who die there. One of the channellings confirmed that The New Jerusalem is, in fact, the physical Jerusalem. If this is the case, I'm curious as to why, over all the centuries, has so much blood been spilled on this land/ground/soil? Why does Jerusalem seem to exact payment in blood—even sometimes from travelers who pass through and are killed? This seems to be a most peculiar thing—it's as if this ground/soil demands human blood for its existence. Why?*

Answer: Your question is truly a profound one. It's against all odds that this would occur, right? It's counterintuitive to the way things work in a divine place, isn't it? This alone should "flag" that there's something here that's different. The reason? Jerusalem is at the heart of the largest religions on the planet (Islam included). It's the center of the "one God" revelation. It's also where the trouble would begin that would end civilization and bring about the tribulation and the end of Earth.

Such a place is filled with the blood of all, even the blood of what you called the Christ. It's all part of a portal that's so strong that it creates human passion, and therefore leads to death (the choice of humanity is what to do with its passion... free choice). God didn't create the blood. Humans did.

The New Jerusalem will be such a contrast to the old one that historians will say, *"How could a place with such a violent history be the portal of peace on Earth?"* This is the potential in Jerusalem. It exists as a "portal to the way Earth will evolve." So far, it has been death and more death. The potential is that it can become the model of "peace and more peace." Can this really occur? Yes. It will take time, but the energy being delivered to the planet from now to the year 2008 will make a difference. Watch the players change. Watch what the children will do.

Question: *Dear Kryon: I'm from Norway. My question: What about organ transplants? What happens to the chakras? I've listened to many channellings (some valuable, others not), and no one except one has pointed out what kind of mess there will be when humans play "God" like this. What will happen on your side of the veil when humans leave part of an organ behind when they die? There are campaigns going on in my country that require people to give away their organs in case of an accident.*

Answer: Dear one, get out of the drama of this entire subject. God/Spirit is not in a vacuum when it comes to these things. Did you ever wonder, in this new energy, if God actually created this so that Humans could help Humans? It is perhaps normal for you to think that these things will somehow affect your chakras, karma, etc. Here is the truth: Through your God-given new technologies, you have permission to save another's life in this fashion. You have permission to use intent to void out the problems of rejection and even to rearrange your own cells! This is not taboo in a sacred journey. It is an extraordinary gift of life! It's part of a new energy science, and it is honored.

God knows exactly what's taking place, and through your new cellular communication, your body does, too. Don't take these things to a place they don't belong, thinking that somehow God will somehow be displeased, or that the body won't know what's happening. Leaving the organ on Earth when you die is an awesome lineage. What a gift to the planet! How many Humans can say that when they die, part of their body remained to give life? The science was actually given to you so that you could have life-saving technology at this time in your history. It's a gift that can and should be used with spiritual integrity and love.

Let's say that someone needs a kidney or they'll die. The one giving the kidney speaks to the organ and blesses the synchronicity that it will supply extended life to another Human. That Human may go on to affect others, and may help the planet. Therefore, the donated organ is not an accident of nature, or a freak of creation, or a mistake of bad science. The very cells of the kidney know of the contract between the Humans involved. Did you think of that? It was in the potentials of both lives all along, cooperating with new science and new energies. The kidney is blessed and is given sacredness, bringing life and contract fulfillment to both Humans.

As for a requirement to donate? Each Human should have free choice over all things. The giving of an organ should be a sacred event, celebrated with intent—not a requirement.

Question: *Dear Kryon, what is the position with people who have had organ transplants and have to take anti-rejection drugs for the rest of their lives? I have read that to achieve ascension status, the cells must not be poisoned by drugs. Does* *this mean that a transplantee cannot ascend in this life, nor do they have to trust that the body won't reject the donor organ if they stop the drugs? I would very much appreciate your answer to this question.*

Answer: Let's engage in some plain talk, and speak directly to those who have had organ transplants (including those relating to the heart) and are existing on drugs. Organ rejection is a chemical attribute of your biology. It has nothing to do with your spirituality. The drugs that are keeping you alive are blessed and God-given. They're not poisons to your system. They are, rather, to be honored and celebrated as the very science that's helping to keep you alive, and one that was divinely inspired.

Ascension status is given to any Human on the planet who will give intent and start on the path. God isn't somewhere behind a curtain! Your divine spiritual family knows exactly what's going on in your body and won't penalize you because you're keeping yourself alive! It's time to use spiritual common sense in these things. See God at your side, knowing all things, and celebrating your life. Then make whatever spiritual decision you wish, knowing that all is perfect within your pure intent.

Question: *Dear Kryon, please enlighten us as to the role of the two great teachers—that is, Buddha and Christ. If one were to literally study each of these two masters' lives and work, it would appear that they're not preaching the same truth. Yet, if there is one God, there should be one truth. What is the truth regarding these conflicting teachings? One appears to teach that the end of desires is the gate to immortality or nibbana; the other teaches that by accepting the finished work of redemption on the cross, we have made peace with God and our eternality is assured.*

Answer: Your question is asked in the posturing of what you've been told today. If you were to understand what both really were about, you wouldn't even ask the question. Today's "history" is one that has been manipulated by the leaders of these two organized religions.

The idea of accepting the redemption of what took place on the cross doesn't even relate to the real purpose of the master of love, who was the Christ. That entire scenario was created later from a false assumption, and did well for those who would control the population with religion (which history will show they did). The Buddha (Siddhartha) also has not had his full true passion revealed. The teachings of both were sequestered early on, and revamped to suit the needs of those who would be in control of the teachings.

The above information may sadden you, but be aware that you can "tap" in to both of these great masters anytime you wish. And when you do, you'll discover that the truth is the same. The ultimate liberation for all beings is within you. You're eternally assured of peace with God because you are a piece of God. Even the master Christ told you that you could be exactly like him... a son of God. How do you justify that information against what eventually became the doctrine? Are you at all concerned that there was no Rapture when it was "scheduled"? Did you know that Christ taught about your past incarnations? Where is that in scripture? Why is it missing?

Things aren't always as they seem, and you must now "look past" what men have given you or taken away. Look past what they manipulated and removed from the teachings of both, and instead, now it's time to pull from the truth within. When you do, you'll peacefully justify all the teachings of the great masters, given from culture to culture, that taught unity for all and exposed the grandness of the Human Being.

Do not let this shake your faith, for the Love of God is still supreme in all these things, and if you seek, you'll discover the true messages, and then you'll love these masters all the more.

Question: *Dear Lee/Kryon, it is with love that the Kryon books have landed in my lap at this time of my spiritual learning. I haven't been able to put them down. The love that I feel when I read is overwhelming. I have a question: In Book Six, you talk about disengaging from your children. As a mother of two boys aged 17 and 19, I worry about them all the time: Will they get jobs, will they be happy in their lives, and so on. Can you please explain to me what you mean by "disengaging" from them? With love from a family member.*

Answer: This admonition is about taking care of you. Every caring parent alive will love and be concerned with their children's lives as long as they live. But many parents live their own lives through what happens to their children. So the instruction is to balance yourself. Be loving and helpful, but don't let what happens to them become your entire focus. If it does, then you'll take responsibility for another's free choice. You'll ignore yourself and your own spirituality and give up your power.

The best thing you can do for your grown children is to love them and send them light all the days of their life. Be there for them, but don't live their lives for them.

Question: *Hi, Kryon, it's Pablo from Australia. My friend Rachel and I believe that it's our job to save the world. We feel like we have a big role to play, but we can't seem to find the exact action to take... as in, should we inform, protest, fight injustice, etc.? Or just chill? I feel that just chilling and fixing the self is the*

way to go, but at the same time I feel we should be doing some-
thing more, Any advice?

Answer: Dear one, you're exactly right. There are two steps
toward doing what you've set out to do, and also a very powerful frustration. Take care of yourself. We've taught this for a
very long time. *"Why,"* some ask, *"would this help anything?"*
We answer in this fashion: If you were going to win a race in a
race car, would you spend any time preparing the car, or would
you just hop in and drive? The answer, of course, is that there
is far more preparation time with the car, than time in the race.
Wise Humans know this principle. The more you're ready to do
what you came to do, the more effective is your performance.
Therefore, prepare yourself. Vibrate higher, become wise, and
spend time on your spiritual being.

When you're ready, begin to develop your light and start the
work. The work is a concentration of consciousness, or sending
light to dark places. Don't send your ideas or thoughts... just
the light. The metaphor is that you're illuminating dark places
so that others may have free choice and see or discover hidden
ideas that may contain solutions for some of the biggest problems on Earth. It's not an evangelistic light; it's a loving light of
wisdom. It honors the free choice of all humanity, but it creates
a more balanced place where everything available may be seen
and evaluated.

In politics, it creates solutions that haven't been seen before.
In disease-ridden places, it creates peace and hope. In scientific
places, it creates ideas and inventions that were "hidden" in the
past. Where there is strife, there can be peace, and where there
is hatred, there can be understanding.

The frustration? You can't see the results of what your light
does for a very long time. There is no instant response, since

you're so used to seeing in normal reality. Since results are the desire of every Human Being who takes action, it will be frustrating not to see them right away. It will cause you to even wonder if anything is working at all.

There's no greater thing you can do for the planet than to hold the energy of hope for your future, and project a divine light to dark places.

Question: *Dear Kryon, are you aware of NESARA? Is this a real law, or a metaphor to help increase consciousness?*

Question: *Dear Kryon, I've been reading a lot these days about NESARA, and I was hoping that you would have more information on this.*

Question: *Who are the "Wingmakers"? What is their role in the ascension process? Do they work with your group?*

Answer: This is a time on Earth where there will be many new systems, laws, and organizations that will intend to reflect the new consciousness that's being built. As you look at them, you must discern for yourself if it's right for you. Here are some guidelines:

(1) What is the greatest intent or goal of the system? Does it promote the individual or a group?

(2) Is it political or affiliated with a bias? If so, it's a mixture of the old and new and isn't appropriate.

(3) Does it ask for your membership? This is an old energy method. The family of God has a built-in membership that's spiritual, understood, and forever.

(4) Is there an underlying monetary or marketing structure? Examine this. Lightworkers must earn a living, too, but does it go further than this and involve your investing? Stay away from

any organization that asks you to follow another Human Being, dead or alive.

Ask yourself do you really need an organization in your life to accomplish your Lightwork?

Question: *Dear Kryon, my question is this: Since we can "channel" other beings of Light from the highest realm, does that mean we can also "channel" God, the Creator? If we are "God" as you say, are we therefore channelling ourselves? Our own golden angels within? It would seem as if we were indeed talking to ourselves. But how can the answers that we "receive" be unbiased? Does that make sense?*

Answer: All of this makes sense when you realize what you're attempting. First, the answer: Yes. The best channelling on the planet is when you get divine answers from the closest God-source around—your Higher-Self. Many are channelling their own Higher-Selves and are finding very profound information there. After all, as you mention, it is God.

The question about being biased is indeed the challenge. It's what we've been teaching all along. It is the new tool set in the new energy that allows you to build a bridge between the duality and the divine. It's a bridge that allows you to step out of the duality and into the wisdom of God, and it's all within you. It's the basis for the "neutral Implant" that we brought to you years ago... the implantation of your intent to eliminate the bias of duality!

So you are indeed invited to find the divine within, and channel yourself. In the process, it may seem like you've found a wonderful angel who is outside yourself, even with another name. That's the perception when you step out of a dimension that features singularity, bias, and linear thinking. Instead, the entity is you, and it's ready to give you answers for you.

Blessed are the Humans who find wisdom for themselves by channelling themselves!

Question: *Dear Kryon, I'm from Brazil and have read some of your books. I have questions regarding the neutral implant. If we come here with karma that has to be lived through to be cleared, when we neutralize this karma (as I understand it, it is not changed but neutralized), what will happen after we leave? Do we still have to clear this karma?*

Another question is that if we neutralize the karma, what will happen to the people who had karma to clear with us? For example, I have a son and a daughter who definitely have karma to be passed through and cleared with me. We surely agreed, or made a contract, before they came to live through the karma. If I neutralize mine, what will happen to theirs?

Answer: Dear one, again you have elected to intellectualize something very simple and basic. When someone says "I love you," do you then launch an inquiry?

Listen: The neutral implant is "permission to neutralize the past." It's a tool of Spirit given to you to use if you wish. It completely changes the parts and pieces of your interdimensional DNA that were scheduled to perform an old energy task of solving (working through) karma. When it's asked for, a process begins that is profound and different for each individual. Some feel it and some don't. The karma is cleared at the moment you ask to personally change. Others who had karma with you are also changed. This may not seem "right" to you, but we've taught you now for the last decade that you are a "group." Nothing you do for yourself is singular. It changes the energy around you. We've told you that if you regularly play tennis with a partner and one day the partner doesn't show up anymore, after a number of broken appointments, you'll stop showing up at the tennis court, too!

Karma is complex, but it indeed works in the way we say. If you clear yours, the one who had karma with you is also affected. It's all part of a grand system that says that if you help yourself, you also help the planet. When you leave and come back, it's still gone. There is no "rule" that you must relive anything. Once you change your spiritual DNA, these attributes belong to your soul and are part of the Akashic Record.

Remember this: There is no predestination, only predisposition. You only have potentials when you come into this Earth experience. These predispositions are generated by what you've done and what you've learned. They lay there begging to be changed! Start getting used to the idea that you're a dynamically programmed angel, living in an appropriate but false belief that you're not in control. Your test is to learn that anytime you wish, you may change your life. The neutral implant is one of the first tools (of many) that we told you about that directly affects the spiritual parts of your DNA.

When this was first presented, many of your established metaphysical leaders balked at it, even calling it evil. Their bias was that you were predestined to "serve your karma." But you are not. Karma is a starting energy, and that's all. Does it make sense to you that God would make you come down to Earth with no choice in your own lives? You would be a slave to the past. Think about it.

You're in charge of everything—your health, your love relationships, your peace, your own life span, and yes... even the energy of your own past. If you wish to buy into anything else, you will never bridge the distance from the place you're now in (4D), to the interdimensional energy that's now being given to you.

You're an enabled and powerful Human Being, a part of God and a part of the grand plan of the Universe.

Question: *Dear Kryon, in 2002 I followed my inspiration and moved to Thailand with intent to create a community (of light). In August 2002, a change in direction (of energy) meant that the community did not manifest. Now I have no job, little money, no partner, no friends, no fun, and no home to call my own. My confidence is low, and my tools for manifestation do not appear to work.*

Answer: All attempts to create communities of this type will fail in the new energy. Your attempt is honored and is seen as pure, but now you might begin to understand.

If you create a community of like-minded individuals, you sequester their light from the rest of the earth. The light is needed to be where the darkness is, not placed in a box so it can attract and live with other light.

Instead, create a community within yourself that is huge and bright, filled with the power of many lighthouses. You will have your "community" as those of like mind bond together within an individual system to help Earth. Meet together, plan together, then go and live apart as synchronicity determines.

You are loved, and there is no problem with what you've done. But now it's time to turn your efforts inward. When you do so, many of the things you've longed for will slowly begin to co-create themselves.

Question: *Dear Kryon, I've always been able to feel people's emotions and relate to them on an emotional level. Last year I began to see different energies and entities, but slowly all of that has gone away. I know I've grown tremendously as a person—spiritually, emotionally, and mentally. Can you help me figure out why these gifts have faded?*

Answer: Yes! You're experiencing what many Lightworkers already know. Your "gifts" were linked to the metaphor of an older radio station. When that station was renewed, it changed its frequency of broadcast to a new and higher frequency. Those who continue to "tune" to the old station will find very little there. Those who seek the new station and the new frequency will find renewed and increased power!

So begin to search for the new station. How? Begin by trying new spiritual avenues. Change your meditation techniques. Throw away procedure. Begin asking Spirit for guidance to find the new energy. You're not in the dark here. As you begin this process, there will be a response. There's always a response to those who ask, *"Dear God, tell me what it is I should know."*

Look for answers in ways you didn't expect. Toss away your biases of what you "think" will be God's answer, or what you "think" should be seen as the answer in your reality. Let the energy flow to you in ways you never thought they would!

Question: *What happens to a person who is old but wants to change? Is the old person still inside? Or does he/she just move on to a new plateau? I've made so many mistakes in my lifetime, but also achieved much satisfaction. I would like to keep the good things I've done or achieved, but I also want to cleanse my past indiscretions and become a person who feels wanted and* *worthwhile. If I change, what happens to the good parts that I wish to keep?*

Question: *Dear Kryon, what's the significance when after more and more effort to find a job, I've found nothing? I've made the focus in my heart to be helpful in this world, and I want to change my life for my children, but sometimes I question myself. Do I have a place in this world?*

Question: *Dearest Kryon, I'm having difficulty with my recent past (which is directly related to self-worth) spilling over into my present so much that I feel like I'm caught in a tornado, unable to see where I am or where to go from here. I'm so confused that I feel I can't move forward. In fact, you once said that not everyone who chose ascension would succeed, and indeed, I feel like I'm failing.*

Answer: There are many, if not most of you, who are burdened by a basic theme. You were born in an energy on this planet that wasn't balanced in the "self-worth" department. Add to that the fact that your religious leaders told you that you were born worthless! This is a mountain to climb, and it affects most of you greatly. I've addressed this in a step-by-step manner, and offer you this message that you might climb out of the hole of depressed self-worth. It's time, and I think you know it. Please see the very recent message that I have offered.

Editor's note: See Kryon's self-worth message in its entirety (Chapter Nine in this book)

Question: *The mystical teachings have urged us to renounce craving for material (and spiritual!) things because craving will never allow the mind to rest and the real self to shine through. Now you teach us to co-create whatever we want. Won't that fan* *up the fire of the ever-thirsting mind and take us farther away from the center within? If someone co-created a lovely big car out of greed, he would only have his greed gratified and enhanced further. How would he profit spiritually from this act? And anyway, how does abundance relate to happiness? In my opinion, it is how much we want that makes us happy or unhappy.*

Answer: These are your own thoughts that have interpreted "co-create what you want" to include a big car or the lust or craving for material things. These were never the teachings of Kryon. The ascended consciousness of the masters (what we teach is the definition of *Lightworker*) co-create spiritual balance. They constantly co-create the love of God within their lives. The goals of co-creation have been listed many times, and they never included material things. They were peace, health, wisdom, happiness, long life, and a sustenance of needed items within a specific culture to exist comfortably. The power of co-creation is something granted to those on a spiritual path who have the wisdom to know what they're asking for. It's not an invitation to collect cars.

If you need to work to feed your children, then a job is within the spiritual purity of co-creation. That is not a craving. If you're having trouble within a family or within a relationship, it's not greed that co-creates peace and harmony there. It's time to use common sense. God doesn't wish you to be poor or in trouble, for that doesn't meet your magnificence as a creature of God on the planet, and it doesn't suit the work you're here to do. To always be hungry or homeless, and in "survival mode," helps nobody anywhere. This is not what any master ever wanted for you.

The definition of *abundance* has been given as "sustenance." You can even read how this worked with the history of the Israelites in the desert. They were fed every day for years by God. If you looked at the storehouse where this came from, you might consider each of them to be abundant beyond reason! You all are, since we see you in the "now." So abundance is the storehouse of God, which is your family. It was never meant to crave and co-create material things. Begin to read the Kryon messages with discernment and spiritual wisdom. It will suit you better... and also those around you.

Question: *Please explain the process of accumulating negative karma. Does an action considered negative by society create dark karma by itself, or is it our attitude that counts? If I were to cheat, lie, or even commit a crime in a detached state of mind (in perfect equanimity, so to speak) or with some noble end in mind, would I still create negative karma?*

Answer: There's no such thing as negative karma. Again, Humans wish to polarize everything and place it into a box. This box is then carried from place to place as a singular and linear process. It isn't.

The definition of *karma*: It is the energy of incompletion. It begs to be solved, and drives a Human being to behave in a certain way, live in a certain place, and meet other specific Humans for resolution. It was created and worked in an older Earth energy as a way to move the energy of the planet vibrationally one way or the other as humanity worked the karma with total free choice.

If you clear your karma, you are releasing an old energy and moving on to one where you are free to help the planet with your light. This is your free choice, and it is driven by your intent. Those with the "attitude" of pure spiritual intent will indeed move into that new attribute of being a Human with no past-life karma. Part of this process is the understanding that becoming interdimensional means blending the past, present, and future (potential) into a new reality called "the now." This "now" leaves no room for "past karmic instruction sets" within the DNA.

If you were to clear your karma, then go on to do what you deem as inappropriate things, then you place upon yourself (free choice) attributes that you'll be forced to deal with immediately, in this life. Creating new karma, the kind that's passed from lifetime to lifetime, is no longer done. Again, these kinds of questions are the result of those who wish to analyze God. To try to analyze God within a single-digit reality is folly. Can you analyze love? Can you set rules for angelic thought?

It's time to grasp all of this as "the way things work." Many use the machines of Earth to get from one place to the other without a full and complete understanding and disclosure of every working part in the mechanism. If they had to have that, no one would ever get anywhere! They would forever be bogged down in study, and many would never understand. Yet there are always those who feel that everything must make 4D sense to move on. If they can't understand it, they're afraid of it. This fear will keep them in one place all their lives.

It's time for you to fully grasp the principle that the mechanics of God are beautiful, mystical, and constantly with you. You're never alone, and you never have to wonder if this or that is "known" of God. All is known, and the system is loving and wise. Now... use this system to move to another place.

Question: *Dear Kryon, who is Lucifer, and what was the purpose of the Luciferian rebellion?*

Answer: We know this will disappoint many and enrage many more, but there is no such thing as the devil, and there never was a real Lucifer. These were all metaphoric stories to help you understand yourselves, patterend upon the Human duality model. The darkest energy on the planet comes from the Human Being as a result of free choice. Even the added metaphoric story of Adam and Eve should have given you that information. Free choice meant that a Human could choose darkness even in the garden of light. It's what "duality" is capable of.

For those who don't believe this and would rather think that there are those who are after your soul, you still have free choice to think as you wish. But it will also keep you from seeing your magnificence within the love of God, as you base your reality in fear of dark entities.

We have given you a full discussion of dark and light several times.

Editor's note: Please see Kryon's discussions of dark and light in this book starting on page 230.

Question: *Dear Kryon, you've presented much information about DNA and the changes we're going through. What role does mitochondrial DNA play in the Human, our development, and in our past and future? What does it really do? Why is it there? This DNA has been traced back to our origins in West Africa by science to about 250,000 years. It seems that we're all related to a virtual Adam and Eve. Is this a marker of our heritage as humans?*

Answer: It is the mitochondrial DNA that has the star-seeds in it. And remember, it only came from Eve (in your example). Its energy is feminine. This is where you will find the attributes of the Pleadians. This is the actuality of your real biological heritage. It's also not an uncommon thing within the Universe for one life form to help another. In your case, it was needed for you to develop.

If you think this is folly and science fiction, then ask your anthropologists why it was that in early humanoid development, there were many kinds of Humans on the planet. Like all other life forms on Earth, many kinds were being formulated. You can see the results of this diversification all around you... many kinds of every animal. In the case of the Human, however, only one developed.

What a coincidence! [Kryon humor]

Editor's note: See Scientific American ~ January 2000.

Question: *Dear Kryon, the theory of relativity is based on three postulates: (1) constancy of the speed of light, (2) the principle of relativity, and (3) relativity of time. What should one think of these postulates?*

Answer: (1) The speed of light is variable from time frame to time frame. It is not a constant of the universe. (2) All is indeed relative, however, and so the theory holds, but the rules are unique to each reality. (3) Time will be relative to whatever the speed of light is within the construct of the reality it represents. That's why you can look out into the Universe and observe "impossible physics." One should celebrate these postulates, for they are the beginning of the explanation of how nothing stands alone. If one thing changes, it changes the whole realty. This is also how it is with each Human on the planet.

Question: *There's so much wonderful spiritual energy/information available. How do we get it (the channellings) out there (to the public) without offending the nonbelievers? I understand that we don't want to intrude where we're not wanted, so how do we reach/teach those inquiring minds?*

Answer: You may feel that the information is sequestered, but it's not. Any Human who's in a situation of searching can find the truth. There's a spiritual mechanism for this, even in the most remote village on the planet. One of the promises of God is that those who seek will find the truth. Sometimes this will be without books, tapes, meetings, or the Internet. Don't be concerned that they might not find the channellings of Kryon. Their own channellings will be just as good. Also, don't be concerned about offending others. Only the ones who seek the information will be affected. The others will be honored within their silence.

Question: *Dear Kryon, I'm a Reiki master, and I've got a question about this energy and other older energies—for example, the Celtic rune. Are these energies changing in these days? Are they replaced by EMF? When I use Reiki as a living holy energy (in German, "Schöpferkraft"),isn't it all the same, then?*

Answer: We have channelled this information many times: Many of the older modalities are just now coming into their own as major players of healing on the planet. Reiki is one. How can you tell if the process is of the old energy or the new? It's easy! Does it still work? Is it being enhanced within your practice of it? If the answer to these questions is yes, then it's very viable and should be continued. If it simply isn't working anymore, then it no longer fits with the energy that you've created on the planet.

EMF is a new and beautiful tool. It doesn't replace anything, however, but rather gives you still another powerful new tool in the tool cabinet of the Lightworker.

Question: *Dear Kryon, just this fall I discovered the Kryon series of books and have been reading them avidly ever since. I read that sleeping patterns can be altered in the new energy. As a teenager, I had trouble with insomnia, which cleared up as I matured physically. Now at 48, it seems to be back. I seem to be noticing a subtle vibration, a tenseness in my body, that prevents me from relaxing, even though my eyes and mind are tired enough to sleep. I'm worried that I can only relax with a glass of wine, even after I've taken a prescription sleeping pill. This has been going on for several months now, and I've been blaming hormonal changes.*

Answer: Dear one, you and many like you are facing the exact same thing. It's tough to sleep when the bedroom is being renovated! Here is the answer: Don't be angry when you can't sleep. You think you need a certain amount to exist? The answer is yes, but Spirit can give you the equivalent of it without your ever having it! It's only energy, you know.

So try this: (1) At a sleepless moment, thank God for this, that you're being vibrated so much that you can't sleep—that the energy of DNA change is so great that sleep cannot be accomplished. (2) Ask Spirit to give you the needed energy as though you had slept. If you need seven hours of sleep, then make a deal with God. You get the equivalent of seven hours of sleep (from Spirit) even though you didn't sleep (in 4D), and you'll promise to just lie there and smile and not get angry or frustrated as they work on you!

Take the rest. Don't get up and do cleaning, or errands either. Don't read or otherwise occupy yourself. Rest and celebrate. Then watch this process reveal itself. The next day you will have more energy than you expected. Repeat this often until it no longer bothers you that you're not seeming to sleep in the way you used to. Just about the time you get used to the whole scenario? ZZZZZZZZZZZZZ

Question : *Dear Kryon:*

1) I recognize that you think it important for where we are now to know that we don't have two or three spirit guides, but rather, an infinite (metaphorical) energy soup of them that act as one and change composition from time to time. My first question is "Why is it important for us to know that the old "2 or 3" metaphor was inaccurate and that the new metaphor is more accurate?

2) My second question is: Don't clairvoyant people "see" two or three guides? What are they seeing if not guides?

3) If guides are more appropriately called "energies" rather than "entities," are there still nonbiologically based life forms that are entities?

4) Are angels such entities, and if not, how would you describe angels relative to guides?

5) What are archangels relative to angels?

6) More recently you said that some of the guide energy is with us for the duration of our Earthly life cycle and other parts of it change composition. But, in the more distant past, you mentioned that during larger vibrational increases we go through, there is a guide change for 90 days during which they "go quiet." So, my questions on this one are why is it necessary for them to go quiet?

And, why 90 days? And, I assume that they're still there just being quiet rather than truly disconnected from us, right? And what triggers this "go quiet" period?

Answer: Dear one, (1) it's important for you to know that you can't count the guides so that you don't "hang your hat" on them, name them, and depend on who you think is two or three entities. If a Human does this, it keeps them from experiencing the reality that there is far more than what they think. It keeps the Human from restricting his sight.

(2) Clairvoyants see the top layer...the ones who are doing the most help at that moment, and the ones whom the Human needs the most at that time. That's also why auric photography (energy photography) differs from day to day. It's the "guide soup" at work, changing what you need.

(3) Our definition of *entities* is any energy that has a consciousness equal or above to what you would consider Human. Yes there are many nonbiological forms called entities in addition to energies called entities. Here again, we have the problem of your 4D propensity to compartmentalize almost everything to a singular source. This is very understandable, and honored. But a true interdimensional being knows that there are no hard "walls" to any consciousness, and therefore the idea of assigning names or even personalities to interdimensional beings is limiting and misleading.

(4) Angels are interdimensional beings just like you, but who contain their entire "group" in their awareness and comprehension. They have no duality, and they have no biological expression.

(5) Archangels are angels who have the energy of many angels. They are not "higher" or "lower" despite the name. They are not "in charge" of anything either. They are instead filled with the

energy of many of the pieces and parts of the other angel entities. This makes them seem like they are more important. They
are not. Think of them as communicating stations, or "hubs" of
energy transference that are more easily accessible to the whole.
They exist to help bring groups of energies together for those
who can't think out of 4D. They also help in the organization of
energy that is needed in the Universe.**

(6) With the implantation of permission to ascend (the implant), there is a one-time shift in the guide energy. It's related
to the activation of the third layer of what you call DNA. What
you call "going quiet" is a process that you will relate to only
metaphorically. It is the changing of the guard. It is that moment
in space and time where one temple is torn down and another
has its foundation laid. It is variable from Human to Human
and also relates to your fears and allowances. It's a one-time
change, and it's profound.

And no... your assumption that they are still here is only
partially correct. The guides actually leave. You are *never* alone,
however, but what remains during this changing of the guard
is far less than what you are used to. When the great Master of
Love thought he was near death, he called out to the "family"
and thought they had forsaken him. He instead was experiencing this exact thing. Even the master was upset with this shift.
In his case, it lasted 90 minutes. In most cases, it is 90 days. The
"9" is completion, and is significant in energy.

** *Here is a discussion on the definition of archangels from
Ronna Herman, world-renowned channel for Archangel Michael:*

The great archangels represent the individualized
aspects, attributes, and qualities of the Supreme Creator.
They bring forth the fuel, or project the "love nature" of the
Creator. The Elohim, builders of form, project the mental

aspect of the Creator, and are the co-creators of manifested worlds using universal Light substance. They are projectors of primal life.

One explanation would be that the archangels and the Great Beings of Light carry a greater amount of "God Essence" and we are refracted facets of these great beings. Each of the seven major archangels of our galaxy embody and radiate particular aspects, qualities, and virtues of the Creator. Example: AA Michael radiates the First Ray of Divine Will and Power. Each archangel and ray overlights humanity and the Earth in 2,000-year cycles. The predominant rays at this time are the Seventh Ray—the Ray of the violet transmuting flame—ceremonial order, freedom, redemption, and purification; and the First Ray of Divine Will to Create is the secondary influence.

The Angelic Host of this Universe came forth under the direction of the 12 great archangels who came from the Great Central Sun. They are the link between humanity and the Creator.

The archangels are the messengers who bear the Divine Decrees of God and come forth in greater force and number to interact with humanity during times of great change/evolution.

Ronna Herman — Channel for Archangel Michael — [www.ronnastar.com]

Question: *Dear Kryon, are microwave ovens really bad for our bodies?*

Answer: Yes, don't ever get in one. [Kryon humor] Microwave energy is dangerous to your cellular structure. Period. In whatever form it is presented in your science, including transmission for communication, it's dangerous. There is no reason to throw away the science; instead, understand it and devise protection that is appropriate.

As for the microwave oven, you would be better advised to know what is happening to the food you ingest that has been cooked with it, rather than being afraid of the oven itself. Microwave energy removes much of the nutrition from anything cooked with it. It's not the same kind of heat you would have from a fire. Therefore, our advice has always been to use these ovens sparingly and not as your prime source of heat for cooking.

My partner says popcorn is okay. (Smile)

Question: *Dear Kryon, this question has to do with sexual energy. I understand that this energy is sacred; however, using it in a sacred way has proven to be a great challenge. In an environment that manipulates this energy in varied and conflicting ways—advertising, pornography, classical religious doctrines, alternative meditative practices, abstinence, celibacy, monogamy, polygamy, etc.—what are the New Age guidelines/practices to use this energy sacredly when a partner is available and when one is not? How does this differ for a single person, a married couple, a male and female?*

Answer: This answer has never changed. You have free choice to do whatever you wish with this. Since it can be used for anything from fear-based religious control to sacred life-giving love, do you understand that it is something that will always be a measure of energy on the planet?

What are the new rules? The same as the old ones: Treat it as sacred, change yourselves, and thereby change the energy around you on the planet. (Again, the parable of the tarpit is in order.) When other Humans see the enhancement provided by adding the sacred attributes to something only seen as biological, they will have the option to follow suit. The end result is a change of consciousness on the planet.

There will always be this balance, since sexual energy is also so related to so many other things that create lessons, drama, and turmoil. But the more it is discovered within a spiritual framework instead of a solely biological one, the more those around will change what they have perceived it to be.

Any powerful energy on this planet of yours can be used to create or destroy. This is the duality of your existence, and is the playing field of free choice.

Question: *Dear Kryon, I'm in the process of donating my eggs, and I'm seriously questioning what I'm doing. Are there any consequences to the child? Is this child my child or the child of the family that I'm donating to? Is this the child that I have a contract with that should be born to me and raised as my child? How will this affect the future children that I have with my partner?*

Answer: Long ago you made agreements to do this, and now here it is. What you do here may be the sacred passion that you have always had to bring others to the planet who otherwise would not have the chance.

It's not about biology. God is not in a vacuum concerning these things. There is no punishment, or karmic payment. There is nothing but sacredness in your decision. It doesn't affect any of the things you mentioned, all of which are concerns of mis-understanding of the real principle at work here.

If this is your passion, then do it. It will result in a completion of a contract that you are well aware of. Your partner, if truly un-derstanding, will also know this. Don't think biologically. Think sacredly. Part of what you "know" will be passed to a Human

Being who needs it. Did you think of that? This is the miracle of DNA... all the layers of it.

Question: *Dear Lee/Kryon, in my psychotherapy practice, I am specializing in menopause and other women's life-transition issues. I am trying to frame menopause as a step within the spiritual evolutionary process, perhaps even part of the female response to ascension. Can you help me with an explanation of what the process of menses means for my clients? And how is it that females seem to undergo this "reverse puberty" process in a more dramatic way than men do?*

Answer: Again we say to you that you must remove the biological from the spiritual. Look at what the body does. It is geared to stop the engine of procreation so that the female will not be harmed. That's why it occurs at all. It is an engine of appropriateness related to age. It's also an old paradigm, however, since we teach that you can extend your life-span, and that also means bearing children longer with safety, if that is part of your life plan.

For a male, the evolutionary process is one where, since he does not give birth, his biology is not one that goes through anything in the birth process. Therefore, age is unimportant to his health when it comes to producing the seeds, which he can do almost until death.

So the body is protecting the females from undue stress, and even from premature death—going through childbirth when the chemistry is not up to it. This should be seen as a blessing, and one that is honored.

However, now we tell you something that is more along the lines of your question. In females, sometimes the process isn't stopped for biological reasons at all, but spiritual ones! In males, sometimes the hormones of desire and performance are also seemingly prematurely stopped.

The reason? Sometimes shamans need to have some of the common distractions of Earth eliminated so that their concentration can be focused more clearly on spiritual matters. Don't read anything into this. It's different for every Human Being, so there is no generality here. But you should know that this is often part of the process of "relief from the distraction of things that are no longer needed," given for spiritual enlightenment. Not for all, but for many. This is often why you perceive elders to be wiser. They don't have that set of very complex and demanding chemicals surging through their body, either giving them pain with each cycle, or the pain of desire without fulfillment, which has its own attributes of psychological frustration and distraction.

For the females: Think of these things as all related. What is it you need? Do you give permission for it? Is it appropriate in your contract? Then when it comes, talk to your cellular structure and replace the chemistry that needs to be there for your energy, and say good-bye to that which is leaving. Give ceremony around it. You may do all of this naturally, talking to your cells. They will respond, and create what is missing.

These are the new Human Beings, taking control of their bodies, and speaking directly to their cells—creating tissue and chemistry naturally, since the cellular structure of their bodies is "listening" to what they need, and is far more capable than any scientist has ever told them.

And this is the truth.

Question: *Hello, Kryon, I appreciate your sense of humor so much; it brings me such joy to laugh with you about our duality. How does humor work between spiritual entities? How does a sense of humor differ, if at all, when we are in lesson versus when we are not in lesson? What other things (besides our duality) prompt laughter?*

Answer: Dear one, thank you for this profound question! Humor is one of the only energies passed through the veil completely untouched. The other is love. They are related, and we cry when we laugh and also in grief. They both affect Human biology, too, and so they are catalysts for chemistry changes.

On the other side of the veil it is there, too. Don't we smile and laugh when we hug you? Yes. Don't we dance when you do? Yes. Believe me, it's very much a part of what you call The Cosmic Lattice of sacredness.

Truly, humor is sacred. It calms the Human spirit and creates the chemistry of tolerance, forgiveness, and even health. Is it any wonder that we make it a staple of this work you call "the Kryon"?

Question: *Dear Kryon, regarding homosexuality or transsexuals, why are they the way they are, and why are they not accepted in mainstream society?*

Answer: [From the Kryon office]:

Kryon has been channelling for 14 years, with nine books covering many, many topics. Homosexuality was one of them from the very beginning.

Here is an excerpt from Kryon Book 6, page 306, Q&A section:

Question: *Dear Kryon, I am gay, and an enlightened man. I live in an American society that barely tolerates me, and actually has some laws against my way of life. The church I used to belong to cast me out as being evil and anti-God. I don't feel that I am violating some human ethic. My love is as true as any heterosexual, and I am a Lightworker. Tell me what I should know.*

Answer: Dear one, less than two generations from now, there will be those who find this book and laugh at the quaintness of this very question. Before I answer, let me ask you and those reading this to examine a phenomenon about human society and "God."

Thirty years ago, interracial marriage was considered to be wrong by the laws of God. Now your society finds it common. The spiritual objections around it were either dropped or "rewritten" by those divinely inspired and authorized to do so. Therefore, your actual interpretations of the instructions from God changed with your society's tolerance level—an interesting thing, indeed, how the interpretations of God seem to change regularly to match a changing culture!

The truth, of course, is that you find yourself in a situation that is known to create a test for you. Right now, in this time, you have agreed to come into your culture with an attribute that may alienate you from friends and religious followers. You have faced fear of rejection and have had to "swim upstream," so to speak, just as an everyday life occurrence. Your contract, therefore, has been set up well, and you are in the middle of it. Additionally, like so many like you, you have a divine interest in yourselves! You feel part of the spiritual family. What a dichotomy indeed, to be judged as evil by those who are the high spiritual leaders—interpreting God for today's culture.

Now I say this: What is your intent? Is it to walk with love for all those around you and become an enlightened human being in this New Age? Is it to forgive those who see you as a spiritual blight on society? Can you have the kind of tolerance for them that they seem not to have for you? Can you overlook the fact that they freely quote the New Age master of love in order to condemn you, yet they don't seem to have the love tolerance that is the cornerstone of the master's message?

If the answer is yes, then there is nothing else you must do. Your INTENT is everything, and your life will be honored with peace over those who would cause unrest, and tolerance for the intolerable. Your sexual attributes are simply chemistry and setups within your DNA. They are given by agreement as gifts for you to experience in this life. Look on them in this fashion, and be comfortable with the fact that you are a perfect spiritual creation under God—loved beyond measure—just like all humans. But then you know that, don't you?

Question: *Dear Kryon, I am a healer/alternative therapist, and I need to know, what is the best way to help people with addictions and compulsive behaviors?*

Answer: Addictions and compulsive behaviors are a result of more than just psychological disorders and/or chemical imbalance. They are a way for the biological-self to distract a Human from completing what it came here for, spiritually.

If you work with addicted Humans, then I don't have to tell you the frustration they feel. They absolutely know what they are doing, yet they can't communicate with their cellular structure enough to stop it. The main part of this struggle is the one where the biology builds a "wall of addition or compulsive behavior" so that the Human does noy have to make the decision they came here for. Worse, sometimes this activity is actually designed to kill them quicker (by their own design)!

Many of these precious souls are very spiritual... have you noticed? They are "on the edge" of complete knowledge, but just can't seem to "go there."

What to do? Your work as a healer is to help them over this hump of fear. They can't stop smoking... or eating... or having overwhelming sexual desires... or doing drugs? These are all classic Human biological ploys that are part of the "seed fear" of enlightenment.

Clearing fear is the answer... fear that perhaps this time they won't suffer and go through torture because they accept the information of the Higher-Self. Many are unconsciously fearful of moving into a spiritual experience. Even those who are healers, channellers, and ministers will also experience this! They don't want to "go all the way," since the last time they did this. they died horribly.

So, healer, help them to begin talking to their cellular structure in ways that will relax the fear of spiritual information and action. The more they can love themselves, the less they will rely on outside stimuli for their peace. The more they can drop this very real fear of theirs, the less they will need their addictions. Behavior will modify, and the addiction will eventually drop away.

Meditation is also part of the key to this... real meditation, with intent and motivation. Finally, self-worth is the real issue (the same as loving themselves). When this is settled, then the addictions begin to diminish and go away. We will give you more on the actual ways to gain self-worth as the months go by.

Question: *Dear Kryon, I found the questions and answers on your Website extremely helpful, but I have a question that has been nagging me, and I can't find an answer for it: Given that our world population is at its highest that it has ever been, with over six billion people, where have all these souls been all this time in the past when the earth was not so populated?*

Answer: In the place you call "the other side of the veil." There are more entities in the pool of "God" than you can conceive. Each star you can see and can't see represents a hair on the head of an angel. We are countless, yet finite.

The earth is populated with these angelic creatures you call "God," and you are one. Many have waited eons to be part of this wonderful test called Earth. Your population increase allows them to join you, and your planet of free choice.

At some point, you will be full, and if Human wisdom is where we expect, you will deal with it in a way that has common sense and honor.

Question: *Dear Kryon, thank you for the many communications you have given. They have been enlightening in many ways. I hope this is not a rude question, but it is a subject that I have not seen addressed in the collection of Questions and Answers. I want to know: What is the morality of stopping someone's new life in the physical plane by abortion? And what is the karma to the person who helps to accomplish an abortion? I think it will depend on when a human life begins. When life begins is a moment that is very important to those who oppose abortion and those who say it is allowable.*

Do you have a decisive response to guide those who receive your words?

Answer: [from Lee Carroll] Many have tried to "paint" Kryon into a corner on this one many times, since it really is an issue in our society. Kryon says this: "Human life actually begins when the intent of the entities involved in the planning session is to create it." It's not a biological answer, and it won't please either side.

This places it far before any kind of biological morality decision. Kryon has said that there is no judgment in the choice of Humans... including this one. When it occurs, there is also no horrible karmic payback. But there *is* energy created that affects everyone around. Sometimes these lives come and go to create lessons for those involved, then these terminated lives return almost immediately, often within the next pregnancy (sometimes changing gender). If there is no next pregnancy, often it's in a very close family group.

Again we say that God is not somehow isolated concerning these things, and often they are setups, and are executed with the agreement of all parties in advance. This is far different than our society wishes to believe, which wants to paint a black-and-white answer to when life occurs, and set rules on what you can and cannot do with it. Instead, it gives honor and validity to the fact that you are not here by accident, and the things that take place in your lives are not random.

So we leave the biological cultural decisions for those who wish to make them, but we have heard the spiritual answers many times... that these things are far more than they appear, and are all part of our spiritual setups, and they are honored.

Question: *Dear Kryon, I was wondering about the way I feel about whales and dolphins. I've had a feeling that I have to go* *to them sometime, but I don't know how or what I'm to do when I get there. Please help.*

Question: *Dear Kryon, I'm a Turkish/Islamic woman of 57. I live in Ankara and work for the European Commission's project in Turkey. I've read almost all of the Kryon books twice, and I'm planning to read them once more. My question is about the whales. Why do they commit mass suicide? What is the reason for this very sad event? Is it a kind of protest against Human Beings?*

Answer: Dear ones, we've channelled many times about the whales of this planet. In review, they're the living portions of an actual grid-system! They contain the "history of Earth" within their beings, and they're sacred for that reason. They coordinate and cooperate with the Crystalline Grid of your planet, which is currently being rewritten.* Doesn't it strike you odd that these mammals are the only ones protected against hunting by more than 90 percent of the countries of Earth... even the places without oceans? Do you think that this is an accident or a coincidence? No. It's cellular information for all humanity to protect the whales and keep them safe. Dolphins are their cousins and support group, and they play a role in the whales' development. This is why you're so attracted to them.

Whales do not commit mass suicide. They have no consciousness to allow for this, and it has never happened. Instead, you see whales often beaching themselves and then being saved by Humans, only to re-beach themselves and die. This takes place mostly on the coastlines of your continents, and often on those areas of topography that "stick out," such as a peninsula or isthmus. Your Cape Cod is a good example in America, and is

---

* See the Kryon channelling on the Kryon Website "What's Next?" December 8, 2002. [www.kryon.com/k_chanelnewport02.html]

also a place where this has recently happened (up to 47 whales on a beach).

The reason is that whales, dolphins, amphibians, birds, and even insects all navigate to their breeding ground or migration areas each year via the magnetic grid of the planet! Each group follows the ley lines of magnetic influence, almost as if they had a built-in compass. In fact, they actually do!

The magnetic grid of this planet has changed so much, so quickly, as we told you it would in 1989, that there hasn't been time for the pods of whales to adjust with time to these changes. Instead, many simply follow the old magnetic lines of migration, only to find themselves on a beach instead of the open ocean, as the old magnetic direction used to take them. They're confused, and they simply line up and try again, just as they have for years. These things are temporary, and as tragic as you might see them, it's all part of "pruning" the system, and the calves will go around in the future, establishing new instinctive information for the new whales regarding the grid changes. This information has even now been validated this year (2003) by your scientists.

Question: *Dear Kryon, for many years I've been remembering many of my (sleeping) dreams, and also have been trying to interpret what they mean and what they can tell me about myself. I had some thoughts today, and was wondering if you could comment on them, and also about lucid dreaming. Here are my thoughts:*

Are my dreams my imagination, and also my reality? I guess, in a way, the continual shifting in dream scenery could be likened to the fact that our true realities are layered and multidimensional and can change in an instant. Furthermore, who's to say that our dreamscapes aren't alternate realities, on different planes/dimensions, which are brought about by choices we've made, or didn't make, in our "past"? Maybe they're playing out in our subconscious, to poke and prod us to learn in this reality what we may have learned, or are trying to learn, in our other realities?

Answer: First, let's give you, as best we can, the reasons for dreams, and the process involved. It's not what you necessarily indicated. This Human dream function is extremely complex. Even after our explanation, you may not fully understand.

Biological: From a biological aspect, dreams are actually a memory release and rewrite. They are a form of mental clearing that the body must perform in order to actually reorganize the brain during the sleep state. It moves things around and prioritizes the places where memory is stored. In the process, you often get flashes of what it's doing. So this is the clinical truth, not yet seen or accepted by science. Soon, however, as you're able to map the energies of the brain in real time, this will be shown. Remember where you read it first!

Psychological: The memories that are moved from place to place are often done in a priority that's driven by your fears, loves, passions, and even your addictions. This is a hierarchy that remains very telling in analysis, and hasn't changed much through the centuries of Human existence. The nonlinear attributes... seeing people in places they never were, or couldn't be within a real 4D time line, are common, since the brain is moving these things in a nonlinear way. Think of it this way: You're carrying a box of photos of all your life experiences. Suddenly you drop the box, and the photos go everywhere. As you pick them up, they're not in any order. The past and present are all mixed up. As you hold the photos in your hand, your Aunt Sally is next to a home that she never saw, visiting your children whom she's never met. In addition, you pick up certain photos first that have more energy for you than the others, since they're going to be filed in a specific place that needs to be more available to the brain for remembrance. So the brain actually prioritizes the memories in an order that's telling. This is where psychological analysis has been so valuable in the past.

Spiritual: With the coming of the new energy, Lightworker and ascension status has changed all the potentials, and a brand new piece of the dream puzzle emerges. Your newfound awareness is suddenly part of this memory rearrangement. In addition, if you're working at it (being a Lightworker), the dream process has changed its purpose. It's now actually a rewrite of the past within your DNA (in addition to the biological sorting of neuron storage, as seen above)! This is very difficult to describe. Think of it this way: Return to the photos on the floor. Now, as you pick up each photo, you get to rewrite the emotions and energies around them with a new, enlightened mind. The father that abused you is now the "partner in karma," and an entity who did a good job of stirring your life up. The brother who committed suicide and shamed the family is now the one who gave you a gift... a kick in the pants to find out more about spiritual things. The partner who loves you, who may be lying next to you, is becoming more precious with your new divine eyes. So you're not just rearranging the memories. The brain is rewriting them. This is a powerful new attribute that shows a new enablement for Humans, and is primal to the teachings of Kryon and the other channellers of the New Age. Now, the photos you pick up first are the ones that you're rewriting, and are thereby changing your very time line in this place called Earth.

The biological and psychological aspects cooperate fully with your enlightened state. They're subservient to the divine plan in your body, and have rearranged the priorities to help you fulfill a change in your DNA.

How to interpret the dreams? Well, those other channellers were correct—if you're working on your enlightenment. For the old interpretations discount the new spiritual aspects of the process. Now you may look at the interpretations completely in a spiritual light. Did you dream of Aunt Sally? Why? Perhaps you're rewriting how you felt about her and bringing her into a new light? Perhaps she's visiting you in an interdimensional way to help you process and rewrite her history within the scope of your life? This is very, very common. Parents return; those you lost during your 4D time line show up. You see, it's very complex, but it has indeed changed. Look for far more nonlinear things in the dream state.

Finally, a hint: If some of you have dreams that repeat and repeat a process or a song or an action seemingly all night (although dreams are actually happening in just a few seconds), it doesn't mean anything. Don't try to read into it. Instead, it's a smokescreen to let the brain and the divinity unify. The brain creates a feedback loop that runs while it does things that are beautiful, out of sight, and filled with new abilities for your consciousness.

Question: *Dear Kryon, I've been wondering about this for a while now. Do we decide how and when we're going to die before we come into the world? Is that why some people live a long and healthy life, while others die from an illness or accident at an early age? Does it have anything to do with our past lives?*

Answer: Human death is not seen on this side of the veil as anything but a transition of energy and a freshening of expression. This is difficult for you to understand, for to you, death is pain, suffering, and grief. Can you even begin to understand why this is the setup? We see it as part of the "play of Earth." In any play, even the Human with the knife in his chest gets up after the curtain comes down and has a party with the cast. The cast members all know that the adventure in the play is not real. But in the play of Earth, your reality says that life is everything there is. Therefore, it's played "for keeps." It has to be this way, to make the challenge and the test... fair.

Yes, you all have a beginning setup contract where your shift (death) is planned. Sometimes it's to facilitate another person (such as the profound energy created through the death of a child or suicide). So it can be part of an agreement with great energy around it, or a simple potential to leave when it's time. Each case is different, and yes, it is often tempered with a balance from past-life experience. It's also entirely temporary and waiting to be rewritten!

All this is changing greatly. With the new energy brings a change in the system of life and death on Earth. Indigo Children are coming into the planet without past-life karmic attributes. They're "clean" of this karma, and also have a very different setup. They still have a potential life line, and they carry information about past-life experience and the wisdom of what they learned, but they're also aware that they can create a change in that beginning contract. This is the biggest difference between the old- and new-energy Human. The old-energy Human somehow feels that the contract is absolute, that nothing can change it. He actually tries to follow this beginning temporary setup to its destination! This is information that has to be unlearned for most of you. The child? He knows better. He can do anything! Did you notice his attitude? He comes in ready to create and manifest. He's frustrated that you don't see the potentials, or that you wallow in some linear system, or that you try to follow an old setup. Did you notice? This is all part of the new Human-life scenario.

Whereas the plan of old created life and death as a cycle in a karmic engine of lesson—creating energy to help the earth—that is now void. The new system is one that encourages a contract rewrite, including death time, age, and even life lesson. It's a startling change, and brings new meaning to death in the new energy.

Also, there's this fact: We told you in 1989 that a great number of Humans might have to pass quickly in these times for the new energy to manifest. You're seeing it now. With war and disease, the numbers are quickly being fulfilled. What does this mean? It means that many actually had the agreement to pass at this time if the earth had accomplished a vibratory rate shift. It did, and the process began.

What is the reason for this? Although you might feel that it's too sorrowful to think about, we give you the truth: The new indigo color of Human Being will do far better on the planet than one with a very old energy. Therefore, many are leaving early to immediately come back as Humans with the indigo color. This will facilitate peace on Earth faster than anything else.

Question: *Dear Kryon, I believe that there's been mention of changing our physical bodies through intent. However, I was wondering about the effect of surgical enhancements on a person—specifically, implants of the silicon variety. I'm wondering how they affect or perhaps interfere with energy and the next steps of our evolution.*

Answer: So, you wish to speak of sexual attractiveness and self-worth? Let's do so. This is not a taboo subject with Spirit.

It's all part of what makes you do what you do. Think of it as yet another tool of life choice, given in an age of technology that would support it, and a culture where it's not unusual.

There's no spiritual judgment around enhancing your looks to accomplish better self-worth. There's also no taboo around it. There might be biological consequences, however (see below). The spiritual attribute is this, however: What does it bring to you that otherwise wouldn't have happened? Did you create a choice that would steer you into a place you didn't prepare for? If so, do you have good solutions? Did it help with your self-worth? The answers to these things are varied and complex, but they're all honored, since they're all part of what you're creating for yourself in free choice.

To Spirit, there's no difference between this and selecting a new color of clothing or changing your hairstyle. It's not seen as a violation of your body for unholy purposes (as some would have you believe). We've spoken of how sex is one of the most respected energies on the planet, and how Humans have a choice to honor or abuse it. But if honored, it creates sacredness in itself, with love and joy at its center. The enhancement you've described is totally a cultural perception, and isn't seen by Spirit as anything more than your becoming more beautiful to a society that wishes to participate in this ritual of appearance.

Since it affects your biology, however, here's some advice: Anything placed into cavities of your body that are foreign to your system will have a tendency to create an energy of imbalance. Therefore, make the alteration sacred. Bless the substance, and tell it how much better you'll feel when it's added. Speak to it daily, and give the body permission to feel that it belongs there. Make it part of the whole.

Question: *Dear Kryon, did a person named Jesus actually exist, or was it a group with the Christ energy that the church made into a person?*

Question: *Dear Kryon, I've looked at birth charts for Jesus over many years and found one which I believe, if not real, is the most intriguing. Therefore, I ask: Can you please reveal the exact date and time of Jesus Christ's birth? And which DNA layer is the "astrology layer" that you've mentioned? I really believe that this may help in realigning astrology with the energy you've talked about.*

Question: *Dear Kryon, when Jesus came here, did he know of our eternal work of Universe building? Does he know how much we love him?*

Question: *Dear Kryon, I'm not a Christian, but am curious as to whether the story of Jesus is accurate. Did he die by crucifixion, or was he spared to live a full life with a family of his own, elsewhere?*

Question: *Dear Kryon, was Jesus nothing more or less than a Crystal Child? Did he possess something that simply wasn't understood during his time? Did he have different DNA or advanced DNA? This time is so exciting, and things have become so clear, that I want to be able to tell others what I now understand.*

Answer: Dear ones, we posture this answer with great respect for those who love this Human master. It serves no purpose to give information that would be detrimental to any study or search for the divine by any Human alive. This is why we often do not give you the actual history of some of the masters who walked this earth. We see the search for the divine as the most important thing a Human can do. Even if the facts of history are incorrect, sometimes the benefits of the search still bring the Human into the light and into the realization that God is inside us all.

Jesus was a real person. His birth and death were far different than have been reported, but he walked the earth as an enlightened soul whose miracles and teachings were the beginning of a new dispensation. He taught unity, and the principle that all men could speak personally to God. He said, "You can be just like me!" and that is what our message is, also... that master-hood is within each of you. If you really want to know more about the real history, it's very clearly in the scrolls, but it's not in your scriptures!

If you feel that Jesus might have had a special consciousness, as many of the new children do, you're right! His DNA was without some of the restrictions that you have, but had those that you're now learning about. The astrological layer of his DNA (the layers that respond to other planetary energy movements) were void and neutral. (This particular layer will be exposed this year for you, along with a name.)

And yes, he knows of your love, and all the things that your divinity knows. Like all of you, he is multidimensional, and is in many places at the same time. Did you know that you are, too?

Spiritual enlightenment is not about following any Human Being or any entity in the Universe. It's about knowing that God resides within you, and that you're an eternal part of His universal plan. This information has been brought to you from many masters and is within many cultures throughout the history of the earth.

Jesus, as well as other masters who walked the earth, not only gave you messages of empowerment, but then "walked the walk" so you could see that a Human Being could actually do what he said could be done. Many of you are poised on the edge of realizing this same thing.

Question: *(about the Mel Gibson movie): Dear Kryon, as a Jew, I'm aware of the danger in allowing the "passion plays" to penetrate the consciousness of those who would believe that the Jews were responsible for the death of Jesus Christ. I'm also sickened by the belief of some that unless we accept Jesus as our Lord and Savior, we're eternally damned. Can you shed some light on this topic and explain why the world is being exposed to The Passion of the Christ at this time in our history?*

Answer: Stay in your own integrity, and don't look to others to define your beliefs; humanity has always had these divisions. There was a time in Europe for more than 30 years when towns were regularly conquered, destroyed, and pillaged by Christians who demanded that you were to believe in a certain way. Today you have the same kind of behavior within a segment of people who are just as adamant about their own belief system.

The truth is that your divinity is within you, and no doctrine on the planet is higher than this truth. If you claim it, then you'll be "above the fray" of those who wish to convert you, damn you, or kill your family because you're not a believer. This, my Human friend, is the war between the old and new energy.

This movie is a dramatic effort to pull humanity back into the suffering and victim mode. Although it's done with integrity, does it exemplify what this master taught? Does the movie, based partially in myth instead of real history, show the joy of Jesus' life?

We told you that there would be a battle between the old and the new. You are in it, and this is just the beginning of a fight that will bring you to the following questions, which will tear you off the fence of indecision about your own spirituality:

"Were you really born dirty? Would a loving God prepare the earth in this fashion? If God created the earth with love, why is suffering often considered a virtue for sacredness? How much of what you have in your scriptures is altered? How much is missing? How much is political? Do you have the entire historic story? If God is family, and divinity is self-evident, why are there hundreds of factions of belief on the planet? How could murder and rape be perpetrated in the name of a loving God? Could there be something far grander and greater about who God really is? Is it time to find out?"

These are the real questions that are creating the battles on Earth at the moment.

Question: *(on Mary Magdalene): Dearest Kryon, over the past few months, many signs regarding Mary Magdalene have come to me. My intuition tells me that she was, in fact, the partner of Jesus, and that the Church repressed and hid away her status for fear that the feminine would be connected in partnership and marriage with Jesus. This belief would then destroy the myth that Jesus was virgin. It is said that Mary Magdalene was the Blessed Apostle and was given the true doctrine of Jesus. Can you explain this theory, and tell me if it will be a part of the New Jerusalem.*

Answer: Dear one, look to your own history: The scrolls—all of them—will reveal many of these answers. Look for the ones discovered in Egypt, too, including the Book of Mary. There is much here that has been hidden, but which is very well documented by your own Earth sources. It has been sequestered, but now is in the open.

Question: *Dear Kryon, in my work, I actually look at the DNA of Human Beings—the chromosomes—which are the visible manifestations of our DNA. You've said that there will be changes in the DNA as it's activated to higher vibrations. Will I be able to "see" these changes? I'd love to be able to detect the changes and know that they are the activations and not some abnormality.*

Question: *Dear Kryon, I read a book called The Power of Twelve by Anne Brewer, and it fired my imagination. How much of this DNA recoding is true? She speaks of different levels, of genetic engineers, of Galactic Councils, and of their work on our astral bodies. Am I being redundant by asking a bit more information on DNA?*

Question: *Dear Kryon, I've only recently found your teachings, but find them fascinating and heartwarming—thank you.*

I have a somewhat bizarre question that I hope you can shed some light on. Shamans from indigenous cultures across the world (Africa, South America, and Mexico) talk about a race of interdimensional reptilian beings that came to Earth long ago in order to escape another race of beings that were persecuting them. They found that they could hide inside Human Beings and avoid detection unbeknownst to the majority of humanity. This concept doesn't worry me, as we are all one and all ultimately part of the divine. I'm curious as to whether these shamanic stories are based in fact, and if so, are these reptilian beings really our fears, our ego that we must overcome in order to reach enlightenment?

Answer: *Physically-* Those of you who actually study the pieces and parts of DNA won't see many physical changes. The changes we speak about are interdimensional. However, for those unbelievers who say, "How convenient," we say this: Even though you may not see physical structure changes, the chemistry itself will change. Immune systems will strengthen, life expectancy will lengthen, genes may rearrange themselves, and other systems will seem to be on a new track. So you'll be able to see the results of something else seemingly affecting the 4D layer of DNA (the Human Genome). When you finally get the instruments that can detect interdimensionality (the shadows of other realities), you'll see it very clearly around our DNA. This will beg the question: "Is there more to DNA than what's under the 4D microscope?"

Answer: *Spiritually-* We told you many years ago that your DNA has been altered by off-world energies. It was on schedule, and we even told you when it occurred within your Human history. Your anthropologists know of the anomalies of Human development, too... asking why evolution provided such a vast variety of all Earth species except the Human Being! They can even point to when it happened (the end of the variety).* These historic facts all point to a truth that we've given you before: You had help, and it came from that part of the sky you call the "Seven Sisters."

*Scientific American, January 2000, Volume 282, Number 1
*Kryon Book Eight, Passing the Marker, pages 367–69

Answer: *Reptilian-* Due to the above-stated truth, which can never be proven but which is intuitive and surges through your DNA, many stories have surfaced within many cultures about wars, battles, good and evil, reptilian origins, and how this could have been. So I will ask you to go inside and ask yourself: How much of this information fits into a loving scenario of the creation of a Human Being who's divine and has a loving role to play within the Universe? Did you ever wonder who you might have been on another planet in past Universes? We told you before that the Humans who come here have done this before (lived in duality) in other places. We also told you that your whole spiritual record is in your DNA. This also means that there's a subtle memory of you being other kinds of creatures if you look hard enough. But this is meaningless within your life on Earth at the moment, and has a "residual" energy that has been obsessive to many, and has even created fear-based teachings.

Think about it, family: Did you evolve as a result of a mistake... or a battle between evil and good Gods... or the spoils of a cosmic war... or secretive reptilians? I think your own divinity will tell you a better story—one of honor, logic, and divine purpose.

Question: *Dearest Kryon, what's the difference between the soul and the Higher-Self?*

Answer: There are many divine ideas and concepts on your planet that have many names for the same thing. This might be one of them, but from our standpoint, they're different. Before we define them, we'd like to give you a brief discussion about names in general.

When you're dealing with interdimensional attributes or intuitive energies that are being revealed, there's no cosmic dictionary to consult. Therefore, those who channel or regularly give this kind of information must deal with concepts that have no established names, but which are still very real. The result is that you may end up with many names for the same thing, depending on the source. This isn't a conflict, but rather just semantics and the result of being in a very new energy where many things are being presented that are unique and unusual.

The soul is often seen as the overview of all that you are. It includes all the "selves" that you have, including the ones that aren't here in 4D. Therefore, it's a name that would indicate a "divine wholeness," and is often meant to reflect the "entire system of you." This would include the "I AM" presence you have in the Universe.

The Higher-Self is a name that's given to the part of you directly involved in communication with God, and the part of you that's "connected" full-time to the family. Therefore, you might say that it describes a part, a section, of you.

So the difference between them is that one describes the whole, and the other describes a part.

Question: *Is there any way a Human can experience their true selves, at least emotionally, so as to be refreshed and to have some peace while we go about the task of multidimensional creation?! I long to do so. I'd like to "go home" and experience myself, intimately acquainted with the divine.*

Question: *Dear Kryon, it's clear to me that one of the greatest achievements of Human Beings in this new energy is the development of The Third Language. Since the language of Spirit is not linear, is the understanding of symbolic information such as archetypes, metaphors, parables, and symbols a way to improve The Third Language?*

Answer: Yes, yes, and yes! This experiencing of The Third Language is what we teach. It's about "talking to your cells." Look at our teachings in 2003 and up through 2005 for these answers, for it's about claiming master-hood.

This isn't something that you have to call the press and stop your life to accomplish. It's about a daily walk that's so loving, peaceful, and different that your cells refuse to go into drama, anger, or worry. You're "connected to the family" as you walk in ordinary places, and you know it.

You asked how: Start with asking for this in the most quiet times you have. Take time to meditate, and ask for nothing but this. Tell your God-partner (the Higher-Self) that you wish to start this connection and keep it. Take the profundity of the emotional feeling you have during these quiet times with God and keep them going! Come out of meditation and walk this 4D earth in an interdimensional bubble of love. Don't close the mediation... just get up and keep it going!

These are all concepts. They don't seem to relate to a linear step-by-step procedure, do they? You may not have received the answer you wanted, either. So many of you want the solutions in a simple way. It isn't simple. You begin a process through divine co-creation, and you stair-step through it as your own process demands it. But you can't climb the stairway until you open the door.

Can you show the color blue to a child? Yes. This is simple. Now, explain it to a sightless person. This is complex. Interdimensionality is this way. You want steps, rules, and procedures, but it's far more complex than this. It's also the goal of everything we teach. Begin with pure intent. Follow it up with joy. Add some wisdom and give it some time. God can hardly wait to fill up your cup of understanding.

Question: *Dear Kryon, I want to validate my understanding of what NOW time really is. I understand it to be that Spirit is in a spot (for lack of a better word) where you can see the potentials of all possible things to come. I can understand this concept because I equate it to looking at a tree and seeing the branches extend out in an ever-increasing pattern. My questions are:*

What happens when events come to pass? Do they form a singular path of reality, similar to the bottom of the tree, where there's only one path back to the ground? Or is Spirit able to see all possible paths that did not come to pass?

This is sort of a linear-time question, but is Spirit able to see all possible things that reach into infinity, or does it become too cumbersome to see after a certain point (such as you would have with an ever-expanding tree going into infinity)?

You say that NOW time is circular, but we are in linear time. So somehow the two must correlate. How long (days, months, or years) does it take in our linear time to complete one circular path of NOW time? Or is that different for each person, based on where they are on their path? Is there a collective correlation of linear time traversed to complete one circular NOW path for the earth?

Answer: Dear one, first, throw away the tree. It's way too 4D for you to relate to it. It may serve to help you with your metaphor, but it's very limiting within this complex analogy.

There's no such thing as predestination, but only predisposition. As events come to pass, you tend to stay in a predetermined groove, much like the old LP phonograph record groove that plays only one song as long as you stay in that specific groove. So watching a Human Being play the song he began when he was born is very predictable and not all that complex. It's when you decide to "play another song" that it becomes difficult to explain to you.

Picture this: Spirit stands in the center of a huge balloon. Inside this balloon your potentials exist. All the "if you go this way, then this is the potential" kind of energy is shown. For instance, if you void a whole reality (in the same way that you might sterilize yourself), then all the potentials involving having more children go away. This means that as you move within your life, this "NOW map" changes depending on what you do. It also shows you where you are now, and the potentials of what's possible at the next step. Although many potentials are there, only the nearest ones are shown, since they are the most energetic ones.

Now understand that this map is not just for God. It's for you, too. This is the "You are here" map that we tried to explain in the parable of Michael Thomas (Kryon Book Five). Becoming interdimensional gives you insight as to which way to turn in order to accomplish what you want. It's also an energy map that gives you the intuition to move accordingly.

You're right to think that time is not linear, and this is what makes it really tough for you to understand. We encourage you to "think in the NOW" and to understand that your path is not what you think. It's not a straight line from one place to another. Instead, this circle of the NOW takes into consideration that you created it, so you have the ability and permission to change it anytime you wish. Want to get off the "road" for a while? It may feel unsafe, but that's because reality isn't what it used to be.

The two kinds of time exist together, but one is an illusion. They're always connected, but this is hard for you to see. For instance, consider that you're on a road that goes to the horizon. It seems to disappear into the distance, straight ahead. Seemingly it goes forever in one direction. But your mind knows that there's a potential that this road could circle the earth and actually be the same road, all the way around in a circle. (Naturally we assume that it goes over the ocean, too.) So instead of what your eye tells you (a straight road that goes forever away from you), it's actually a circle, and therefore the road in back of you is the same as the one in front of you.

How long it takes to travel over the same spot in the road (that is, to complete the circle) depends entirely on you. If you tend to revisit the same thing over and over, then the circle is fairly small. However, for some, the circle is a lifetime. It just depends on your own path. Even the earth has a path, and has the attributes of this same circle. One of the most interesting things is that when you traverse the same path again (start to go over the ground you already covered), the energies you laid down before are now enhanced, and more apt to manifest themselves than when you first traveled the road. Metaphorically, this is why a past life often leads to a current life that has more resolve, or more manifestation than the last. It's also why Lemurians know they are Lemurians!

Question: *I'm having trouble knowing "who" to pray to. Slowly over the years I've come to believe that we are all a "piece" of God" and that the Human on Earth is only one of a "group." You've told us that you are part of a "group." There are angels like Michael and Gabriel, and masters like Jesus and Buddha, and I assume that they are "groups" as well. I know that we can confer with our Higher-Selves and our guides, but is there any one group or entity In charge? Is there a "Father"? Is the Universe a big democracy?*

Answer: Your question not only shows intuition and wisdom, but also the limitation of what you have placed upon yourself, called duality. No matter what is explained, Humans wish to compartmentalize and build organizational charts around everything. This is a totally linear process, and doesn't represent the reality of the way it is on the other side of the veil.

Take a large bowl of soup. It has organization, taste, matter, nourishment, and form. Yet there's nobody in charge of the soup. Now you might say, "Sure, but there's no consciousness in soup. It doesn't have to think or make decisions and is not aware of itself." You think not? Do you think all those molecules just happened to create themselves and organize themselves into intricate structures that combine in complex ways that are so involved that science doesn't even understand them? Were you aware that even in something as simple as soup, there's a plan, a system, and coordination? If so, then who's in charge? Where's the democracy? Who gives the orders?

What if, instead of a linear order of command, all the pieces had full knowledge of what the plan was, and without any inter-facing, just fit into what they all know? Not only does soup do this, but so does the Universe and what you call God.

Yes, you are all pieces of the whole. But all the angels and other entities that have identified themselves through the ages, have this in common, also: They're all reading from the same script... one that is one consensus, and that updates itself all together. This is like nothing you've ever experienced, so you can't really imagine it. You've even built mythology around "wars in heaven" so that you could somehow justify why things were as they are, thinking that only a conquering energy could be a certain way. These Human actions are all about trying to linearize God.

Your DNA contains a divine code that says it all. You are divine, and also included in the "knowing" of this map. The closer you get to your own divinity, the more this is evident, and the greater your wisdom is. We've encouraged you to find the prophet inside, the rule book inside, and the compass of who you are and why you're here. Critics say that this is also what serial killers have done, mocking the process as something that's unbalanced and even evil. "Just think," they say, "if everyone had their own rule book, it would be chaos!" Then they give you their rule book, often in full integrity, explaining what they say God wants you to do.

The truth is that this "rule book" is individual, but like the soup, it's something that's common to each molecule of the soup. So it's the same script for everybody! It has to be, or what you call "nature" wouldn't work at all. It's the book that says that the "group" is all one family. The organization portion (explained for the benefit of your linear reality) is one that speaks of specialists. Some of your family is dedicated to working with the 4D interface between you and us (guides). Some of the family is dedicated to being angelic before you, and some, like me, are involved in your physics. But we're all involved in the love of God, the support of humanity, and we're all a group... your group... the family group called God.

Who should you pray to? Start turning inward. Instead of praying "to" anyone, start to understand the wisdom of where the power actually is. Then create what you need, apart from any thought of sitting there hoping that God might give you something—like a dog sitting patiently on the floor under the dinner table, hoping for a handout. It's not that way! It's the grace of your own existence, which is the essence of God on Earth, and which drives all creation. You are your own master, a fact hidden completely within the face of your duality. Join the group called God. Pray—not to a higher supreme being—but as a family member who's writing home during the front line of a battle. You're part of God, and are a family member. You're also a Human Being, one of the few entities in the Universe who lives and works in a place where you can't know the truth, since it would spoil the fairness of the test.

... And you wonder why we support you and love you so?

Question: *Dear Kryon, I've been pondering your statements about light and multidimensionality, and something occurred to me today. I'm not sure if this is a flash of insight or just plain crazy. I'd appreciate it if you could tell me if I'm on the right track. Have we missed something about light that's blindingly obvious? We live in 4D space-time. Does light experience time? Light is a massless particle, according to physicists. My "insight" or "crazy idea" is that light is in another dimension than 4D space-time. If this is right, then is it just our perception that needs to change?*

Answer: Yes, the perceptions need to change. Instead of seeing light outside of time, you must start seeing light as controlled by time. It may not experience time, but its attributes (speed, especially) are controlled by it. Why does light travel at all? What is the engine behind it? When you look at the core energy of reality, it demands that light be related to time. But since time is different for many parts of the Universe, then light is not the constant you think it is.

Your insights are good, but you need to carry them still further. Light is indeed partially interdimensional, but it's forever locked to formulas about the reality of where it is. Each time-frame will create a different "speed of Light." This is perhaps the most difficult part of what we teach in astronomy and physics. When you look into space, the light that has come from a far away place is seen as traveling at a constant speed to get to you. . . the same speed as the light that came from the bulb over your head. In fact, this isn't so. Instead, think of this faraway light as having made a long journey through "light roads" where there were construction delays, stops, and even expressways! It didn't get here in the simple linear fashion you think it did. Along the way, it reacted to the time frames that it passed through. This will also give you pause to wonder if your distance measurements are accurate, too.

When you begin to discover more about the dark energy (not negative, but unseen) in your Universe, you'll have to conclude that it's interdimensional, and therefore some of it's even in a quantum state (all together, without distance). As soon as you add this attribute to the reality of space, you then must consider that what you're seeing and measuring as light might actually be far more complex than you thought.

What scientists call the "big bang residue" is an energy left over from a dimensional shift, not an explosion. It creates a reality where you can only see part of it in 4D, and where the energy doesn't "add up" to the whole you know is there. This will lead you into interdimensional math and eventually to also discover the vents we've spoken about. More is coming on this.

Question: *In one of one books, you mentioned that the flow of charged particles interacting orthogonically with a magnetic field can induce zero and magnetic mass. (I hope I got this right.) Could you kindly elaborate more, and hopefully predict when we can expect this kind of technology?*

Answer: The creation of massless objects (what you call anti-gravity) is the insertion of specific multiple dimensional attributes within 4D. It can be done when you understand some very specific and easily accomplished relationships of magnetic fields within magnetic fields. We told you to look for clever ways of spinning fields within fields, and attuning them to certain levels of gauss. These are definitely "designer fields" and not stray ones, and they must "see" each other in a certain way. When you do that, suddenly you get a massless object. If you do it inside an object and follow some specific alignments, the object itself will become massless. You can also "steer" it with the very magnetics being used to create the massless attribute.

But the "steering" is about "where in space" it must exist, rather than what you consider "turning left or right."

Although only a few will understand what I'm speaking of, later some will read this and they will absolutely "know" that this is accurate and therefore must be channelled. For there are only a few scientists on Earth right now who could read this and relate to my next statement: The "magic" of a massless object is contained in the energy artifacts of what's remaining after magnetics voids magnetics. These artifacts of energy are interdimensional gold (as far as you're concerned), meaning that they're the essence of what you're looking for, and what they contain is what will change the "rules" of your physics, causing you to revamp your understanding of matter.

Know that even interdimensionality can exist in 4D (gravity and magnetics are examples), yet be part of your system of 4D physics. But they remain only reactive physics, in that all you can do is see what happens around them. The magic will happen when you can begin to understand what actually creates them, and manipulate that. Then you begin to see beyond the 4D, and begin to manipulate the attributes of the other dimensions and get reactions.

All dimensions are in your lap for you to work with. There's nothing hiding, or against some spiritual law. Magnetics is only the first area of interdimensional physics, but it's the most obvious, since it exists in 4D in a way that can be seen and manipulated. Be careful not to have too many presuppositions about what might or might not be the results of experiments. Remember one of the most basic quantum rules: When you get into interdimensionality, distance isn't a factor.

Question: *Dear Kryon, The question I'd like to ask is, what information do I most need to know?*

Answer: The thing you need to know right now is how to create an energy around you that keeps you balanced and joyful, no matter what's happening in your life or the world. Can you see things in a sacred light? Can you send light to the places that need it the most, allowing for free choice? Or do you wallow in the drama of the politics? The biggest thing that you're learning right now is how to become interdimensional in these things. Learn to see appropriateness... the overview... and to then get to work and send the light to the most needed places on Earth—the Middle East, Africa, and the places of leadership and government. Send them light with spiritual integrity, not bias. Illuminate their areas, giving them a better choice to see things they never saw before. Be as the lighthouse that stands on the rock and helps to steer the ships into a safe harbor. Don't take sides. Don't judge the belief system of the ships. Just hold the light and anchor yourself. Let Spirit do the rest.

Hebrew DNA Names

A Discussion of the Hebrew Spelling
and Meanings of the First Five DNA Layers
As Presented in Chapters 9 and 12

-

Ilan Vainer-Cohen & Levia Valero

Appendix A

Hebrew Spelling and Meanings
of the DNA Layer Names
Ilan Vainer-Cohen & Levia Valero
Appendix A

According to Kryon, the *literal* meaning of the Hebrew names is not essential for understanding the names of the DNA layers, and in some cases the Hebrew meanings are different. Kryon presents these Hebrew words as "sacred names" of the layers of the DNA, and explains their meaning in the context of sacredness. Kryon refers to the Hebrew language as being the... *"core spiritual language of the earth"* and *"each name is meant to be heard as a spoken phrase, strung together for the full meaning in Hebrew."* According to Kryon, *the meaning of the spoken Hebrew word lies in its energy*, and therefore these Hebrew names should be spoken or heard as intended in Hebrew.

Guided by this approach, the spelling chosen for the Hebrew names is as close as possible to the phonetic pronunciation of the Hebrew words, with the intent to maintain the energy that these words carry when spoken. There are several ways of rendering Hebrew vowels and consonants into *Latin* letters. As a result of Jews originating from all over the world, the individual's native tongue exerts considerable influence on the spelling and pronunciation of the Hebrew words. In the process of transliterating Hebrew words into the English alphabet, some form of compromise was required. We did not go into an academic discussion on the subject and kept the explanations regarding the pronunciation as simple as possible for the reader. The main guideline we followed was to reflect the pronunciation of these names in English rather then having them written "correctly" grammatically. For those of you who wish to expand your knowledge of the Hebrew language and its various pronunciation styles, you will find numerous books on the subject and various resources on the Internet.

The following is a simple guide for the pronunciation of the Hebrew DNA names. Letters that are not listed are pronounced approximately the same as in English.

כתר עץ חיים
Keter Etz Chayim - Layer One
Kryon's interpretation:
"The Tree of Life"

Pronunciation:
Ke-ter:
e as in *met*.
r - Pronounced as something between the English *r* and the guttural French *r*.
Accent first syllable.

Etz:
e as in *met*.
tz - Like *ts* in *cats*. Pronounced like a strong "tz" or "ts", as one sound.

Cha-yim:
ch = (guttural) A sound produced through the use of throat and back of the palate, much like in the pronunciation of *Bach* in Johann Sebastian *Bach* or the Jewish holiday *Hanukah* (this *ch* sound is not in standard English).
a as in *bard*
Accent second syllable.

תורה עשר ספירות

Torah E'ser Sphirot- Layer Two
Kryon's interpretation:
"Divine Blueprint"
or
"The Blueprint of Law"

Pronunciation:
To-rah:
o as in *core*
r - Pronounced as something between the English *r* and the guttural French *r*.
a as in *bard*
Accent second syllable.

E-ser:
e as in *met*
r - Pronounced as something between the English *r* and the guttural French *r*.
Accent first syllable.

Sphi-rot:
phi like *feel*
o as in *core*
Accent second syllable.

נצח מרכבה אליהו

Netzach Merkava Eliyahu - Layer Three
Kryon's interpretation:
"Ascension and activation"

Pronunciation:
Ne-tzach:
e as in **met**
tz - Is like **ts** in **cats**. Pronounced like a strong "tz" or "ts", as one sound.
a as in **bard**
ch = (guttural) A sound produced through the use of throat and back of the palate, much like in the pronunciation of **Bach** in Johann Sebastian **Bach** or the Jewish holiday **Hanukah** (this **ch** sound is not in standard English).
Accent first syllable.

Mer-ka-va:
e as in **met**
r - Pronounced as something between the English **r** and the guttural French **r**.
Accent third syllable.

E-li-ya-hu:
e as in **met**
li like **Lee**
a as in **bard**
hu like **hoo**
Accent third syllable.

אורים ותומים

Urim Ve Tumim - Layer Four
Kryon's interpretation:

Layers four and five together are the essence of your expression (this specific life on Earth), and your divinity on the planet. They represent the "name" on the crystal on the Akashic Record. Together, they can be understood as: *The primary and most important spiritual attribute of all is the tree of life, which is family.* These are names of God and should never be thought of as separate layers. They are part of *the divinity group*, (pages 296 and 297).

Pronunciation:
U-rim:
u like in **tool**
rim like **reem**
r - Pronounced as something between the English **r** and the guttural French **r**.
Accent second syllable.

Ve:
e as in **met**

Tu-mim:
u like in **tool**
mim like **meem**

אלף עץ אדוני

Aleph Etz Adonai - Layer Five
Kryon's interpretation:

Layers four and five together are the essence of your expression (this specific life on Earth), and your divinity on the planet. They represent the "name" on the crystal on the Akashic Record. Together, they can be understood as: *The primary and most important spiritual attribute of all is the tree of life, which is family.* These are names of God and should never be thought of as separate layers. They are part of *the divinity group,* (pages 296 and 297).

Pronunciation:
A-leph:
A like *ah*
e as in *met*
Accent first syllable.

Etz:
tz - Is like *ts* in *cats*. Pronounced like a strong "tz" or "ts", as one sound.

A-do-Nai:
A like *ah*
do as in *doe*
Nai like in *night*
Accent third syllable.

Although, according to Kryon, the meaning of the Hebrew words in this context is not of paramount importance, for those interested we give the literal meanings of the words below:

Keter - Crown

Etz - Tree

Chayim - Life

Torah - Torah (The Law), Pentateuch, Five Books of Moses

E'ser - Ten (#10)

Sphirot - In Jewish mysticism: spheres, levels

Netzach - Eternity

Merkava - Chariot

Eliyahu - Elijah (The Master Prophet)

Urim Ve Tumim - From *The Concise Oxford Dictionary*: "Objects of now unknown nature, worn in or on breastplate of Jewish high priest. (Exod. 28:30) [Heb. **urim pl**. of 'or' a light, **tumim pl**. of 'tom' completeness]."

The *Even-Shoshan's New Hebrew Dictionary* adds: "(1) With the aid of these holy objects (maybe stones) the high priest gave God's reply for any question that was asked. (2) A reliable, unquestionable source."

Ve - and

Aleph - The name of the first letter in the Hebrew alphabet

Etz - Tree

Adonai - My Lord. God

As we gradually expose all 12 layers, don't be surprised if we get to the ones that will be the imprints of your past life experiences. Even your karmic attributes are there, and all of them are *changeable!* The most confusing part of all of this for you will be something that we haven't discussed yet: As you change one of the layers in any way on any plateau, all of the others "know" it! Like complex chemistry, you cannot change one thing without the reactions of the others also changing something. In this chemistry metaphor, DNA is the same. If you activate the third layer, all 12 know it.

Drop By and visit our
HOME - *page*

The award winning Kryon web-site allows you to find the latest in-formation on seminars schedules, and Kryon related products. Browse through portions of Kryon books, read some of the most profound Kryon channellings, reference, inspirational and educational material. Read some of the hundreds of answers in the Kryon Q&A section. Also, enjoy the Kryon on-line magazine, *In The Spirit.*

Kryon's Website offers the latest in technology and is easy to navigate. Our main menu allows you to view in an animated or non-animated format allowing for maximum Internet speed.

Find the latest Kryon information at:
www.kryon.com

www.kryon.com

The Kryon Cassette and CD Series

**ASCENSION
IN THE NEW AGE**
Live channelling
ISBN 1-888053-01-1 • $10.00

**NINE WAYS TO RAISE THE
PLANET'S VIBRATION**
Live channelling
ISBN 1-888053-00-3 • $10.00

**GIFTS AND TOOLS
OF THE NEW AGE**
Live channelling
ISBN 1-888053-03-8 • $10.00

**CO-CREATION
IN THE NEW AGE**
by Lee Carroll
ISBN 1-888053-04-6 • $10.00

**SEVEN RESPONSIBILITIES
OF THE NEW AGE**
Live channelling
ISBN 1-888053-02-X • $10.00

**THE
LEMURIAN TAPES**
by Lee Carroll
ISBN 1-888053-08-9
$10.00

Crystal Singer
by Jan Tober

**CRYSTAL SINGER
MUSIC MEDITATION**
by Jan Tober
ISBN 0-96363-4-1-3 • $10.00

**GUIDED
MEDITATIONS**
by Jan Tober
ISBN 1-388053-05-4
$10.00

**COLOR AND SOUND
MEDITATION**
(ENGLISH or FRENCH)
by Jan Tober
ISBN 1-888053-06-2

**TEKNICOLOUR
TAPESTRY**
by Jan Tober
ISBN 1-388053-07-0
$15.00

**I HAVE THE FEELING
I'VE BEEN HERE BEFORE**
JAZZ! by Jan Tober
ISBN 15882-008722 • $15.00

**THE WAY YOU LOOK
TONIGHT**
JAZZ! by Jan Tober
ISBN 34479-05472 • $15.00

**THE
JOURNEY HOME**
Jan Tober and Mike Garson
ISBN 15882-01432 • $15.00

The Rest of the Kryon Book Series

THE END TIMES
ISBN 0-9636304-2-3 • $12.00

DON'T THINK LIKE A HUMAN
ISBN 0-9636304-0-7 • $12.00

ALCHEMY OF THE HUMAN SPIRIT
ISBN 0-9636304-8-2 • $14.00

THE PARABLES OF KRYON
ISBN 1-56170-663-9 • $10.95

THE JOURNEY HOME
ISBN 1-56170-552-7 • $13.95

PARTNERING WITH GOD
ISBN 1-888053-12-7 • $14.00

LETTERS FROM HOME
ISBN 0-9636304-2-3 • $14.00

PASSING THE MARKER
ISBN 1-888053-09-7 • $14.00

THE NEW BEGINNING
ISBN 0-9636304-2-3 • $14.98

THE INDIGO CHILDREN
by Lee Carroll/Jan Tober
ISBN 1561706086 • $13.95

AN INDIGO CELEBRATION
by Lee Carroll/Jan Tober
ISBN 1561708593 • $13.95

Books and tapes can be purchased in retail stores and by phone: **1-800-352-6657**
Also through our Website store at: **www.kryon.com/store**
Credit Cards Welcome

Other Products

"BUBBLE BOWL MAGIC"
by Jan Tober
$6.00

"HOLES IN HEAVEN"
DOCUMENTARY
VHS Format • 51 Minutes
$25.00

PRAYER FOR EARTH
Mediation by Jan Tober
VHS Format • 18 Minutes • $20.00
(Shown in Kryon seminars)

THE KRYON CARDS
50 inspirational sayings from Kryon
ISBN 1-4019-0050-X • $15.95
(50 card set)

UNDERSTANDING YOUR LIFE THROUGH COLOR
by Nancy Ann Tappe
$14.95

THE JOURNEY HOME - CHILDREN'S EDITION
by Theresa Corely
ISBN 1-56170-987-5
$13.98

ELEGANT EMPOWERMENT EVOLUTION OF CONSCIOUSNESS
by Peggy Phoenix Dubro & David Lapierre
ISBN 0-9711074-0-8 • $22.00

THE RECONNECTION-HEAL OTHERS, HEAL YOURSELF
by Dr. Eric Scott Pearl
ISBN 1-4019-0210-3
$14.95

Books and tapes can be purchased in retail stores and by phone: **1-800-352-6657**
Also through our Website store at: **www.kryon.com/store**
Credit Cards Welcome

At Home
with
Kryon

Get together for a personal afternoon or evening with Kryon and Lee Carroll... in the comfort of a cozy community center or intimate hotel venue with a small group of dedicated Lightworkers. It's called *At Home with Kryon*, the most popular venue for joining in the Kryon energy. The special meeting starts with an introduction and discussion by Lee Carroll regarding timely New Age topics, then it continues during the day with profound, inspired teachings from the Kryon work. Next comes a live Kryon channelling. Group size is typically 50 to 70 people. Often lasting up to five and a half hours, it's an event you won't forget!

To sponsor an "At Home with Kryon" event in your home, please contact the Kryon office at 760/489-6400 - fax 858/759-2499, or e-mail <kryonmeet@kryon.com>. For a list of upcoming At Home with Kryon locations, please see our Website page [www.kryon.com/schedule].

Kryon at the United Nations

In November 1995, November 1996, and again in November 1998, Kryon spoke at the S.E.A.T. (Society for Enlightenment and Transformation) at the United Nations in New York City. By invitation, Jan and Lee brought a time of lecture, toning, meditation, and channelling to an elite group of U.N. delegates and guests.

Kryon Book Six, Partnering with God, carried the first two entire transcripts of what Kryon had to say... some of which has now been validated by the scientific community. Kryon Book seven, Letters from Home, carries the meeting in 1998. All three of these transcripts are on the Kryon Website [www.kryon.com].

Our sincere thanks to Zehra Boccia for her help with introducing us to the presidents of this organization over the years. We thank the S.E.A.T for the invitations, and for their spiritual work, which enlightens our planet.

(Lee Carroll was also invited back in September of 2004)

Would you like to be on the Kryon mailing list?

This list is used to inform interested people of Kryon workshops coming to their areas, new Kryon releases, and Kryon news in general. We don't sell or distribute our lists to anyone except our Kryon presenting partners.

If you would like to be included, please simply drop a postcard to us that says "LIST," and include your clearly printed name and address.

The Kryon Writings, Inc.

1155 Camino Del Mar - #422
Del Mar, CA 92014

The truth is that your divinity is within you, and no doctrine on the planet is higher than this truth. If you claim it, then you'll be "above the fray" of those who wish to convert you, damn you, or kill your family because you're not a believer. This, my Human friend, is the war between the old and new energy.

Index
A New Dispensation

Index

Index

Index

Index

Index

Robert Coxon

Prelude to Infinity
Robert Haig Coxon

Robert Coxon, best-selling musical artist, Kryon international team member, and composer extraordinaire, has at last released a new, much awaited album. Best known for *The Silent Path*, Robert has gone to the next step in his musical evolutionary process with *Prelude to Infinity*.

With sacred composition and strong inspiring melodies, *Prelude to Infinity* paints on a canvas that is interdimensional, out of the normal expectations of New Age music. Think *healing....*

Books and tapes can be purchased in retail stores and by phone: **1-800-352-6657**
Also through our Website store at: **www.kryon.com/store**
Credit Cards Welcome

And so it is, dear Human Beings, that another time has passed when you let us hug you. There's such a difference between when we first started and now. For this day we can actually feel the hugs in return. We feel open hearts... open minds... family hugs. And we are so looking forward to doing this for a very, very long time.

And so it is.